Wildflower Seeds:

the Beauties of a Reflective Life

Cat Charissage

Cat Charissage

Cover image: Cat Charissage

Cover and interior design: Beate Wichmann

Author photo: Teri Petz

ISBN 978-1-7380037-0-9

To all those who wander,

*who yearn for a more meaningful life,
and who yearn to find that which is worthy
enough to dedicate your life to. I hope these
ideas help you know that you are not lost;
that you know that you, in all your gifts
and individuality, are so deeply needed here
in this world with all of us.*

Table of Contents

Introduction

I am awakened by the sound of the gas-powered lawn mower. Again. It's 9:01 a.m. on Saturday morning, and next-door Mr. and Mrs. Lawncare are doing what they do best: cutting and pruning and shaping and pulling and moving every living thing that they can control in their tiny tidy yard next to my tiny shabby yard. And I despair, again, of sleeping in. This is one of the strongest memories I have of living in that long ago home.

My neighbors were, in reality, truly lovely people, and eventually I gave in to the culture's demand for tidy lawns and hired them to cut my own grass and prune my own bushes. They were delighted. I sighed and mourned a little.

The sound of that lawnmower, of the lawnmower this morning, of every lawnmower I hear, has become to me the symbol of how we — and by we I mean our western culture for sure, but possibly most humans of our time — have gotten it so wrong, bringing our planet and ourselves to the very edge of survival. In a desperate attempt to control all that is around us, we've disregarded the earth's natural rhythms, re-routed and dammed up waterways, pulled down mountains mining for coal, and paved the meadows and the forests with concrete and grasses not native to the land they cover. And then as soon as the grass grows, we grab noisy engines to hurriedly mow it down. It's enough to make you wonder why the grass doesn't just give up and die when their every urge to grow is thwarted, over and over again!

I paint this metaphor of the lawnmower destroying that which is natural and growing in very broad strokes, and of course it is not true in every detail. Yet it is an image that has stayed with me throughout my adult life as I've witnessed the ongoing destruction of the earth's health and the ongoing destruction of the mental, physical, and spiritual health of so many of us humans.

We're living so quickly, going so fast that we barely have a clue as to where we are actually headed. So many of us live frantic lives filled with other people's voices, from the never-ending news cycle on our phones to our boss's demands or our family's latest crisis. We're quick to dash off a response to any query, and know how to get dinner on the table in 20 minutes. Then, after all the "have-to's" of the day, we're tired. Netflix beckons – just let me throw a few things into the washer first. Tomorrow it's the same thing all over again.

At the same time, we're worried about the state of the world and the state of our own communities. Will there be another pandemic? What about climate change, wildfires, and the very weird weather? Our hearts break to see those who are unhoused trying to cope with the cold, and young mothers struggling to pay for diapers at Walmart, not to mention the corruption and hypocrisy we see in too many political systems around us. But in response, what can we do to help?

When do we figure out what we really think about things? When do we stop to breathe? Or wonder? When do we work through those difficult conversations that weren't quite finished? There are so many causes, so many needs, where do we put our support and our energy? How do we know what is meaningful to do or have time to prioritize these sorts of non-urgent, yet oh so important activities?

Can we reflect upon life while we're living it, when we feel like we're the ball in a pin-ball machine being batted from one obstacle to another? Most of us can't take days out of our lives to step away and ponder the deep and real questions of life, and most of us don't want to live in monasteries or ashrams away from the "real world."

Let me take that metaphor of the lawnmower and turn it over: most of us have been to or at least seen photos of a meadow in springtime filled with wildflowers blooming. The colors are natural, not neon, predominantly light green with soft blues, pinks, and yellows. The bees are busy and buzzing. The edges are filled with blooming lilac bushes. Just thinking about that meadow, or hillside, or mountainside of wildflowers invokes a sigh of pleasure, release, relaxation. How can we feel that release and relaxation more often? How can we "breathe easy" and really think about how to live in cooperation with that kind of natural beauty? Can we plant more wildflower seeds?

While those of us with land might be able to transform our green lawns into wildflower lots (if city bylaws allow it), I'm concerned here with how we can live like the wildflowers I'm bringing to mind. How might we live so that we're confident we belong where we are? How might we live where we fit into the ecosystem of the earth, where just as the wildflower roots hold the soil from being blown away, our own roots, that is, who we are deep down, are protecting the resources for our children's futures? How might we live where we can bring beauty into the world alongside others bringing beauty into the world? How might who we are be nurturing to ourselves and others? How might our own roots, leaves, and flowers provide food, medicine, and a home for those living around us?

How can we live intentional lives that contribute to our own well-being and the thriving of the life around us? It's not easy to leave the rat race when it seems we must keep running just to survive. These problems of excessive speed, greed, over-control and domination echo through all the systems of our lives, and feel almost impossible to address. But I do think that each of us has some choice to do what we are able to do, here and now, today, in our own imperfect, full lives. By that I mean that we ARE able to move to a more life-enhancing way to spend our lives, investing ourselves into creating a world where we all can live freely and with integrity.

We may not be able to change laws or unilaterally reallocate corporate priorities, at least not today. Yet, almost all of us can carve out twenty minutes today to rest, think about things, and listen for what we might do next. We can stop at a park for 20 minutes at lunch or on the way home from work, or take 20 minutes away from scrolling social media, or get up 20 minutes earlier or go to bed 20 minutes later. One 20 minute session here or there won't change your life, but the accumulation of these sessions, daily, over time, can. They can create enough breathing room to take charge of our lives by renewing our strength, asking important questions, and imagining a world worth living in. We can discover what is most crucial and discern how to live this, now. It is a false dichotomy to think that we must choose between either political action for what we believe in or being a calm and enlightened person. Each 20 minute session plants another wildflower seed into our lives and into our world.

This book is intended to help you plant those seeds, to develop the habit of a daily 20 minute reflective practice, what I call a "Depth Dimension Practice." It offers dozens and dozens of ideas of what to do during those 20 minutes in order to explore these important questions. The resources in this book go in two directions: the first is to come to consciousness and understanding about yourself in relationship with the world and your cultural voices, that is to say, to find clarity and discernment unraveling internalized oppression. The second direction is to encourage you to come into silence, to rest, to restore and balance your mind/body/spirit, and to hear the inner nudges towards wise actions.

A Depth Dimension Practice can calm you to hear the small voice inside. It can help your inner spirit heal and renew. It can help you distinguish your own thoughts and beliefs from those that are blasting all around you. It can help you question received wisdom on how to live, and help you identify how other people's values have taken up residence in your deepest self. It can deepen your confidence and your self-sovereignty. It can help you know where to invest your limited energy for yourself and for the common good. And it can bring a bit of joy and perspective to each day.

As humans, there's more than just keeping ourselves in shape to tackle the daily work cycle. There's something within us that is concerned with questions that seem to be unanswerable, questions such as "Why are we here?" "Why is there something rather than nothing?" "Why did my brother die when he had his whole life before him?" "Does war ever really solve anything?" "How is it possible that I can love so deeply?" "Why is there such suffering?" "How is it that in the midst of all the chaos and ugliness, the sunset is so breathtakingly beautiful?" "Is there really a God who will stop suffering and bring justice to all someday?"

Alongside the suffering and confusion, we also have experiences of wonder, and awe, of beauty, of transcendence, even of deep fulfillment. There is music that penetrates deep into the heart, poetry that can completely change our mood from despair to hope, artworks that leave us speechless. Photographs of deep space boggle the mind and remind us of just how big life, the universe, and everything is. These experiences hold a sense of something that cannot even be put into words that is yet perceptible in this human life.

It's part of being a human being to be able to explore these questions and ideas — but when, and how? Life is so often clumsy and difficult. We need to process the daily bumps to meet the next challenges, and our holidays are filled with even more work than our non-holiday days. The struggle is real. But so is the possibility.

I wrote this book for those of us who want to explore our inner lives more deeply, to discover our own beliefs free from our culture's expectations, to know where and to whom we belong and who and what to work for. I wrote it for those of us who wonder about the big transcendent questions in life whether or not we find help in the traditional religious teachings many of us grew up with. And I wrote it as well for those of us who just long for moments of restorative rest and inner peace.

Many of us don't have wise persons in our lives to talk to about such things, and it takes time and effort to find a compatible and ethical teacher or group. For many of us not in big cities, these communities and teachers may be impossible to find. This book offers plenty of no- and low-cost ways to explore some of the most important things in life, even if you don't have a community to do it with. I wrote this book to show how a daily depth dimension practice will cumulatively allow each of us to live a deep and meaningful life of authentic self-expression and communal participation in supporting life-honoring ways of being — in other words, how to plant wildflower seeds.

After reading widely about self-empowerment and social justice, seven years of academic study of theology, extensive study and experience in mystical theology and contemplative practice from Christian, Buddhist, Jewish, and Islamic traditions, half a lifetime of working with people in trauma recovery, education, and now accompanying others in the depth journeys of life, I have some experience in approaching these questions. I want to share the ways I know that will help us deepen this engagement with our own humanity, to deepen our relationship with our inmost self and with that which is as wise and transcendent as we can imagine — whether we are involved with religion or not, whether we believe in a "God" or not. By doing so, we then discern what we can and will do in our daily lives to make a world worth living in.

As you read this book, I strongly encourage you to read the first and the last chapters before you read the chapters on the practices. That way you'll get a sense of the "parentheses", or the context, in which this book is situated.

In the first chapter I discuss what I mean when I claim that developing an inner life is a political act, and why these Depth Dimension Practices are useful in creating ourselves and in changing the world. In the following sections I offer a series of practices that will help us live meaningful and authentic lives through five modalities of Word, Image, Dream, Silence, and Embodiment. *Word* encompasses practices around reading, writing, and journal keeping. Image invites us to examine the images that commodify us and how they offer a supposedly desirable way to live, plus the practice of making images and using color to create environments that support our true values. *Dream* attends to night dreams, daydreams, cultural stories, and the stories we tell and are told about us, and how we can analyze their power to influence how we live each day. *Silence* includes many types of meditation and other practices that help us to slow down the chattering of the monkey mind, and ways to listen to ourselves and to that which is beyond ourselves. *Embodiment* asks questions about how we learn about our bodies and how to care for ourselves, and offers practices to do things with our bodies that bring us into deeper consciousness. Finally, the last chapter is a reminder of why this exploration can be so important and what is possible when we do live our lives with freedom, consciousness, and intention.

While I offer many suggestions for practices, none of us needs to explore every last one. Not only would that be a lot of distracting work, but it would mistake the means for the ends. We each only need one or two practices for our entire lives, but I have heard from so many good-hearted folks that they "can't meditate," or "sitting still brings up so much anxiety," or "I don't like nature — there are too many mosquitoes!" And they give up and pull out their phones without experiencing the beauties of a reflective life. There are so many ways to restore ourselves, come to clarity, or listen for wisdom, and this book collects a huge variety to help you find your way. In fact, there are many other practices, such as music, relationships, or sensuality that I don't talk about. I hope that you will find here both the encouragement and the practical ideas to help you plant your own variety of wildflower — to continue in exploration, and to expand your reflective practice to more than a simple 20 minutes a day. Come for the adventure! We all need you.

catcharissage.com

1 What Are We Doing Here?

Developing an Inner Life is a Political Act

When I was a little girl, I thought that the world was run by a group of wise leaders who knew what to do about the problems I'd heard about. I thought these people were leading us all toward a better world of providing for all people's needs, and bringing justice into the chaos. The idea of a United Nations inspired by "liberty, and justice, for all" completed the image (yes, it was easy for my young self to merge the U.S. with the U.N.) Well, I grew up and found out, probably just like you did, that we're it – ain't nobody in charge of it all, though some people do grab whatever power they can and think they're in charge. But it's still up to us humans to create a world worth living in. Many of us hope for a God who will make it all alright in the end. But God or no God, I've always felt that I can and must do all that is possible to create harmony and justice in this life now, in myself and in my community.

Sometimes, though, just getting through the day in one piece seems challenging enough, and sometimes, it's the best that can be hoped for. As I struggled through early adulthood, I pondered various visions of "the good life" and "the healthy community". At the same time, I realized that most of the people I encountered, though often well-intentioned, just couldn't get it together to be effective for very long in bringing justice, teaching liberty, or sustaining hope. I saw the occasional victory for social justice often sacrificed in the next election cycle. As my disappointment threatened to turn into jadedness, I realized that the old elders' wisdom quoted by my teacher Dr. Clarissa Pinkola Estés was right in defining a cynic as "a disappointed idealist."

In the midst of all this, I found both solace and inspiration in my 20 minute a day practice of reflection, rest, and dreaming of the best I could be and do. This practice sustained me in both the high times and the low times. I saw other activists whose practices also sustained them, and I became very curious as to what it was here that was helpful. We didn't have the same practices, and I have certainly changed what I actually do during those 20 minutes as different seasons came and went; it couldn't be a strict "do this" to "get that." I knew it didn't necessarily rely on a faith in God, as several of us had left traditional notions of God. I also knew it wasn't positive thinking, as others of my colleagues were on the edge of despair much of the time. My curiosity led me to suspect that the help the practices brought had to do with the consistency of coming back after whatever lapses we had, which in turn led to the accumulation of insight and wisdom over time. We also had a willingness to listen to our deepest selves, in addition to whatever inspiration we found. This book is my attempt to put all of this into words. This is a book of practical suggestions that will help you to be sustained in high times and low, and to come to know that having an inner life is a political act. So much around us attempts to colonize our minds, telling us what to think and what to do; finding and listening to our own inner wisdom is as important an endeavor as any war in the name of freedom. As more of us are able to sustain ourselves and free our imaginative spirits, we will be more equipped to do what we need to do to make a home for all of us in this fragile world.

This book invites you to begin a practice that will bring immediate calm, comfort, and depth, and, in the long term, bring insights and habits that can move the entire course of your life into one of meaning, intention, and authenticity, both in your individual life and in your life with others. You can discover your own greatest gifts for yourself and the wider community, and develop them into effective strategies to bring more wisdom, light, and love into this needful world of ours.

This book will guide you to building a 20 minute daily practice of reflection and exploration into the deeper aspects of your life. In this practice you will get to know your deepest self in all the wonder and contradiction that you are. You will develop inner knowledge to become grounded in your unique ideas, and strengthen your inner sovereignty in order to transform your deepest desires into reality. The way to get there might seem surprising; there are myriad entry points, from watching deer eat leftover crab apples outside your window, to writing in a journal in response to selected prompts, to the embodied movements of dance or chi gong—and much more! The catch? You actually have to do the practice and develop the habit. This book can help you all the way through. This chapter will talk about many of the "why's," and the latter chapters will give you enough "how's" for years to come.

How do we explore the deepest questions of life if the only language we typically have for that is religious language – especially when that language is no longer relevant to vast numbers of people? I offer here ways to investigate meaning in daily life which primarily sidestep talking about "God." I start by asking what almost every human wonders deep down: What are we looking for in life? What is life for, if it is "for" anything?

I'm sure there are as many answers to these questions as there are people, but there are also some common answers: happiness; a sense of well-being; a sense of being part of something bigger than oneself; a belonging-ness, whether within a family, a country, a religious group, humanity, or life on planet earth inclusive of other animals, past, present, and future; or being part of the "all"; or part of "God". Similar to that, many of us seek a sense of interconnectedness or, to use Thich Nhat Hanh's word, "Interbeing." Most of us also seek hope, open-heartedness, joy, equanimity, gratitude, justice and a sense of goodness, the ending of suffering and the presence of justice. And all these qualities, senses, or feelings are part of the treasure that being human allows us to experience and reflect upon. It seems that a human life, lived reflectively, can be a source of endless mystery, endless questioning, and possibly, endless meaning.

The only place most of us learn about these things, the churches, the mosques, the synagogues and meditation halls, are often not particularly helpful in answering the questions many of us have these days. I've observed that many of us don't know what to believe regarding God, the Sacred, the Holy. Perhaps we're no longer able to believe the miracle stories we were told as children, or we question how science and religion can be truly reconciled, or we struggle with how a good God can exist when there is such great suffering in our world. Some of us are trying to heal from deep betrayals inflicted on ourselves or a loved one by persons representing religion. It's confusing, complex, and unsettling. Many of us have tried to just not think about it very much and have simply surrendered to the demands of our busy lives. And some of us who do find our spiritual needs met by the religions we were born into or have chosen still want something more and deeper, something more tangible than what we have experienced so far.

I call these areas of life where we confront great mysteries that are usually the purview of religious communities the "Depth Dimensions of Life." These are areas such as love, awe, birth, wonder, chronic illness, suffering, justice, and death. They are what I call "Soul Matters" and "Soulwork," the aspect of self that is concerned with what is deepest within us, and which also reaches out for "More," or the greatest that human beings can imagine. Sometimes we're forced to wrestle with the more painful of these areas just through life circumstances. But this intuition that there is something More or Beyond is an intuition that has persisted throughout human history. Oftentimes we yearn to explore these mysteries precisely because they ARE mysteries and somehow, they just feel very important. These depth dimensions of life are where we find meaning and authenticity, questions and experiences I often call the "D & R's" (the Deep and Real things) of life.

I have found that many people feel adrift in how to explore the D & R's of life, especially if they don't find resource in a religious tradition. Yet I also see that so many people would like to explore these D & R's and how they relate to their daily lives and the world around them. What I have noticed is that when people do engage in depth dimension practices and this kind of seeking, they tend to live more authentically, creatively and joyfully within the mysteries of life. They are often more engaged in their communities, working on issues of equity and justice. One can certainly live a soulful life without having to make a choice between a religious point of view or total secularism. It may sound paradoxical, or even selfish, to suggest that we sidestep questions of faith, religious doctrine, and even who "God" is in order to focus on our own soul lives. But starting with who and where we are, turning towards our own inner soul life opens us to wonder and a desire for authenticity. And so we will begin the journey by exploring, and living out the questions and qualities that must not be allowed to be forgotten in the pragmatics of struggling through daily life. There are ineffable questions and experiences in life, whether we describe them as religious, or a function of imagination and metaphor.

These are questions and observations that can bring inner freedom and, consequently, can bring about political freedom to think and express one's own thoughts while respecting the thoughts and beliefs of others. They can bring about practical actions that create a world where we do indeed belong with each other. And along with the questions, we will explore practices that, in themselves, enrich our lives while deepening our engagement with life's depth dimensions.

I use the word "Mystery" with a capital "M" to refer to this ineffable "something more," that points to the unanswerable aspects of human life, as a reminder that I'm endeavoring to speak of the depth dimensions of life without the human and historical misunderstandings that are attached to the word "God." And I use the term "depth dimensions" or "soul life" to refer to that which humans usually mean when we use the words "spiritual" or "spirituality", again as a reminder to question and reexamine our conventional understandings.

Long ago, one of my professors in college was trying to teach us the nuances of the word "mystery" as used in theology. She acknowledged that many people think of mystery as something that one can never understand, like a puzzle that no one can ever solve. But she said that mystery is rather something that can be infinitely revealing, always having more for us to know and to understand. She likened mystery to a rose slowly blooming, filled with beauty and wonder at each moment, though it was always changing and opening even further in each moment. If we could imagine that process as infinite, she said, we would understand better the essence of Mystery.

So, while this book is not explicitly about spirituality, it is about soul life, a soul life embedded in our human lives and communities. I offer ideas for practice, invitations in five different areas to engage in inexpensive or no-charge activities that can take anywhere from 5 minutes to a week to a lifetime. Many invite you to look at familiar things in new ways, to imagine what it would be like if…

They are also designed to evoke critical thinking and to help you articulate your own questions and sample different ways of approaching those questions. The different areas in which we are going to play in the mystery of it all are 1) Word, 2) Image, 3) Dream, 4) Silence, and 5) Embodiment. *Word* contains ways we play with language, in journalling, dialogues, poetry, and collections of luscious and provocative words. Image has us paying attention to photographs and the advertising we're immersed in, creating simple graphics and drawings, and doing experiments with color. We'll explore the power of symbol and archetype for a multileveled understanding of the depths we're moving in. *Dream* covers all kinds of stories, our night stories and how to work with them to find meaning, how to remember dreams, uncovering the main story of our lives, or the stories of different eras of our lives, such as the stories we grew up with, and the stories we now tell each other. *Silence* explores simple musings, from looking out our living room windows to different types of meditation, to the intimacy of silence when shared with another. *Embodiment* includes reflections on where our body begins and ends, how we move through our lives, how we express meaning through our bodies, and how to come to terms with our bodies in a world focused on comparison and perfection. It also offers ideas on what we do with our bodies that deepen our soul lives.

A primary question the activities will address is how we figure out what we have control over and what we don't. We will be looking at how in *responding* to our environment we also create it. When must we accept what is, and when can we imagine and then build something else? These practices also work as peace bringers, in that they work as a pause between stimulus and response to aggravations in life that might otherwise bring out our anger and derision. A thoughtful response is almost always more compassionate than a defensive aggressive response. These practices can serve as creative alternatives to counting to 10 when responding to the provocations that life brings. They remind us of our values and how we really want to live our lives, and give us the strength to respond rather than to unthinkingly react to life.

The activities are designed for you to do on your own, sometimes calling for very little energy, other times directing an enthusiasm of energy into inquiry and discovery. Many times we don't have others who share our interests and questions, and I focus on activities that are actually within our control to do and explore without having to wait for the right group, the right teacher, the right course. Many practices, however, can be done with others for a different, and often deeper experience.

Another primary question we will explore is what makes a life worth living? As none of us is in complete control of our lives, how do we dance with reality in joy? Are we choosing our priorities or are we simply following the values we've been handed? Are the values we've been handed worth keeping and developing, or is there something more pulling at our edges that is begging to be articulated and lived?

What I want for you with this book is to have a variety of practical tools. I wish for you a sense of deep belonging, to know that you've come out of this world, and that by the fact of your coming out of this life on earth, you are at home and profoundly acceptable as part of it all — just as the wildflowers are. You belong here. We belong with each other, here, now, on this earth, even if we don't have to sit at the same table with those whom we deeply disagree with.

I hope that the practices will help you access the much larger world of symbol and archetype, and allow you to recognize how you already have been co-creating much of your world view, to recognize what power you have to create and influence not just your own life, but life with others. I want all of us to also discern clearly how much is not under our influence or control, and to not blame ourselves for every condition we find ourselves in. I want us to explore how we can live peacefully in the midst of so many other people. All of us both intentionally as well as unconsciously use symbol and story to inspire and fuel possibilities, as well as to limit our worlds to little more than a prison without bars. Examining this increases our freedom to know what is possible. I want to share techniques to release useless anxiety, guilt and shame, discerning what is ours to wrestle with and what is best walked away from.

The inner life, the life of the soul, is not valued in most of our contemporary societies. Yet it is through developing and nurturing this inner life that we find the ways to live that bring life, joy, and meaning, and that motivate us to work for justice. If we unquestioningly follow the cultural norms, we almost always end up exhausted, ill, and burned out, with little energy to heal ourselves, much less the systems and institutions that profit from our lack of power. So many forces around us would prefer us to shut up, stop thinking, and get with the program to be good little soldiers, and they use indoctrination, then coercion, then force and violence to create the world that they want. They have an interest in keeping us exhausted and disheartened, and feed off our feelings of helplessness. To have an inner life is a political act when we examine, understand, and break out of those internalized forms of oppression, when we wake up and refuse to wait for joy until earning heaven in an afterlife.

In a world that could be one of cooperation, respect for all, and deep beauty – at least more than we experience now, I ache that people are not taught about the potential and imagination of the soul and soul life. I hate that children and young adults are not given, as part of their birthright, relevant entryways into an interior life or taught how to navigate our inner lives. As a result, especially for those of us who do not find resource in traditional religious teaching, many do not have a soul life that will guide them as well as nourish them. This is a grave injustice when everyone can potentially have access to these depth dimensions, and have access without giving up our own sovereignty.

We really can develop our souls without having to sell them first.

So, Who am I to Talk About This?

These practices and questions touch on the deepest aspects of our lives; what gives me the authority to talk about these things? It's my own experiences, both painful and ecstatic, and my education and training. It's talking with and working with hundreds of people for over four decades about these depth dimensions of life, about trauma, about abuse, about existential questions – primarily, the "Why?" question: *Why do bad things happen to good people?* It's conducting Story Circles to facilitate critical thinking through listening to others explore deep questions and challenging readings. It's companioning beloveds in their own lives' journeys to meaning, belongingness, a larger self, and to the core of what it means to be alive, here, now. It's spending hours and hours and hours in my own practices, in silence, listening, writing, reading, and painting, in what many would call prayer.

I graduated from university with a degree in theology, hoping to go on for a doctoral degree. I wanted to teach theology at a university. I'd always been good at school and wanted to help other young adults explore deep questions and develop a mature understanding of their religious beliefs. I knew that most people – at least most Christians in North America – do not actively focus attention on their faith after adolescence, often stopping their learning after "Confirmation," the ceremony in which one is confirmed as a full member of their Christian religion. I wanted to help students to learn about other religions and to learn to be a respectful guest when invited to other places of religious worship. And I wanted to help young adults combine their passions for social justice with what it was that was deepest within them, to see that loving God and others also meant living that love out in their daily lives of seeking justice. I wanted to help them to live lives of reflection and integrity.

I moved from the United States to Canada, and received a wonderful education that, unfortunately, did not include finishing that Ph.D. I'd hoped for. Although studying at the Toronto School of Theology was initially exciting, in the afterhours talks with new colleagues, I began to see the world with new eyes, and to deeply understand the struggles of sexism, racism, and other "-isms" that dehumanized different members of this world and denied justice to so many.

A number of my depth dimension practices came out of those times and questions. For example, in my exploration of gender equity, I began to notice that most of the images I was seeing of women were of a certain kind: young, slim, always conventionally beautiful, almost all white and middle-class, and made up with lots of cosmetics. I would see these women in advertisements, in movies, TV and magazines. Then I'd look up and notice real women in the subway or on the street.

They seemed "uglier," less colorful; they were often heavier than their television counterparts, and many looked like they were having "bad hair days." I include myself in the real women description! Through this new awareness, I realized that the media and advertisers were showing us images chosen for their own purposes, which did not include giving real women a reflection of their reality but rather an image we were supposed to aspire toward. As a result, I started to collect images of real women and put them up around my room. This was in the 1980s; the internet was not yet around and making and collecting images was much more difficult than it is today – color photocopying was rarely even available. Nevertheless, there were small presses that published postcard photos of accomplished women from the last 150 years of history, as well as art cards that profiled women with a different kind of beauty, often in museum guides to historical exhibits.

Little by little, I amassed hundreds of images of women that looked like the women I would see in my daily life and who populated the real world with different shades of skin colors. As I lingered with these images, I noticed that my own self-image was changing from feeling fat and disheveled, to being someone who was doing interesting things, like someone friendly with whom you could have a great conversation. I started seeing the women on the streets and on the subway as interesting. They greatly expanded my definition of beauty – women with full lives who worked hard and showed their emotions on their faces and in their bodies. I gradually came to critique new images of women with the question, "Can I imagine this woman as a physician or an experienced worker? A teacher or a trucker?" If the only job that I could imagine the manufactured image of a woman to be doing was modeling for the male gaze, then I knew that I was being given those images by someone who wanted me to aspire to be someone they could sell their products to.

In the early 1980s, besides gender equality, I became involved in women's health issues and the peace movement. I grew to understand that so many of the atrocities that had happened throughout history were not just unfortunate exceptions to my naive younger belief that history progresses towards greater justice and development. I began to understand that the beliefs and policies of nation-states often reflected religious beliefs that actively supported the violence against whomever was labeled "other" in that particular age. While studying for my bachelor's degree I had been taught the best that Catholic Christianity had to offer. In Toronto, I studied its history and was deeply troubled. It deeply shook my faith not only in the Church that I had been loyal to, but also in God. How could there be a good God who just lets these atrocities happen without stopping them?

As a result of these realizations, I left my studies and spent many years working in a variety of advocacy groups, including six years at a sexual assault center. Much of my work was in public education around social justice and violence issues, and so I learned much about how different people in my audiences understood or did not understand these issues. I also witnessed the passion and devotion of people doing committed social justice work, along with the anger and burnout that often accompanied it. I began wondering what could support these exhausted people who started out with such loving hearts, and what could help us to keep on with it.

I wanted to know how we, with humility, could teach people not familiar with these issues and their negative effects to understand their importance and impact. I wanted to understand how to encourage persons who feel powerless to see and to commit to the myriad ways of bringing more justice and compassion into the world, as well as how we help people think for themselves, question what they've been taught, and speak their own truths with confidence and power.

While working at the sexual assault center I completed a Master's in Education degree focusing on adult education for critical consciousness. It was during this time that I reflected on and discussed many of my experiences with others who were also working in social services or advocacy organizations for social change. Life was busy, but by that time I had several personal practices that kept me relatively balanced and mostly energized to do the work I had chosen. Yet meanwhile, a chronic illness began to manifest itself in my body.

Even during spiritual crisis and difficult work in social justice areas, I continued the meditation practice that I had developed years before. Much of the time I wondered if it was just a waste of time, but I also noticed that when I quit my practice, life was harder. Despair was closer at hand. I figured that even if my 20 minutes a day was a waste of time spiritually, it wasn't a waste in terms of the general benefits to my own life. The meditation practice grew and evolved into different areas such as journal writing, collecting images of symbols and studying their multivalent meanings as doorways into a larger world, doodling with mindfulness and, eventually, painting and poetry. I also took up Tai Chi and began to understand movement as a way of shifting energy in my body. Many days I spent more than the minimum 20 minutes a day in these kinds of depth practices, especially in reading depth dimension books, but I still found that the 20 minutes, on a consistent basis, was enough to nurture my own depths and bring balance into my life of outward-focused activism. It was much more effective to do a little bit every day than to go months without a practice and try to catch up on a weekend retreat.

I also observed my colleagues who seemed to be able to carry on in this work and stay sane, kind, and purposeful. In almost all cases, each had their own versions of 20 minute a day depth practices. Whether running, writing, meditation, walking a dog, or crafting, there was a small window every day into joy and depth that was sustaining and nurturing.

In 1995 my spouse and I resigned from our stressful jobs, moved to the Alberta Rockies, and began to write the books we'd dreamed of. Within six months of making the move we had the surprise of our lives: I became pregnant for the first time, at 39 ½ years old! It was a very welcomed surprise, but as you can imagine, it changed our plans. This started an entirely new journey for me regarding teaching a little person about the D & R aspects of life. Switching from adult education to teaching my own child had its challenges, but I learned so much especially because while raising our son Liberty, we were also living in locations with predominantly evangelical conservative Christians. We wanted to be respectful and community minded, even though we did not share those exact beliefs.

By then I had come to a truce in my own anger against "God" for seeming to stand aside when bad things happened, allowing any number of injustices and atrocities to occur. I use quotations for "God" because at that time I couldn't have told you if I believed in God or not. I had not yet developed a different way of speaking about the spiritual, or what people refer to when they mean something much greater than anything human or in nature. I had given up using God-talk, and my continued explorations into what I now call life's depth dimensions were primarily silent and wordless. My truce about the presence of evil consisted of ignoring "God" and God-talk, while still exploring the capacities of myself and other humans to be loving, compassionate and helpful – capacities that I used to attribute to the God of my previous life of faith. But raising a child meant that if I wanted to talk to that child about the religion of many of the people around me, or about many of the qualities and behaviors that were most important to me, I'd have to figure out a way of talking about spirituality without using "God" and traditional religious language.

I taught my son about how we humans deal with both mundane problems and the mysteries in life, including that many people believe in a loving, all-powerful and all-knowing Father who created us and everything around us, even though no one knew for absolutely sure. When he was little, I started with folk-tales from around the world, then moved into fables and then myths from around the world. The world of children's picture books had exploded with variety and beauty, showcasing beautiful artwork and poetic renderings of traditional stories. Reading with my son was a deeply pleasurable part of being a mother, and I loved having a front row seat to observe the everyday wonder of growth and human development. We were able to continue reading together long past the time that most parents are able to because my spouse and I decided to home educate our son, and reading was a foundation of that education

Teaching my son about the search for meaning in life, and about unseen realities such as love, kindness and empathy led to many conversations with other parents as well. Often, the first question after meeting someone was "What church do you belong to?" My usual response was "Oh, we're not a church-going family," even though some people assumed that if we didn't go to church then we must be immoral, and possibly dangerous.

After getting to know them, though, through homeschooling activities, we often became "Exhibit A" when families wanted to show their children that even people who didn't attend their own church could be good people, too. But that entailed me developing a comfort with talking about values and choices about how to live "good" lives. This further sparked in me the need to articulate why I do what I do in my depth dimension practices, and what I thought they accomplished, if anything. Comparing the practices to certain kinds of prayer practices and mindfulness practices began to provide a shared language in the communities we lived in.

As Liberty matured and needed less of my daily attention, I was able to get back to my own work in adult education. This took the form of facilitating Story Circles, mostly with women, where we explored in small groups important questions and reflected on our own life experiences. The groups explored various topics such as poetry, journal writing, dreams, and living lives of depth. Along with this, I often accompany individuals as a spiritual companion and witness their navigation of the depth dimensions of their lives. As well, I am a poet and a painter and mixed-media artist.

Over the years I have had deepening health challenges including persistent and debilitating chronic pain. This gave a certain personal immediacy to my questions about why bad things happened to good (or at least trying to be good) people. I have worked to develop some wisdom about these things, even though some of the best wisdom I can offer is a sincere "I don't know why bad things happen, but I know we can make things better if we respond with compassion, as well as reach for whatever joy we can find in our everyday." This is quite a shift from forty years ago when, deeply immersed in my theological studies, I certainly could give you answers!

So even though I don't have many answers anymore, I love to explore questions. I know that reflecting on good questions, along with exploring many non-verbal ways of being human, can help us to make meaning in our daily lives as well as discern the actions that will lessen suffering and bring more justice. This is the best definition of soul-life that I have right now, the openness to and the reaching for More than the daily grind. It leads to a full and enriching life, a way of living more comfortably, creatively, and joyfully with Mystery. It is a life worth living and sharing with others, in whatever ways we do that as humans. And that's why I invite you to make meaning, and make soul, through consistently practicing depth dimension activities.

Infinite Interconnectedness

I live now out of the idea that we all are immersed in absolute interconnectedness with all of reality. At its simplest manifestation, rather than being self-contained boxes of organic material, our bodies are semi-permeable, self-ambulatory condensations of matter constantly taking in our environment with each breath of air, and leaving behind our bodies as we shed breath, hair, and skin cells. We move the muscles of our throats and mouths into vibrations that are taken in as meaningful sound by other condensations of matter. We take into our bodies each day the liquids and solids of food and drink, and we leave behind us these liquids and semi-solids that our bodies do not need or cannot use in the reproduction of cells, that is, in keeping us alive.

Even just physically, we are embedded in circles within circles of care and influence, nourishment and danger. And going out from there our minds and thoughts interconnect with others, from the books we read, to the Facebook comments we write, to the shouts of warning we yell out. While our locus of action is the present moment, we extend backwards and forwards in time. We receive influence from civilizations that lived thousands of years ago, and what we do now with this earth will reverberate in its ability to support human life, or any life, a thousand years from now.

If we keep extending that interconnection outward to the complexities of social interaction and the psycho-spiritual effects of trauma and projections, how does this all interact with love? There is familial bonding and sexual need all the way toward, and mixed deeply within, unconditional love and generosity. There is taking and destruction within this circle as well. I don't pretend to know how all this works, especially when one adds life's depth dimensions, spiritual knowledge and practice to this. But I do know that we are embedded in circles within circles within circles. And that what we do matters, more than we can imagine. We belong here, with each other, for better and for worse.

Given this, what we do can make a profound difference to ourselves and each other, for good or ill. What we do is influenced by what we think and feel. And though we do not have total control over what we think and feel due to past traumas, current gut biomes, the people we have to live with or work for, etcetera, we definitely have some control over our thoughts, feelings, and actions. We have choices about what we pay attention to in our environment, and the ability to contribute to environments that can enrich our lives. We are not completely at the mercy of our bosses, our political leaders, or social media. I think we have, therefore, some responsibility to not just "do no harm," but to help when we can and within our reach. I've come to see that there are huge untapped resources of meaning, connection, inspiration, healing and possibility within our lives, just as we have huge resources for destruction. I know that many of the practices I will talk about in this book tap into those resources for possibility and hope, that it is possible to live with purpose, and to move into happiness.

We live in a world that has more than enough for our needs, but not for the greed that is so present in all this interconnectedness. The abuse of whatever power we have is a constant temptation as seen in the dominator mentality, the patriarchy, and the many "-isms" we are increasingly becoming conscious of. There are many forces that feed on our unconsciousness and our depressions. These forces are rampant, almost universal, and there is a huge need to examine and develop our inner freedom in order to lead to outer freedoms, and to nurture our own enough-ness in order to create enough for others as well as ourselves. It is necessary to recognize, escape, and strategize to disempower both inner and outer predators, to sensitize ourselves to any abuse of power around us, including that which we ourselves perpetrate. Depth dimension practices help us to do this, and it's worth the time, energy, and commitment to do these activities for ourselves and all the others with whom our lives are so deeply embedded. Wherever we have choice, let us not unconsciously mow down the wildflowers.

2 Before We Start…

Re-examine all you have been told
In school or church or in any book,
Dismiss whatever insults your own soul;
And your very flesh shall be a great poem.
… And have the richest fluency, not only in its words,
But in the silent lines of its lips and face,
And between the lashes of your eyes, and
In every motion and joint of your body.

WALT WHITMAN, *preface to Leaves of Grass,* 1855 edition

Getting Started – the Short Version

Take a deep breath and gently relax your body. What's on your heart right now, today? Do you have an intention for your depth dimension time today? Note how much time you have today for this. Grab a notebook and pen. What other supplies do you have available? How much privacy do you have? How much of a mess can you make right now? Can you leave your work out overnight to dry, or do you need to clean it up all in the time that you have? Browse through the practices in this book. Choose your practice, and go to it!

Getting Started – the Longer Version

The goal in exploring our life's depth dimensions is not to add *another* thing to do in your already busy life. The goal is to live a life of engagement with all that is in your world, both your inner and your external world; and if your world is now not a place you want to be in, to be able to little by little change either your life or yourself so that you do like it. It is to become an agent of peace and stability in your world by tapping into the deep wisdom available to you, part of your birthright as a human being. But it doesn't just come to you without being deeply present to your inner self or curious about how you are embedded in the world around you. You need to be conscious of your fundamental connectedness with all of life, in fact, with all that is. While there may be difficult or sad emotions along this exploration, it is ultimately intended to allow you to choose possibility and joy, and to become a change agent.

We are not routinely taught this, or are only taught this partially, in certain circumstances, with certain people. We're taught to be willfully blind about much ("I don't understand why you're not happy, you have it all: spouse, children, good job!" "We're only engaging in war in order to bring peace to the region!"), to not trust ourselves but to defer to "experts" who are too often just another name for the "authorities" — whether or not there is anything authentic about those decision-makers. We're under deep social pressure to disregard our inner lives, to never know the connectivity or the energy of our inner worlds in relationship with the world around us. We're not taught to notice or to work with other concerns or other realities outside of our daily work or our current roles. But what is healing and wholeness, if not the coherence of all our layers of reality?

If there is a lack of frequent, regular interaction between our interior and exterior worlds, we feel the "blahs", a lack of animation, a lack of meaning, a deadened, sometimes agitated ennui of situational depression. We are often successful in our daily work, yet the question niggles: is that all there is?

Let's do something right now to begin to cohere all the layers in our lives. Before you read more, look around the room you're in and remove something that bugs you or depresses you. You may not have the freedom to get rid of your computer (or your spouse – I hope you're laughing with me!) without more consideration or consultation, but the little stuff — the poster your "frenemy" gave you that you never liked anyway, the newspaper story about the criminal behavior of a public figure, that hole puncher that never quite works right – take it down and put it aside. Decide later whether to throw it out or give it away. If you cannot change your environment, try moving your chair so that what is directly in front of you is pleasing or neutral to you. Start doing what is possible for you to do to create harmony and beauty around you.

Putting things in a box, either literally or figuratively, is an excellent option when first considering whether to keep something in your life or not, and is, in fact, a depth dimension practice. Putting something into a box gets it out of your immediate consciousness so that you can get clarity away from the in-your-face quality of so many disturbing objects, memories, tweets, news updates. Of course, if you put things into a literal box, you (or your heirs) will have to deal with it someday.

Put a reminder on your calendar and if you haven't needed whatever it is by then, donate it or throw it out. None of us need any more baggage to carry around.

As an example of baggage we no longer need, many years ago I had carried around with me, through four moves, something that was a physical artifact of some of my childhood wounds. In my closet was a pair of sexy red satin slings with 4-inch stiletto heels, complete with cute little bows, that had been an extremely inappropriate gift from a close male relative. I'd worn them only once, when coerced to do so. I'd kept them as a reminder of how far I'd come in my healing, how much I'd worked to recover from the past, and how I had become committed to preventing and healing sexual violence. But realizing that they depressed me as well as having fueled my eventual empowerment, I finally gave them away. Those shoes would not take up any more room in my life. I did take a photo to remember the story, however. The photo, a small slip of paper, is now one piece of a large journal, and large life, of many photos, many papers, many stories.

In these practices, there is little that is new that I suggest, but it's the putting them together, you choosing how you will try the different behaviors, you feeling the connections among them in your bones, you realizing deeply that having an inner life truly can be a political act, and you then taking action in the world as a result of new awarenesses – that is what is unique about these offerings. I want you to use your inner exploration, plus your external observations, combined with your expressive creativity, all done consistently over a period of time, to come to know deeply your unique self and what you can do in your life, now, to express your unique self within your embeddedness in the life around you.

As I described in Chapter One, I have divided the practices into five different ways that we humans know and interact with the world: practices of *Word, Image, Dream* (including *Narrative and Story*), *Silence, and Embodiment*, practices that you can explore by yourself, and start anytime. The five divisions are somewhat arbitrary and many practices incorporate two or more of these categories. They are not at all exhaustive; I haven't included music, relationships, or writing poetry, for instance. What most have in common, though, are noticing, reflecting, savoring, bringing into consciousness what you are experiencing, and bringing your whole presence into the now of what you choose to pay attention to. You do this 20 minutes today and tomorrow, and as time unfolds, more and more of your life will reflect what YOU choose to pay attention to, how you choose to live, and a coming to peace with what you cannot control.

The practices come from a variety of religious traditions as well as secular mindfulness practices and creativity exercises. I describe all of them in a secular manner, but all are also appropriate as actual spiritual practices as well. Feel free to adapt any to your own circumstances. Use my examples as suggestions for starting points, but expand them in ways that call out to you. I've minimized the "do it exactly like this" instructions as a deliberate way to encourage your own choice and assessment of what works in your life, now. I have experienced every one of the practices I include, as well as having used them with the people I work with and the small groups that I've run over the years.

I've come across most of these practices in several sources; it's impossible to track down the original creator of any particular practice. Many practices I've created myself from my life experience. I invite you to read through the description of the practice to make sure of a good fit for your particular day: to see the supplies you will need and the kind of space that is needed (for example, if you need access to water for cleanup, if you need silence or privacy, or if you can do them while commuting by train or bus). I suggest a minimum of 20 minutes for each practice because it takes about 15 minutes for our brains to relax and move into the rhythm that is more conducive to creativity and problem solving. Also, our world seems to organize itself into half hour chunks, so one way to find the time for a practice would be to switch it for a ½ hour program or podcast, or while waiting for a child at music lessons, for example.

Barriers to This Practice

The usual barriers for starting these practices are not enough time, not enough money, or not the right group of people to do them with. I'll offer a variety of ways to make these practices accessible, but we all have unique circumstances. If you're dealing with disabilities, chronic illness, many young children, or too many responsibilities, you may have to make a 3-day a week practice instead of a daily one. Try not to let your circumstances define you totally, but also do not compare yourself against others with fully healthy bodies or totally flexible schedules. Assess with utter honesty, without shame, blame, or excuses, the general conditions of your life, and figure out how to include what you choose. Explore your limitations, figure out what you can and cannot do, and live accordingly.

Try to find a regular time for your practice. When it becomes part of your routine, it tends to happen more regularly. Attach your depth dimension practice to something else that you regularly do so as to more easily make it a habit. Can you do it after work at a coffee shop or at the library before you even go home to other distractions? Can you do it while your children are doing their homework or watching a favorite program or having their computer time? How about right after the evening dishes before getting into other chores or turning on the tv or scrolling your Facebook feed? Can you pick up your children from daycare a half an hour later, or ask the babysitter for some extra time? Maybe you can start your bedtime routine a half an hour earlier and do your practice before crawling into bed. How about lunchtime at work, or in a corner of the public library after your regular errands? By far, one of my favorite places is in university library stacks, especially since they now allow you to take a coffee or beverage in with you! What about every Sunday morning, instead of sleeping til noon, or every Monday evening? Sometimes it's a matter of subtraction rather than addition. Note where you might find your inner self more by taking away something that doesn't serve you well, than thinking of this as adding just another thing to do into your already busy schedule.

This attitude of subtraction works when thinking about spending money for supplies, too. Please don't use starting these practices as an excuse for a craft store run! I know how some of our brains work, and I have been guilty of this more than once! Eighty dollars later, and I've used up my allotted time for my practice as well. My favorite phrases (excuses) are "I've never been depressed in an art supply store!" and "It's cheaper than therapy, and a lot more fun!" And sometimes that actually might be true, with something having more value than you immediately realize.

Perhaps it serves as a kind of "artist date" for you, where you lose yourself in new colors or supplies and fill your well of inspiration. I used to love to go to Liquidators stores, where there would always be a new mixture of organizational helps, office supplies, household gadgets, totes and boxes for storage, etcetera. I used to get down on myself until I realized that I felt rested and more effective at working afterwards — I needed the time to let my brain wander and to imagine different ways to organize my personal or work life, away from whatever concerns were imminent. Now I'm tempted to wander in dollar stores. And thrift stores! Don't get me started! Just be honest with yourself. These practices truly need only a minimum of supplies that are inexpensive and easily accessible, often already in your home.

Actually limiting your supplies consciously may be a depth dimension practice in itself. After all, the fulfillment of life is letting go of it all in death, and we can start practicing now. No need to accumulate and accumulate, adding to the clutter of our lives.

And so many lifestyle helps are monetized far more than needed — since when did most people need select athletic gear to go for a walk around the block? I talk about depth dimension practices as leading you to know the *More*, or the *Greater*, in life, but it's not about consuming more. It's about discovering, and enjoying, the more that is already here within and around us. As a depth dimension practice, think about how you and your family use your resources: there's camping in the national parks, and then there's flying to exotic eco-tourism lodges. There's mountain biking, and then there's quadding. There's scrapbooking for those of us who didn't get enough kindergarten, and then there are art retreats in Bali. We don't *need* to be flying all over the world for special experiences while ignoring the wildflowers in our own backyards.

Another consideration is to be mindful of when you schedule your depth dimension practice. What activities might you be doing just prior to engaging in your practice? For instance, you may not want to scroll through the news just before you open your notebook or journal. All of us have to be conscious of how we negotiate our relationship with keeping informed about the wider world these days. No news is good news, and if it bleeds, it leads. With "news" available to us 24/7, and as close as the palm of our hands, engaging in doom scrolling rarely actually helps us to know more useful things about the wider world and what our role can be to make it better. Yet we're encouraged to keep informed, and social media sites hire the smartest of psychologists to figure out how to keep us addicted to staying on site to enjoy the dopamine hits of each new update or "like". This is tricky for all of us, and it changes, too, at different times of our lives. Just try to be conscious of how you use the news and social media and of its effects on you, and to remember that you do have a choice.

Consider the idea of a Sabbath day. Do you have a day to truly rest and restore yourself? When you say you don't have time for it, is that *really* the truth? What would it take to have a day to nurture the deep and real parts of your life? I call my version of the sabbath a DDD, a Depth Dimension Day, where I fill my well with spiritual and/or creative ideas and practices. Some days it's merely looking through a book filled with photos of art, other days it's a concert or a meeting with an inspiring friend. On DDD's I try to keep the computer to a minimum, or at least to use my computer time very consciously, very intentionally. I remind myself that I can't drink forever, nor give forever, from a cup that isn't filled regularly. A daily 20 minute practice keeps me basically nourished, but the luxuriousness of a sabbath is what keeps me moving forward into new areas, new tiny adventures.

A sabbath is, in truth, at least theoretically available to each of us. It might take intentional decision-making, some work, and a fair amount of perseverance to actually make it happen, but it is usually possible. For those of us with church families, I know that Sundays are not always very restful days, what with ministries, obligations, committees, getting kids dressed and out the door in time, and making sure there's food to greet us and our guests when we get back home – not to mention the socializing with people who we might not necessarily choose to otherwise be with. For others of us who do not include a worship service on our Sundays, if we were raised in a religious tradition, there's often an ambivalent feeling of restlessness, perhaps even guilt, as we sleep in or find ourselves wandering the house on Sunday mornings, not exactly sure what we should be doing. Sometimes it's easier to just take on the extra shift and work all day instead.

Perhaps a different day of the week would work better for your Depth Dimension Day. Be honest about how much rest and nourishment you get in your life, and come to some acceptance and peace with our human bodily, psychological, and spiritual needs. It has literally taken me years to accept and to accommodate my limits and my needs. Identify what's working, and guard that from being encroached upon.

Supplies

Now that you have a tentative time marked out for you to do the depth dimension practices, you need to get set up with some supplies. All you really need is a notebook and pen, but you'll want some way of adding color, and you should use nice materials to honor the time, energy, and intent that you're expending in this endeavor.

Assemble a small tote to carry your supplies. Keep it portable, unless you have a room of your own that you know you'll be doing these practices in. Something like a canvas briefcase or cloth tote bag is perfect. Ziplock bags work well for small items. Don't invest much money in this when you first start, because as you take up these practices, you'll find the types of supplies you like best, which may suggest other ways to carry them around. If you need to start inexpensively, most of the supplies can be gotten at a Dollar Store for less than $15.00. I get my supplies at one of the big craft stores, like Michaels. To start, include

- ◆ A journal or notebook you'd like to write in. I prefer it not to have lines so that I feel free to doodle, add color, or glue papers into it. The paper needs to be thicker than typing paper or even a sketch book, and it's helpful if the pages lie flat. The Canson XL Mixed Media spiral bound notebooks, 90 lb. weight, 9 in. x 12 in. work well for me. If you prefer single sheets of paper, I recommend watercolor paper or mixed-media paper at 140 lb. weight.
- ◆ Pens or pencils you like. Include a waterproof black pen or marker. Pigma micron pens work well. Gel pens are great, especially from the Sakura brand, which come in a variety of types of inks, metallic and textured as well. Inkjoy pens are of good quality too.
- ◆ A timer. You can use the one on your phone, but if your phone is nearby, it's easy to be distracted from your depth dimension practice. Have you ever gone to just look up the spelling of one word, and an hour later "come to" after you'd checked your email and Facebook? I have. Don't place distractions in the middle of your supplies unless you have the requisite willpower! Ideally, the timer should have a gentle ring or quiet buzz so that it doesn't cause your adrenaline to soar when it goes off. Don't ever do to yourself what you wouldn't do to a baby — don't scare yourself or unnecessarily stress yourself.
- ◆ A set of colored markers, or colored pencils or pens. There are dozens to choose from, but Crayola kids' markers are inexpensive and work just fine.
- ◆ Watercolor pencils or watercolor crayons. These look just like colored pencils or crayons, but when you brush across your writing or drawing with a wet brush, the pigments dissolve and they're like watercolor paints. The Caran d'Ache Neocolor II water-soluble crayons are a delight to play with, giving deep

rich color with ease and no mess. But Crayola or store brand watercolor pencils will still give you options to play with even if their colors are not very deeply pigmented. As you go on in your practice, you may want to include a watercolor set and a few bottles or tubes of acrylic paints in your favorite colors. Regarding acrylics, you'll need to have access to water for clean-up. If you're new to acrylic paints, the inexpensive craft paints work just fine. The best artist brands are Liquitex and especially Golden paints. The quality is very apparent, but they are also comparatively expensive. Acrylics wash out of brushes and off hands with soap and water, or with just water in a pinch. Try to keep them off of clothing as they sometimes are hard to wash out. If you use the higher quality acrylic paints in a notebook, be aware that your pages may stick together. Just place thin paper between your pages, or wax them to keep them from sticking.

- Paint brushes, 2 or 3, plus a small jar of water. Make sure the jar doesn't leak. A 1-inch flat brush, a small round brush, and a ¼ inch flat brush are all you would need. Even just a round brush is enough to start. Or you can get a waterbrush. Waterbrushes hold water in their barrels so that you only need to gently squeeze the barrel to get the brush wet. They greatly reduce mess, and are easily portable.

- A glue stick or tape. Can be transparent tape or even masking tape. Washi tape, available at craft or art stores, comes in dozens of designs, and is fun, but not needed. When using glue sticks, be generous and apply a thick layer. The UHU brand works very well.

- A few pages of scrap paper, for notes and for testing pens or markers.

- Scissors or a 6-inch ruler, preferably a metal ruler, for tearing out photos or words from magazines or old books.

- A few paper towels or a small package of wet wipes or baby wipes.

For Later, as You Become More Experienced:

File folders, or one expandable file folder with many pockets, in order to collect fodder for including in your journal. You may collect images from magazines or old books, or print images from the internet. Sometimes old calendars have images or cartoons that are great to save. Here is also where you can save poems and quotes you like. As well as positive images, you can have a file for images that disturb you, of things you don't want in your life, or images that are deeply thought provoking. Another important file to create is an ideas file. This is where to collect things like the names of books you might want to read, things to look up, poets, artists, or musicians you want to check out, websites with great images for printing out, and any other miscellaneous information.

A large plastic tote or bankers' box to store your journals when you've completed them.

As an alternative to glue sticks as an adhesive, get a jar of Matte Medium in the Fine Arts section of a big craft store. Matte medium, and the thicker gel mediums that are available, dry into a type of plastic that bonds things together permanently. If you have a collage held down by ordinary glue sticks, sometimes the glue dries out. Your images then separate from the page they are pasted on. Though this doesn't happen often, it can be disappointing if it does. Using matte medium circumvents this problem. It is a thick liquid applied by brush or an old credit or gift card. It is also a much stronger adhesive than a glue stick. Gel medium is like a thick paste, and can hold down small items such as charms, beads, and other items that are heavier or 3-dimensional. It comes in either a gloss finish or matte finish. Both matte medium and gel medium can be painted over an entire page to make the page waterproof and ensure that there are no corners that will lift up. They dry clear. They can also be mixed with acrylic paints to create "colored adhesives."

Finally, be sure to have a "capturing system" for catching ideas on the fly. I always carry a small 3" x 5" notebook or index cards with me, along with my phone. Or you can just email yourself a reminder on your phone or take photos of ideas. In any case, as time goes on, replace your pocket-less clothing with clothing that has large pockets. You may become like a raven or crow who collects shiny tidbits to include in your journal. Myself, I'm a magpie. It can be a joy to wonder about what catches your eye, and to notice more and more the small beauties in your everyday life.

You'll also need a comfortable place to sit when you're working in your journal. Lap desks, a large book, or even just a doubled-up piece of corrugated cardboard on a pillow will provide a flat surface to write on if you're not at a table. And of course, a nice beverage is always pleasant.

Privacy Concerns

One important thing to consider is your privacy, and especially the privacy of your journal when you're not using it. Doing your practices in solitude, even in the middle of a library, gives you the freedom to express yourself fully. Give some serious consideration as to where you will keep your journal, though, because it's really important to feel that you can be totally honest in your writing without worrying about someone accidentally or intentionally reading it later. Of course, you can choose to share if you want to, but the point is that it should be your own choice as to who reads what you wrote.

Some people just need to explain to their family what they are doing and ask them to not touch your supplies or journal without your permission. Other people find that their spouse's or older children's curiosity is just too much for them to control, or that younger children like to disappear their supplies without permission. There's also a difference between innocent curiosity and an intrusive curiosity. Adapt accordingly. You can keep your bag from being a temptation by keeping it in your own car or in the trunk of your car, especially if you think you'll be working in it when you're out of the house. Sometimes just keeping it in your purse or tote bag is fine. Or, you can find an out of the way spot in your home to "hide" your bag. Top shelves of closets work well, so does storing your bag underneath your underwear. You could store it in an old purse or gym bag, or in a suitcase under your bed. You could use a cash box or lockbox that has a key for access.

However you manage this, don't just leave it sitting out on the kitchen table or on the couch and then get upset when family members or roommates get curious and read your journal. One woman I know distrusted her boyfriend enough that she kept her journal in the locker that she rented at the university library, and only used her journal when she was supposedly studying. Also give a thought about how you will store your work when complete. I have seventeen bankers' boxes filled with my "archives", as I call them, stored under the stairs in our basement, inaccessible enough that no one in my family is tempted to look in there, but still accessible to me when I want. Or, you can also do what I did for many years: write on the opening page of each new journal "This is my PRIVATE JOURNAL. Please do not read it. If you are looking at this journal without permission keep in mind that I sometimes express my feelings in impolite or even mean ways, and that that may include my feelings about YOU. However, feelings pass, and I probably don't feel that anger now. But if you continue to read, you just might get what a snooper deserves, so BEWARE!!!" It was always good for a laugh whenever my spouse happened to see it!

Put the date on everything you write or create. Make it a habit to include the date in a consistent, inconspicuous spot. Trust me, you'll appreciate that in the future. And *please* don't throw away anything that you write or create. If it's ugly, turn the page and do something you'll like better. Or throw it in a box and label it "Archives". If it's written, you can tear it out, put it into a sealed envelope, and tape it into your journal. Don't torture yourself with something that brings up unpleasant feelings, so get it out of your immediate vision. But if one of the goals of these depth dimension practices is getting to know yourself well, what you like, what you dislike, and what you value, then it's important to keep these clues as to the magnitude of who you are and what is within you. They might bring great insight into your struggles many years later as you reread them. Honor yourself by accepting who you are at any point in time, and enjoy discovering how you change as time goes by and we learn more. Old journals can teach you to be compassionate towards yourself. The best training in becoming compassionate towards others is to be compassionate towards yourself, you being no less a person deserving of kindness than anyone else.

Sometimes you may want to ceremonially burn something that you have written or created. As a ritual of release and "turning the page in your life" this can be quite powerful and personally meaningful. If you plan on doing that, though, photocopy or take a photo of your original beforehand. Do your ceremony with the originals, and then later, write up a page in your journal about it all. Include your copies or photos, and include how you now feel as the ritual is complete. Our intentions in our ceremonies and rituals are strengthened by this kind of reporting. It's an honoring of ourselves and our inner lives.

People often ask me what the difference is between a ceremony and a ritual. There is no exact difference, but rituals are regularly done actions, like brushing your teeth or writing in a gratitude journal. Rituals often become habits, and include things like daily prayers or depth dimension practices. Ceremonies are less habitual, but are special times alone or with others, usually planned in advance, often involving words, actions, and things that include several of our senses. They often commemorate something important to an individual. Burning old writings or documents can be done in a ceremonial way. Life transitions such as weddings and new baby blessings are certainly ceremonies.

Dealing with Anxiety or Fear

It is probable that engaging in these depth dimension practices will be pleasurable, joyful, and often inspirational. However, some people experience anxiety when they sit down away from their ongoing everyday concerns and activities. While normal, it can definitely be a huge disincentive in doing these practices. There are a couple of ways to approach this. First of all, if you can put this anxiety into words, write about it in your journal. Sometimes the anxiety comes from a fear of forgetting important tasks, or from an unfinished interaction that is bothering you. In either of those cases, use your time to note the dates and tasks, or write about the unfinished interaction in order to bring it to completion or to discern the concrete steps you will next take to bring completion and resolution.

Other times the anxiety is wordless, in which case I recommend that you try the depth dimension practices that use your mind in reflection, recording memories, and answering questions. As you do this regularly, it's as if you're training your anxiety that there's nothing to worry about here, that you can handle the exercises that ask you to write about your life, that you can take all this a tiny piece at a time. Once the anxiety is calmed – and it may take 3 days or 3 months – you can try the depth dimension practices that are not as directive that bring you into silence. Use your timer here, and enter silence for only one or two minutes. Explore your inner self slowly, knowing that you can come back to consensual reality and everyday life any time you wish. Slowly increase the time that you sit in silence. If the anxiety persists despite your best efforts to titrate your experience, consider talking with a wise person or counselor.

If you are someone who has a fierce inner critic, then doing something new may bring up self-criticism, memories of old failures, or voices of people in authority who have criticized you in the past. Ask yourself who the criticism reminds you of. Whose voice is it? Is it something a parent or a teacher used to say, or is it a fear that is trying to warn you about something. Write it down. Look at the criticism in the light of your life, now. Is there any truth in the words now? If so, write out what that truth might be, separate from any mean or shaming phrases attached to it, and then consider how to respond in yourself to that truth. Incorporate the insight into your life. Identify clearly to yourself that while there might be that truth in what the critics say, the shaming and meanness is not okay, and you do not have to accept any shame nor tolerate meanness.

When there is no truth, no fair warning in the critical voices, write down your refutation of their message. Write down that you will not listen to those comments anymore, and whenever those thoughts come up again, refer back to this refutation in writing.

Remember the truth, and claim your inner sovereignty. It might take coming back to the writing twenty times before you can dismiss those criticisms as soon as they come up, but be persistent. When possible, talk with a good friend or wise person around you so that they can reflect back to you the truth. Whenever we deal with criticism, we should listen carefully, once, to see if there is any truth in the criticism that might be of help to us. There is no use in letting the words circle round and round in your head draining your spirit.

Many of us have been taught that our inner voice is the voice of God. When we've also been raised in a climate of criticism and exacting expectations, though, we very often internalize the criticism and perfectionism and know them as inner voices. When this happens, we end up thinking that this self-criticism is the voice of God demanding that we do the right thing, that we be perfect in all ways, and that this is so important that our lives and eternal salvation depend on it. This is an extraordinarily painful introject, an idea put into you by someone else when you were young and did not have the resources to know that it is not true. It is spiritual abuse. If you think that this is the case for you, please speak with a wise person or counselor about this. This is usually way too painful to try to sort out on our own, but also, sometimes it is impossible to find a wise person when you need them. Please treat yourself the way that a healthy mother would treat a dearly beloved child, with love, with kindness, with patience, with understanding. Many people believe that the source of that kind of love is God – that who God is, is love. Keep treating yourself with this kind of lovingkindness and know that cruelty and ridicule is never deserved, never the voice of a loving God.

Sometimes the anxiety can be very strong, and mixed with fear or dread, and sometimes you have no idea what it's about. If this is happening to you, the first thing to do is to bring yourself back to consensual reality by grounding yourself in the here and now. Look around the room and notice the colors around you. Tap your thighs and arms, perhaps walk around the room and stretch. Recite the alphabet, count aloud, or recite your phone number to yourself backwards. Remind yourself that here, in this moment, you are safe, and that you will not push yourself any farther than you are comfortable with. All of this brings your brain back into an alert, present, and problem-solving mode. When you feel present and centered, try to identify what's going on and what triggered the difficult emotions. If you feel up to it, write all this down.

Ask yourself whether or not you can do something about whatever the difficulty is, either right now or in the future. If you can do something to immediately take care of the difficulty, do so. If you don't know what the anxiety and fear are about, though, or if you are experiencing painful memories, you might not even know if it's fixable. If this is the case for you, try doing the depth dimension practices that use your mind and intellect to reflect on your life, as I mentioned above. If you can do these without distress, keep on, and slowly begin the depth dimension practices that move into silence and letting go of thought. Go slowly, a minute at a time, and always stay within your experience of safety. However, if this remains difficult for you and the anxiety is accompanied by intrusive thoughts, then please consult with a counselor.

And if you find that dealing with daily life becomes very difficult or overwhelming, especially if you can't seem to make it to work or do your daily activities, for example, or if you aren't able to feed yourself well, or care for or feed any children you are responsible for, then reach out for help as soon as possible. Call your doctor, ask a librarian for the number of a crisis line and call it, or go to a hospital emergency room. Treat yourself with as much care as a healthy mother cares for a beloved child.

In all cases, be aware of what you take into yourself, what you consume in terms of food, of information, of visual imagery. Pay attention to where you place your attention, and to what the world around us pushes at us to see and know. Too much bad news is bad for us, and when is the news good? Yes, it may be helpful to have an idea of what's going on in the world, but having bad news repeated over and over 5, 10, or 15 times a day, with no information as to what we can do to actually help, is exhausting and depleting. And then there is the "entertainment" of action games, horror movies, and the like. We are bathed in actual and fictional images of horror all the time. The mind is so much more complex than we understand, and it's not surprising that if we slow down enough to process what's going on inside of us, then we will need to process the actual and fictional horrors to which we've sometimes become desensitized.

Another kind of anxiety is when you're obsessed with a memory or worried about a seemingly insurmountable problem and you just can't stop thinking about it. Perhaps you have a family member dealing with serious illness or addiction. Perhaps your job is under threat or you are fearful that your pension will not be enough to live on. Of course, strategize, collect information, plan whatever action you can, but after you have done whatever you can do, you may still be constantly fretting about something you can't do anything about. In these cases, a useful way of dealing with it in the moment is to "containerize" it — to put it aside literally or imaginatively and to deal with it only when you have something that you can clearly do. Sometimes called "God Boxes", or "Treasure Chests", you could have a literal box: shoe box, locked strongbox or cash box, or plastic tote you keep on a top shelf of your closet. Anytime something comes up that you just can't deal with at the moment, make a note of it and put that note in the box.

People I know have used them not only for bad memories or disruptive thoughts that get triggered, but for times when there are problems they've felt helpless to influence. The idea is that we ask, or intend, that forces stronger than us, or stronger than we feel at the moment, will help us to deal with those ideas or worries. Then later when we're feeling stronger, we either by ourselves or in the presence of a counselor or good friend go through the box to assess if there is anything helpful we can do next, and/or whether we need to get some expert help in the situation. Some things in life can't be changed or are unanswerable, and feel beyond the reach of any help. Those things stay in the box with the intention or prayer that we surrender them up to greater forces of Love. Those things are "God's business", and keeping them contained in the box helps us to move forward with the things that we can do something about.

Besides a literal box that you put notes or symbols into, you can keep a computer file to contain these things in. Or you can just take a selfie and send it to the file. All of this is using the power of our intention and imagination to focus on those things that we want to focus on, rather than being thrown into a swirl of chaotic emotions that can escalate into our becoming incapable of any good thought or action in the moment.

After "containerizing" the emotions or worries, I suggest taking a few centering breaths and grounding ourselves in the here and now. Notice your senses, and consciously count 3 things around you that are yellow, then blue, then red; notice your feet on the floor and your bottom in the chair, or hold onto something that is meaningful to you such as a charm or piece of jewelry you carry with you, some sort of a talisman — use it as an anchor to keep you here in the present moment; squeeze your hands, or put your hand on your heart.

Notice what you hear around you. People talking, the radio, elevator music? What do you smell? Can you chew some gum, or take a drink of your beverage? You can recite the alphabet slowly, one to a breath, and remember happy memories that begin with that letter, such as Arizona, the beach, coffee, deer, etc. My mother-in-law, a devout Christian, used this idea to help her calm down during a time of panic attacks, only she used bible verses suggested by each letter: "Abide with me", "Be not afraid", "Come to me, all who are weary and need rest", etcetera.

As I mentioned before, though, engaging in depth dimension practices will usually be pleasurable, joyful, and inspirational. At times, you may even experience moments of ecstatic joy and profound belongingness. When this happens, ponder these experiences for at least 30 seconds with gratitude and perhaps awe. It takes a few moments to incorporate these moments into ourselves, into our bodies, mind, and heart, soul and spirit. Into our memories. If we don't mark these moments when they happen, it's too easy to later dismiss these profound experiences and to forget about them. But there's no need to go too far in the other direction, either, and proclaim yourself as now either fully enlightened or a holy mystic. These moments of joy, ecstasy, and profound love are our birthright — they are what is possible in a full human life. The very best thing to do is to ground yourself and ask yourself how to put these experiences to good use in your life, now, in becoming a compassionate and wise person.

When you finish with your depth dimension practice, ask yourself a couple of questions by way of reflection and evaluation. You can write down the answers, or just be thinking of them as you move on to your next adventure of the day:

- Did I like the activity?
- How did it feel?
- What surprised me?
- What do I want to remember from this?
- What do I want to know more about?

In summary, there is truly very little you have to do to prepare to do these practices. Enter with a spirit of curiosity and play. I sincerely hope that you will develop a regular practice of reflection, creativity, silence, and wonder. Plant a wildflower seed, and enjoy what blossoms.

3 Word

The kinds of practices described in this chapter include many that you are probably already familiar with, such as writing in a journal and responding to prompts that solicit your point of view on a topic. It's well known that we often learn what we think by actually writing about it, wrestling with words until they truly communicate what we want to say. There are more than journal prompts in this chapter, however.

By 'Word,' I am including the practice of everything having to do with reading, speaking, writing, and pondering (thinking in words). The aim of these practices is to bring you more deeply into yourself, whether that is your deepest inner self, or the deep connections you have within you with the people you have around you, or with the nature and earth around you.

People have often asked me if it makes any difference whether we read or write online or offline. Are real books and the slowness of writing instruments and paper worth it any more in terms of speed or ease of organization and storage? Although some may disagree with me, I want to strongly state that when it comes to depth, analog is always better. Analog includes more senses, more of the things that make us embodied humans rather than a disembodied mind. For an example, think of the images in the movie *WALL-E*, or think of how it feels to receive a note from a lover that's written in her or his handwriting on a beautiful card, rather than receiving a text or even an email. The text or email is certainly better than nothing, but a card gives our fingers something to touch, the beauty of the paper or the image on the card gives our eyes something to enjoy, we hear the scrunching of the paper as we pull it out of an envelope, and oftentimes there's a slight fragrance of the paper, or of a spritz of scent intentionally included by the sender. It's a deeper and richer experience all around.

So, when possible, read from real books rather than computer files, especially when you're reading things like books of reflections, scriptures, books of quotations, or meditations. In addition to a fuller bodily experience, you're not fighting the in-your-face distractions of the beeps of notifications, or of checking your email yet one more time. Part of depth and focus is one-mindedness, a psychological willingness to listen deeply, whether to self, another person, or the other who is the author of whatever you are reading.

The same things go for writing: there's the feel of the pen, the feel of the paper, the crispness of the line of ink on the paper, and then there's all the other visual input from the design of your handwriting interspersed with when you choose to print, to adding images you've already printed from the computer or clipped from magazines, to the manipulation of glue and the stimulation of the colors and the symbolism of the images. Using more senses makes something feel more "real", and "real" fosters reflection and depth.

For most people, the computer is associated with work, entertainment, and with communications with others. With these practices, we're looking for a certain kind of quiet and a looking within to notice what we think, to articulate what we believe, to discover what we love — all without an audience or your public persona. Computers are just too distracting, too fragmented, too other-directed, and too unpredictable ("you mean Joe is texting me?! What would he be wanting from me now?!?")

In any of the practices having to do with writing, except for writing poetry, I suggest using "free writing" with or without a timer. If timed, set your timer for 1, 3, 5, or up to 15 minutes. The idea is to take your idea or prompt, put pen to paper, and keep your hand moving until the time is up. Don't worry about spelling or grammar, don't cross things out, don't self-edit. It doesn't have to be in sentences, just get it out. Single words or phrases are okay. As much as possible, you want to get away from your performative voice, where you are always modifying, even censoring what you want to say depending on who might be listening. If you're not using the subtle pressure of the timer to circumvent your inner critic or inner censor, just keep writing until you run out of what you want to say.

Then say to yourself "Drop deeper!" and write some more. Try to express the energy underneath the topic. If you find yourself going round and round in circles, or can't think of what to say in response to a prompt, use this prompt: "What I really want to say is …" And go for it. If you surprise yourself with what you write, so much the better.

Of course, to write like this, you need to have confidence that no one will be reading your writing without your invitation or permission. In Chapter Two I've written a lot about privacy for your journal and expressive work, but here are a few more ideas specifically for excerpts from your journal that when you reread them, you're surprised by how shocking or incendiary they are. Try not to just throw it out as fast as you can. You might be telling yourself some truth that your mind isn't quite ready to know, but if you keep denying these ideas by destroying them, you might be causing yourself unnecessary difficulty. You can paste another page or an image over your writing to keep it away from casual reading. If you do this, glue, staple, or tape the new page or image just around the edges so that you yourself can go back at a later time to look at what you wrote. If the previous page in your journal is blank, you can hide your writing by taping your page to the previous one, this time taping just over the edges. You can also carefully cut out the page and insert it in a pocket you make by taping pages together with only the top open to slide the page into. You can fold the page into a regular envelope, seal it, and glue or tape the regular envelope into or in the back of your journal. Think of old movies where there are secret messages enclosed in books, and let your imagination fly!

If you know in advance of writing that you want to express yourself completely freely and don't want to keep the writing, the next best thing to invisible ink is to write using a watercolor pencil. Write what you want, then take a wet paintbrush to activate the color in the pencil. You will end up with a page lightly colored, but unintelligible. Or you could write with any tool across a page, then turn the page 45 degrees and write right over your text. Then turn your page again 45 degrees and continue to write. You will have a page of obvious writing, yet you won't be able to read anything except a word here and there. These two techniques are excellent for when you know you want to rant about something, or just express and get anger out of you. You might know that you're not going to be writing anything that is worth reading later, but you want to honor your need to get it out. When you look at that page later, you'll remember the release of your emotions, but won't embarrass yourself by reliving the rant. Don't underestimate the value of writing something that you will immediately "destroy". Catharsis is very useful. In general, however, I encourage you to make it possible for yourself to read your writing again in the future in order to benefit from hindsight and to mark your change and progress in ideas and attitudes. One practical tip is to use initials or code for the names of other people in your journals. You'll remember who they are, but it might save hurt and hassle if your journal were to fall into the wrong hands. Yes, careful readers might guess at who you wrote about, but at least the names aren't there drawing attention to those particular passages.

Writing regularly in private journals is the easiest, most accessible, and least expensive tool we have for getting to know yourself and exploring your depths. You can very often write even in the presence of other people; most people are very unlikely to ask what you're writing about or ask to read it. Of course, keep your privacy needs in mind and store your journal as you need to. Write your thoughts spontaneously; don't worry about contradictions, don't write for an audience, don't worry about whether what you're saying is right or wrong. Go for the jugular. And finally, you have complete permission to write the worst junk possible. Just like in an old second-hand store, you never know when you'll find the smallest little treasure mixed in. And if there's no treasure, just turn the page and write again, just as you would leave the store and check out the next one.

Within each of us is a treasure load of creativity, images, and ideas which can animate us to live an authentic, meaningful life, one that can begin to kindle healing, transformation, and sustainability in all within our reach. By documenting the stories of our navigating these profound difficulties, whether the pain be disappointments, crises, spiritual doubting, or chronic illness, this documentation is an honoring of your unique life. By reflecting on all this data, then, you can discover the portals in wounds and challenges that will take you to a deeper, more soulful, compassionate life. Now, to the collection of that data!

Books to Inspire You

There are all sorts of books full of quotations or short meditations that are now available, compiled specifically for people who don't have a lot of time to read, but who still want an inspiring thought to begin their day. There are often daybooks with a quote for the day all by one person, usually entitled something like *A Year of* _____, or *365 Days* with _____. They have short chapters, or one page a day. Books of short vignettes are in this category, too, books like the *Chicken Soup for the* _____ series. What's great about these books is that you don't have to think a lot about what you're going to read or write in response to it. Just turn the page and there's an idea. The other great thing about these kinds of books is that they are everywhere, easy to access and often free or very low cost. Besides the library, they're easily gotten from thrift stores or borrowed from friends who received them as Christmas presents. Or you can raid my bathroom! I often have a few in the magazine rack I have in there!

The quality of the books vary, of course, but if you're just using them as a starting off point, most any of them will work unless they are sarcastic or satirical. Read the page or the quotation, and then free-write in response for 10 or 15 minutes. Start out by writing out the quote or the topic, then respond: Do you like it? Does it speak to your situation in life? Does it leave you flat or even aggravate you a little? Why? Go off on a tangent and write whatever comes to mind. When the timer goes off, reread what you've written, and let both the quotation or meditation piece and your response to it roll around in the back of your head as the day proceeds. If you have more thoughts, add them to your journal whenever you get the chance. Ask yourself "How does this apply to my life, now?"

Quiet Books, or "Underlining Sentences"

When I was a teenager, I was a fan of political thrillers and spy novels. But I found that if I read them just before going to bed my brain was often too revved up to go to sleep, and my dreams were just one chase scene after another. I stumbled upon a good solution that has served me well since then. I keep a "quiet book" on the go, reading it for 15 - 30 minutes before bed. A "quiet book" is any book that settles you down into a thoughtful or mellow mood – for me, a book of essays does it, a non-fiction book from authors I like, or some biographies. A "quiet book" is NOT a book with an exciting plot line, or one that relates one adventure after another. Some quiet humor is good, but a laugh out loud book doesn't do. Almost any book of poetry is great.

Use these books as you would a book to inspire you. Read a short portion, then write, either in response to what you read, or about something completely different. The idea is that the book serves to separate you from whatever you were engaged in before you sat down to read and write, setting the mood into a quieter or more reflective feeling, releasing you from anxieties or obsessive thinking. Some of my favorite authors in this category are Annie Dillard, Anne Lamott, Richard Rohr, Thich Nhat Hahn, Natalie Goldberg, or Joan Chittister. You'll have your own favorites. If you don't yet, look these authors up on Amazon, and check out the further selections they advertise until you find authors you love. Ask friends for suggestions, or spend a glorious afternoon browsing in a bookstore.

There's a story told about the mythologist Joseph Campbell that when he was asked by various gurus and yogis, spiritual teachers, or monks from a variety of religions what his own spiritual practice was, he responded by saying that he "underlines sentences." So this is the "Underlining Sentences" practice.

Sacred Scriptures of the World

If there's one place in this world where the wisdom about life's depth dimensions may be found, it is in the writings that come from the communities of people who have founded the major world religions. The reason that I'm suggesting first the major world religions is that they have stuck around in this world over long periods of time, and many people throughout history have found inspiration and instruction in these writings. These religions are still here, and still influencing their followers. And, in an intercultural, diverse, interfaith world, it's only polite to have some familiarity with others' spiritualities. You don't need to access their Sacred Books first; perhaps just finding some literature that explains their beliefs would be most useful. These can be found on the internet, of course, but ensure that you are reading something that originates within the religion itself, not simply a Wikipedia article or, for instance, a Catholic's commentary on what Buddhism is like. Those writings may well be worth reading, but for here, I'm inviting you to imagine what the world is like from inside another religion, to explore the worldview and beliefs in as accurate a way possible. For instance, my family is not Muslim, but we are reading *The Study Quran, ed. Seyyed Hossein Nasr*, a translation with commentary prepared by an Islamic scholar first for Muslims but also for a general public. Sometimes it is very difficult for an outsider to understand a religion's sacred texts if we don't have any knowledge of the context in which they were written, or how a text is generally interpreted by believers themselves in the present age. So be as careful as you can that you are not reading just a few verses out of context of the whole's meaning, and not reading commentary written by someone who is negatively critical of the religion.

Another way to begin to understand another religion is to read introductions or instructional material aimed toward children written by the religion's leaders to teach their children the faith. It's easy to feel overwhelmed, and sometimes when I suggest this to people, I get comments such as "But I was raised Christian, and I haven't even read the Gospels fully myself!" Remember there's no hurry, and there's no "finish line" you're trying to reach. We all have the rest of our lives to explore these things. Find some sources that are authentic and respectful, then read a little, write a little; read a little, write a little; and repeat as many times as you want.

If you find things you don't understand or that you disagree with, make note of these things and as time goes by, be open to finding the answers from reputable sources. Really try to imagine how the writing makes sense to someone from that religion or culture, but don't get agitated if it all seems so, well, *foreign*. Some religions actively discourage their followers from learning about others' religions. For our purposes, however, we are not reading in order to be converted, we're reading for breadth and understanding. A useful perspective is to not assume that other religions are completely *"Other"*, but may be "in addition to" what we already know, perhaps thinking of them as different parts of ourselves that we haven't yet come to know. And remember, of course, that as a sovereign soul you don't have to believe anything you read! Be curious and respectful, and you may find that the whole world opens up for your exploration.

Along with Sacred Scriptures, you can read the texts of holy persons, especially world mystics. Read a passage, write in response. Repeat. There is a wide variety of places to start; several authors or texts that are readily available are the *Tao de Ching, The Conference of the Birds by Farid ud-Din Attar*, poetry by Rumi, writings by Francis of Assisi, Teresa of Avila, Hildegard of Bingen, Meister Eckhart, Rabia, Tagore, Hafiz, John of the Cross, and many, many others. We live in a time when there has never been so much available to interested explorers. I often begin to despair of the junk that is sometimes pushed at us, but then I remember that there is so much treasure as well.

With any of these texts, you may not "get it" at first reading. If that is your experience, go back to something that you have some familiarity with: read the Psalms contemplatively, if you are familiar with Judaism or Christianity, or read through the Wisdom books of the Bible. Our western culture has primed us all through our literature to understand the books of the Bible more easily.

Always, read a little, write in response. You can make this a kind of formal study, but don't keep it just on an intellectual basis; write from the heart, asking what kind of wisdom might be there for you, now.

Lectio Divina

Lectio Divina means "sacred reading", and is a very ancient practice in taking the word of God into our hearts. Originating in Catholic Christian monasteries, it was referred to as "chewing" on the word of God, or ruminating or savoring God's gift to us of God's wisdom. This practice can be done, though, with any kind of written quotation or section of poetry as a way of internalizing it and finding out what message there may be for you, today. Start with having chosen your quotation (perhaps from another day's depth dimension practice), then settling into your chair with a couple of deep breaths, inviting silence. The length of the selection should be short, from a few lines to a short paragraph.

There are four movements in Lectio Divina, each more or less lasting about 2-5 minutes. The first, "Lectio," is reading the selection slowly and mindfully, noting its general meaning and also noticing if there is a word or phrase that sticks out to you. Give yourself a couple of minutes to sink into this. You're not reading here to get to the end of the chapter, but to savor just these few sentences with the ear of the heart.

In the second movement, "Meditatio," read the passage again and ask if there is something here that speaks to your own life. Are the words a comfort, an answer to something you've been wondering about, or perhaps a challenge to you in your life now? Meditate on the meaning of the selection for you personally.

In the third movement, "Oratio," traditionally you would move into prayer, or a dialogue with God, or Source. Read the passage for the third time. If the idea of praying feels strange to you, just imagine having a discussion with a wise person you know about the passage. If you have any questions or concerns about the passage, imagine how your wise person would respond. If you don't particularly like the passage, or what came up when you were meditating on how it might relate to your own life, acknowledge that here, and ask yourself and your wise person if you might be missing something.

The fourth movement, "Contemplatio," is a time of silence, of just letting the passage work its way with you, wandering around in your brain and heart, without intentional effort on your part. Read the passage for the final time, then relax into whatever happens next. As thoughts arise, make note of them, but let them go without grabbing onto them and wrestling them down. Just "be" with the passage, letting your intuition receive whatever comes.

When your time is up, there are several ways you can end. You could smile and end with thanks for however your experience went. You could copy out the passage in your journal. Or you could write out any thoughts, insights, or new understandings that occurred to you, including the content of the dialogue with your wise person.

Variations:

—When you're first getting started with this practice, it's good to have the four movements written down in your journal in order to remind you to move through each. As you get more familiar with the practice, though, you can go back and forth among the movements, weaving your thoughts and questions through the four ways of engaging with the text, almost "dancing" with the wisdom it offers. It's not a formula, but rather a suggestion of how to interact with a text in order to extract its wisdom through respect for the text itself and for your unique life that comes to that text.

—The text need not be words on a page. There is Visio Divina, Musica Divina, and also examining your own life in a sacred manner. You might do this practice with a piece of artwork, or an image or photograph, whether one of your own or a historical photograph. You might listen to a (short) piece of music and go through these movements. If you are looking at your life in a sacred manner, it's most useful to either pick a short vignette ahead of time, or to just see what arises as you sit down to do this practice. The temptation is to spend your time reliving the scene, thinking of what you could have or should have said or responded to, and otherwise getting lost in the memory. Resist that temptation. Keep the four movements of the practice in front of you, and remember that your intention is to mine the memory for what wisdom there might be now for you in looking at it. Think of yourself as reporting the incident, not reliving it.

—When revisiting memories of your own life in this practice, if you get caught into reliving an unpleasant experience, immediately try to see the experience from the point of view of the compassionate Divine or of your wise person with unconditional love for you. If that proves difficult, ask whoever or whatever might be of help to assist you in seeing the past experience in a different way. Imagine the Divine or your helpful wise person being right there with you, either revealing any wisdom that can come of the incident, or leading you away from the incident that is from the past, reminding you that you are in a different place in your life now and that it is not happening to you at this moment. Tread cautiously and compassionately, but there is no need for fear.

—While it is optional as to whether or not you record what comes to you during this practice, remember that good insights are often lost in the busyness of daily life. Try to record at least a few words so that you can keep the wisdom and insights that come to consciousness.

Collections

Once you start finding poetry or quotations that are meaningful to you, you'll probably want to keep a copy so as to enjoy it again. Of course, you can always google it, or keep your poetry and quotation files on the computer, but if you do, and want to access them during your depth dimension practice time, you expose yourself to the distraction of the computer. Who can resist checking your email — just for a second?

Also, there is something about writing down the pieces in your own hand, or in nice lettering, that helps to incorporate the writing into your whole self. It slows you down, helping you to memorize the piece if you wish to, and helping it live in you so that the words can come up to remind you of their wisdom in the moments of everyday life when you might need them the most. Writing in your collections is a peaceful, reflective activity.

There is no end to beautiful blank books that you can purchase for your collections, and later in this chapter I will give instructions as to how to make a simple pamphlet blank book either from plain copying paper or from fine watercolor paper.

Give a little consideration as to if and how you might want to decorate the cover or the pages in the future. Know that if you plan to use markers or watercolors in the future, the colors might bleed through the paper to the other side. Colored pencils and colored gel pens are usually fine, even on plain copying paper. Otherwise, use quality paper.

Also, consider the size of the book you will use. I have often chosen to create larger notebooks of 7 in. by 9 in. or 8 1/2 in. by 11 in. This allows me to print out something on the computer, trim it, and easily use a gluestick to include it into the notebooks.

Over the years, I have collected many books filled with quotations and poetry that have meant something to me. It's a joy to revisit them and to remember where I was in my life when I wrote them down, knowing how full a life I have lived. They are also a source of ready material if I need a poem to include in a card for someone or for preparing articles or talks.

If you personally copy out other people's work, be very exact and accurate. It's a matter of respect and courtesy, but it can be very helpful if you decide to include their words in your own writing. Also include, if you have it, full bibliographical information so that you don't need to look it all up again. If you're not copying the words from a book or article that the author has written themselves, if you want to use your copy of their words in your own work, it's worth doing a search to clarify that you have their work accurate and complete. People like Rumi, Abraham Lincoln, and Albert Einstein have had all kinds of quotes attributed to them that they never ever said!

We can also hear something very different from what was actually said or written. Just in the last few months I have mutilated a couple of quotations that I read on billboards. One said "Be willing to leave what you know," but I remembered "Be willing to believe what you know." I heard what I wanted or needed to hear. The other was a poster with some street people pictured who were obviously suffering with the cold. I thought it said "Poetry is real," but couldn't figure out why they used that image with that quote. On further examination, the poster actually said "Poverty is real."

Another thing to collect, whether in a separate book or just in the back of your journal, are words that strike you in some way. You can collect words that "shimmer" for you, words that you've overheard, words that make you wonder, words that annoy you because they've become such buzz words, words that suddenly come up, out of the blue, or words that you've heard in your dreams. Collect words that make you smile, that sound fun, that are puns. You could write them in list form, or you could also write each one on half of an index card and store them in an envelope. Here are a few just to get you started: love, whole, cave, rose, sunshine, star, smell of cigarettes, fear, vulnerable, impact, shimmer, tremble, fullness, burble, murmuration, ululation, onomatopoeic, matter, slight, embodiment.

These collections of words can also launch the writing of your own poetry, and any prompt can be responded to in poetic form rather than in prose. There are many ways to inspire the writing of poetry, but that, alas, would be another book!

Creating a "Book of Books"

Since 1992 I've filled several blank books with the titles and authors of books that I have read, audio programs I've listened to, and some of the videos that I have seen. I start a new page at the beginning of every month, and truly, my only regret about doing this is that I didn't start years earlier. It's wonderful to look back and see the stages I've gone through, the "obsessions" I've followed. I only write down the title and the author, but of course you could include a short review or some quotes from the book, or note how you discovered it, whether out of your own interest or someone's suggestion. I really advise you to not make this burdensome for yourself in any way. You want to ensure that it's easy to do so that you'll actually do it, and then you'll get a fairly accurate record of what you've taken in.

It's easy to be overwhelmed with ideas that sound so appealing, but then feel bad when we've set ourselves up with too much to do. Keep your expectations small and doable. Whenever I finish something, I write down just the title and author. Anything more is dessert.

Yearly, or at the completion of a volume, I look over what I've recorded and reflect a little: was I happy with what I ingested that year? Are there other genres, or types of authors, that I want to include in my reading? Is my reading fueled by obligation, by book club membership, classes, or by my own curiosities?

So often, we just consume whatever is in front of us, whether that's our phone (there's a reason it's called a "feed"), Netflix, or the Internet, and we are therefore constantly exposed to certain kinds of advertising telling us what kinds of things we're supposed to want, and what kind of life we're supposed to live. It all has a cumulative effect over years of taking this stuff in. Ask yourself if this is the effect that you want in your life. Are you directing your life energy, or are you brainwashed only by what "they" (advertisers, influencers, producers, industry) want you to know and to be? Just as you read the labels on your food to know whether what we're ingesting is healthy or not, why not take a look at what we're putting into our brain? We're not born consumers, we become them. Wouldn't you rather be a self-directed creative, a one-of-kind original?

Encouragement Files

Over the years, almost all of us have received notes or official letters that thank us for a job well done or for our thoughtfulness, or that have given us a compliment or an appreciation. These can be anything from a positive Job Evaluation to an email where your friend notices your great sense of humor. It's nice to keep copies of these "love notes" for the days when you're feeling emotionally fragile or you've received criticism. They can remind you that it's just a bad day, and that you're not really a major loser.

I've found it effective to make a photocopy of whatever document holds the positive affirmation, so that I have two hard copies. I put the original in an official external file folder that is titled "Encouragement File," and I glue the other one right into my journal. The one in my journal has all the historical context of my life surrounding it; the file has the simple pile of positive letters. Be sure that they have the date on them.

Sometimes, when someone has said something positive about me in a verbal conversation, I will write about it in my journal, with a marginal note saying "Encouragement." So many of us have been taught that we shouldn't accept or focus on compliments, but I think there's a place for the honest appreciation of your good qualities. It's basically a truthful acknowledgement of the fullness of who you are, and noting them can help you learn to accept compliments realistically and gracefully with a warm "Thank you." So many of us work so hard to do the right thing or to complete a job well, and it's so wonderful when someone else notices your efforts or your accomplishments. It reminds you that the effort is worth it, and that your efforts and work do matter in this world. It's encouragement to continue on to create the kind of world you want to live in, the kind of world that so many of us would like to live in.

Gratitude Journals

These have become quite popular, and research has even shown the good effects of such a practice. One of the reasons as to why they are so effective is that humans have a tendency to remember more easily the negative things that happen than the positive things. We must make a conscious effort to overcome that bias, just to remember a somewhat accurate picture of what our days were actually like.

These Gratitude Journals need not be kept daily in order to do their good work. A couple of times a week works well, or even once a week. Creating a habit of doing it regularly, though, keeps you at it; it's easy to forget one day after another until you just don't have a Gratitude Journal. Some people keep it in their regular journal, adding the gratitudes right in among the other entries. If you choose to do it this way, I suggest having some way to set them off in the text so that you can look through them without needing to read the entire journal. You could circle or box them off, use arrows in the margins, or use a highlighter or colored pencil over what you write.

Another habit that works well is to have a dedicated notebook, and keep that notebook and pen in its own place, perhaps by your bed or even in the bathroom. You could attach writing in it to another habit you do regularly, say brushing your teeth before bed. This makes it much more likely that you'll actually write in it, and it also sets you up for falling asleep more easily, remembering pleasant things from your life as you relax in bed.

Try not to write the same three things every day, such as "My spouse, my children, my health." Think of recording events unique to that day, rather than just nouns, or things that you have. "When Joanne brought me a coffee back from her break" or "Grateful that the election turned out the way I wanted" are examples of how to remember the richness as well as complexity of your daily life. When you reread your Gratitude Journal, you will have a collection of vignettes and the people who make up your life. If you record the good times, no matter how small, it will be evidence that even during the hard times in life, you were able to have encouragement and kindness. It's well known that for people who keep journals, they often work through problems and conflicts in its pages. A Gratitude Journal balances out the negativity with positives as well, reflecting a fuller truth.

The Examen, or Examination of Conscience

From St. Ignatius Loyola in the 16th century to Benjamin Franklin in the 18th and on to Stephen Covey in the 20th, many sincere people have encouraged some sort of regular examination of how successful we are regarding our attempts to live well and kindly. When I was growing up as a dutiful Catholic girl in the 60's, we were taught a version of The Examination of Conscience where before bed we were to look over our day and notice where we had sinned against God or our neighbor. With a "firm purpose of amendment," we were to ask forgiveness for our transgressions and resolve to do better the next day. It came across to me at that age as a "do-it-yourself Confession," and I "confess" that it never appealed to me very much.

As I think of things differently now, I've found that I have taken up my own version of this. I keep the good intent of the Examen while dropping the guilt-producing message of constantly never doing, or being, enough. Near the end of the day I spend a few minutes listening deeply to the inner unfolding of my day.

As I'm clearing off my "mental desk," I go through my activities of the day, asking where there were events or interactions that need clarification or some sort of resolution. Oftentimes these are undone tasks that I need to make note of, but just as often they are memories of my harsh impatient words, hateful, or angry thoughts that I fueled way too long, or promises unfulfilled. And, just as often, too, there are the wonderful memories of the friendly interaction with the check-out person at the grocery store or the planning of an event with a co-worker that went blissfully smoothly, leaving us both with a sense of camaraderie and efficiency.

I don't look only at what happened outwardly during that day, but in stillness I contemplate the inner movements of the day as well. I consider each movement or event, my emotions, desires, anxieties, hopes, plans, fantasies, memories, and relationships, even how the dreams of the night before might have colored my day. I'm looking to be aware of the formation of my life from the inside as well as from the events that anyone could witness. And that often has practical results: I've found out that if I read a novel or watch a movie before bed, I never remember my dreams on that night, because I'm reliving the adventures of the novel or video I'd taken in. I've found out that when I wake up naturally rather than by an alarm clock, life is just so much sweeter. I've also found out that a light alarm rather than a sound alarm is a much kinder way to awaken when I do need an alarm. And, I've discovered that some interactions are so complex or hurtful that they won't be resolved with an apology or any one action. Those events I imaginatively bandage up, hoping that they will heal, and resolving to look at them again soon.

It's not so much that I examine my day with my datebook and journal in one hand and a magnifying glass in the other, it's more that I sit quietly and notice what arises. What's left undone, what brings me a smile?

Just as I make note in my Gratitude Journal of the things that went well, I make note, sometimes in my head or sometimes as a note in my journal, of the open loops that need to be resolved. An apology, a follow up — whatever is needed to try to match my life with my intentions, I figure out what I can do and find a time when I'll do it. If it only takes a short email to resolve something, I do it right away, and go to bed feeling a little more successful in living the life I want to live. Sometimes I need to give myself a little slack for not focusing on what I needed to do that day, sometimes I need a pep talk so as to generate a needed attitude adjustment.

One way to remember to do this is to give yourself a metaphorical rose every evening: the flower part of the rose is something to be grateful for, or something good that has happened that day; the thorns are the difficult, unpleasant things that we regret, that we really don't want in our lives but often can't help; and the buds are our good hopes, and planned actions, for what happens next — the promise for our future. You can draw a very simple rose in your journal and label each part with a word or two that reminds you of what has filled your day. But also remember to note your good intentions where you will be reminded to do them the next day.

This practice is helpful in several ways. Not only does it help you align your life with your intentions and how you wish the world to be; not only does it remind you of the mending of your life and therefore your part of the world that you can actively restore; not only does it help you fall asleep with a "clean conscience;" but thinking about these things, your good intentions and how you're not yet the perfect specimen you aspire to be (I hope you're laughing with me!) will fuel your dreams to come up with new ideas, new initiatives, and creative ways to solve problems that may have seemed intractable.

I recommend the practice. Not only daily, but monthly and yearly. Our own lives are at least as important as anyone's we might read in a biography, with the added advantage that we can actually act in our own lives, and influence the future for ourselves and others.

Lists

In the back of every one of my journals, I have several pages of lists: shopping lists, especially for places I don't go to very often; lists of places I want to visit; lists of videos I want to see, or books that I want to read; lists of topics I want to research more online; wish lists. Sometimes the lists are positively entertaining to compile: wish lists for a political rival, or for a difficult person in my life. (Try to keep the venom out!) Others are fanciful, but can get your imagination going, or be a form of brainstorming: wish list for a better world; wish list for your city; what is needed to make recycling easier; what I want to bring up at the next meeting; lists of wacky ideas to celebrate a birthday. Sometimes I like to write a list of things that I want to list: strong women to inspire me; historical indigenous events of this city; the number of ethnicities in the neighborhood. I may not have time to compile the list then and there, but the ideas aren't lost.

Of course you can write lists right in the middle of your other writing. If you want to find them later, use a post it note for a label. Keeping lists in your journal is a great place to store them — little pieces of papers aren't lost the next time someone else cleans off the table!

Lists help you acknowledge what you want in your life, or what you think is important. They make note of these things without you having to commit yourself to getting them right now, or making them happen right now. After they are written down, they can work in the back of your brain to help you align your life more closely with how you really want to live it.

"Muddy Angels"

This is another version of a list, but includes more than simply words or phrases one after another. Here you include the people who inspire you, or have influenced your life in some positive way, even though their whole lives may not be inspiring or anything that you would want to emulate. Dr. Clarissa Pinkola Estés uses the term "muddy angel" to describe these sorts of people and energy in our lives. I don't know all that she means by this term, but when I heard her say it, I immediately knew in my life who I would include in this category.

These could be people who might inspire you even by their bad examples, or by just one or two aspects of their characters. Who have you come into contact with who is outrageous, but makes you happier to be a human being? Who would never be canonized as a "saint", but still is someone who inspires you to let your soul shine?

They can be people in your family — often the "black sheep" in our families teach us a lot without ever even trying. They can be celebrities or characters in books. They can be street people who you witness being kind, or humorous in their requests for money. They don't even need to be people; have you seen animal or bird behavior that strikes you as hilarious, or touching?

At the minimum, list these characters so as to honor them for what they've brought into your life. You could go on to draw them, include their photographs, or find an image that reminds you of them. Try to describe in words, or in image or colors, the influence they've had on you, the feelings that they evoke in you. There are a few people in my life who will always be yellow people to me: bright, sunny, cheerful, noticeable. Think about the qualities that you're documenting, and see how you might express that quality yourself. How might you express even more of it?

If it's appropriate, think about letting them know the influence they've had on you with an appreciative email or card. Spread the joy around.

Perennial Quotes

Previously, I suggested writing in response to quotes that speak to you in some way, whether you agree with them or not. Here, I suggest you begin a list of quotes that you think would be interesting to revisit, say, every three years. These quotes should be thought provoking, and ones where you can lay your own life alongside of them to see how you are, now. When you make the list, note after each quote the dates that you wrote in response to it. Make this list on a separate piece of paper that can travel from journal to journal as you finish one and start another, or find a small blank book in which to collect these kinds of quotes. It is fascinating to reread your responses and see how you have changed (or not) over the years.

Here are three, just to get you started:
- "You need chaos in your soul to give birth to a dancing star." (Friedrich Nietzsche)
- "What is it you plan to do with your one wild and precious life?" (Mary Oliver)
- "Though her soul requires seeing, the culture around her requires sightlessness. Though her soul wishes to speak its truth, she is pressured to be silent." (Clarissa Pinkola Estés)

Affirmations

Much has been written about the power of affirmations, and many people feel very strongly that they either love them or hate them. I use affirmations as reminders of how I want to live, as reminders of things that I've spent some time thinking about, things that are different from the obligations and urgencies of daily life.

I find that the important thing is to write affirmations for yourself, rather than borrowing ones written by someone else, for someone else's life. Writing your own takes a little bit of time, a little bit of reflection, and a good dose of reality. And once you know what you want included in an affirmation, it's nice to summarize it into a pithy short sentence or two. This is why I recommend composing them and refining them in your journal.

Affirmations such as "I have the job of my dreams, I am wealthy beyond anything I could have hoped for, and I'm gorgeous — and thin, too!" are humorous fiction writing, not useful phrases that fit my particular life. When writing your own, think about what qualities or things you wish to exhibit or manifest in your life and why you want them.

Write them in the present tense as if you were already living those qualities or you already have those things. Most importantly, though, note how you feel when you state your affirmation. Do you have the response of "Yeah, right! Well, that's never going to happen, but I might as well go for it anyway"? Or do you have a sense that "Yes, this is who I really am, who I truly want to be, even though I'm not living it consistently in my life yet"? Or do you feel "I don't have this yet, but I know that I'm capable of working for what I want and I'll be able to get it sometime, maybe even sooner than I expect"? You want to craft your affirmation so that it reflects what is really important to YOU, and that you feel that even though it's not in your life at the present moment, it's possible to attain.

If it really feels impossible to attain, yet you really badly want it, you can still write an effective affirmation. It will take a little more self-examination, though. Ask yourself why you want it. Do you really want that exact thing, or do you want it because it will make you feel a certain way, or say something to other people about who you'd like to be? Getting clearer helps you hone a more effective affirmation. If it's a certain feeling that you want, say, for example, to feel successful, then you ask yourself what kinds of ways of living would make you feel successful. Don't just affirm what the media or the culture or your parents say is success, really examine what the conditions are that would give you that feeling of success. Perhaps it's not having a new car, but it is being admired by people whom you respect. Perhaps it is having financial security. Perhaps it is having a particular educational attainment.

Even if you don't know what would give you the feeling that you want, you can make an effective affirmation out of that. You could craft something like "I am learning what I need in my life to feel confident and strong." As you recite the affirmation, ideas might come that reveal some of those needs. Make a note of them and when you next sit down to revise your affirmations, incorporate those ideas. An example of how this affirmation could evolve is "I am physically active and my body is getting stronger each day" or "I speak up for myself at work with politeness and clarity."

These are just a couple of examples, but they illustrate how necessary it is to write affirmations that you believe are possible. If they don't feel possible, rework them to something along the way towards your seemingly impossible goal. Think of what the next step would be, or what kind of a person would make that happen.

Affirm the next step along the way, or affirm becoming the person who could make your goal possible. Always keep revising your affirmations as you and your life situation evolves.

And finally, once you have crafted an effective affirmation, copy it out onto a few pieces of paper or onto your computer. Put them up in places where you will come across them on a regular basis, but not where you will see them so often that they just become part of the wallpaper and you don't really notice them anymore. For instance, the inside of your bathroom cabinet will work, but probably not on your refrigerator. Setting your affirmation up as a screensaver could be helpful. Seeing them intermittently will surprise you a little every time you come across them, reminding you of desired goals. As they then sit in the back of your mind, your brain works to align your behavior with your goals, and you will see opportunities to either behave as the person you want to be, or you will notice and move toward the new opportunities to get what you're hoping to have. I don't believe affirmations are magic, but they can work as good reminders at regular intervals to work at what you've already identified as your most treasured goals.

Letters, Sent and Unsent

Oftentimes our correspondence says a lot about our lives and about the times when we wrote it. Letters are one of the primary resources of biographers, especially when they're sent to friends or relatives. So, collect the letters that you write and the emails that you send. They usually include a summary of what we've been up to, how we're feeling about outside events, and what we're thinking about or planning. These are all the things that many people record in their journals; only with letters, we don't need to rewrite all of it. You can keep them in a separate file, but I've found it helpful to immediately copy my letters and emails, and glue or tape them into my journal. It's easy and fast to do, and I know immediately where they're stored. I can also add notes about any of them right in my journal. For instance, if I've included a letter to an elderly relative, I may not want to burden them with some of the negative events in my life at the time of writing, but nevertheless want to note that I was thinking of those negative events the whole time I was writing, figuring out how to be both truthful and protective about personal events that I didn't want to share. That conflict and my attempts to resolve it in my letter might be something that will prove interesting to me when I reread the journal years later.

Letters that you don't intend to send are really useful, too, and may be easier to express than just an entry in your journal. They can help you to articulate your thoughts to an imagined correspondent, and are valuable resources as you imagine how your imagined recipient might respond to them. You can write a letter to a politician with all your passion and anger intact, and only later decide if you want to send it, or revise it before you send it. In any case, you have documented your feelings about a particular issue. Whether I write these by hand or on the computer I include them in my journal. You can also write to people who are not available to you anymore, such as deceased loved ones or historical figures. As you craft your words so that your imagined recipient can understand you well, you gain a new perspective on whatever you are writing about. You've kept a record of your issues, of your loneliness, or of your love for a departed one. Considering how much we don't know about whether we can communicate with the deceased, you may have had a real conversation. Letters to the Great Mystery that many call God are just as powerful, as well. I had one friend who "couldn't" write a journal, but she had a huge selection of letters she wrote, but never sent, to her sister and to others.

Dialogues

This depth dimension practice is similar to writing a letter that you do not intend to send, but here you write back to yourself from how you imagine your interlocutor would respond to you. When we admire someone, we often absorb some of their world view and values without being aware of it. When we allow ourselves to imagine how they would respond to questions from us or to our plans and dreams, we can access all that knowledge that we have unconsciously picked up from them, and benefit from their wisdom in our lives as combined with our own.

In other situations, we sometimes have leftover business that cannot be resolved in this life. An example would be an apology we never delivered before the recipient passed away. Or, not ever knowing why a parent acted the way they did; you can't ask now because they are in the wilds of dementia. Or, perhaps you never were able to confront an uncle or neighbor about how they abused you as a child.

Discern whether an unsent letter might be effective in bringing something to resolution, or if a dialogue might be better. Is it most important that you have your say, or do you really need some sort of response? Remember that this is not a reliable way to get information that you can be absolutely certain is accurate in consensual reality, or that could ever be used as evidence in a court of law. It is, at base, only what you intuit or imagine they would have said in response to your queries. However, when done in deep reflection and open heartedness, enough information can come to be both helpful and comforting. It might also give you a clue as to where you might find the actual answer you're looking for. Even the lack of an answer tells you that perhaps the person themselves wouldn't have an answer to your questions.

Go about this slowly and with great respect for yourself. Set an intention that this will not be just a hashing over of an old grievance that you've hashed over for years, but that you are sincerely asking for something new to be revealed to you. Ensure that you will not be disturbed for 20 minutes or half an hour. Center yourself, take a few deep breaths, and hold your other person in your mind's eye. In your journal, fold or actually draw a line down the middle of the page, then assign one half to what you say, and assign the other half or page to what your interlocutor has to say. Start by greeting your person and asking a first question by writing it on the page. Be open to an answer suggesting itself to your mind. Some people hear words; other people just get a sense of what the other person is saying even though they don't hear anything. It might even feel like you're making it up, and that's okay. It gets more comfortable after the first couple of questions. At this time don't question too much what comes. Allow yourself to give this a try, even if you feel it's probably just a waste of time. Once you have an idea of the words they would or might say, then using your non-dominant hand, write out what you "hear" or imagine that your person is saying. Yes, it's difficult to write with your non-dominant hand, but doing so allows you to access a different part of yourself, of your brain, that can communicate more than just what your rational self is thinking. You might surprise yourself in that your hand goes to write something a bit different than what you thought you would write. Go slowly enough for it to be legible enough for you to get the meaning, but other than that don't worry about how nice it looks or how tidy it comes out. Anytime I use this Dialogue practice, it takes pages and pages, and looks a mess. Yet, it's helpful.

Go on, back and forth, until you come to some completion as conversations often do, or else you run out of time. You may want to close by thanking your person for talking with you, and asking if you can come back again to talk with them. It's also customary to give them a gift, and then to ask them for a gift. These are not literal, material gifts. They can be things such as a sunny day, or an imagined apple or leaf. This gift is to symbolize good will and respect, and the sense of exchange that you are having with your interlocutor.

It's pretty normal to wonder afterwards if you made it all up. It took me years and years before I ever told anyone that I would sometimes do this in my journal. Ultimately, though, so what if you "made it up"? In this dancing world of particles that are at the same time a form of light, what do we really know about where thoughts come from? For me, a common sense way to interpret this is that, yes, I may be imagining what their answers to my questions are, but as long as I hold open the possibility that I may be interpreting it wrong, I accept whatever information comes. In "real" life, that is, in consensual reality, when we have conversations with others, communication is so often muddled. It's hard to know if you understood the other person perfectly, even *if* they themselves were clear about what they wanted to say to you.

The questions to ask are: *Was this helpful?* and *Of what use is this in my life now?* Helpfulness and usefulness are the criteria to assess whether or not this technique is a good one for you. If you hear abusive or unkind responses, interrupt the conversation immediately and say (and write down), "I will not accept any abuse! Please tell me what you have to say in a respectful way so that I can hear it, or this conversation is over." If you continue to hear abuse, stop the dialogue, go wash your hands, drink a glass of clean water, and/or take a shower. Care for yourself well. You are in control of these dialogues, and you do not have to tolerate anything that is abusive or frightening. Tell it to be gone!

Assuming, though, that you had a more or less good conversation, you can leave it for now, or you can reread it immediately. At some point you want to revisit the dialogue to see if you have any more information than you did before, or if you feel any differently about either the person or the situation you talked about. Ask yourself if there are any actions that you could or should take to really take in the new information or feeling, such as visiting a gravesite, talking to someone about this all, making a craft or talisman to memorialize the conversation, or writing an unsent letter to the person. Trust your intuition, but also remember that there's no need to act quickly or rashly in any way.

Variation:

Consulting Your Board of Directors, or Checking in with Your Elders
You can have an inner conversation with people whom you admire where you ask for advice or wisdom about what's going on in your life at a particular

time. Imagine who you would invite to your personal Board of Directors or Mentorship Group (usually assembled for outer world or career advice), or to your Circle of Elders (associated more with your inner life, your spirituality, and your relationships). These people can be historical figures, some of your beloved dead, or even people who are alive whom you respect. Do not include people whom you can actually access in your daily life. Go to see those people in person as you can, and ask for their advice or guidance. In your journal write out their names, and why you've invited them for your meeting. After a time of centering, imagine them sitting at the table surrounding you (or wherever you would want to have your meeting), and then write down how you are opening the meeting. Try to involve all your senses when imagining the meeting, and be in it with as many details as possible. What are they wearing? What did you bring with you? Is it during the day or in the evening? Etcetera.

Write down the discussion you are having at the meeting, again using your dominant hand to write your part and using your non-dominant hand to write their responses and contributions. You can write it down word for word, or in summary form.

Then close the meeting and analyze as you would a dialogue with one person.

Brain Dump

There are just some days when you feel like you have weasels running up and down your veins. Other days it feels like a riot is going on in your brain. Sometimes I can listen to a friend full of anxiety starting to list what she's worried about and what she has to do, and her eyes get wider while her speech gets faster and faster. It's almost as if I can see her getting wound up tighter and tighter and tighter, ready to explode like a rocket and chaotically fly away! Those aren't happy moments.

While some physical activity might be a good way to bring some relief, sometimes a brisk walk or run just isn't practical. As well, if the chaos is predominantly in your thoughts, you could just end up taking your brain for a run and come back even more agitated. Instead, just dump it all out onto the page. Write about anything and everything that you're thinking, as fast as you can. Don't slow down to make complete sentences. Make lists all over the page; use abbreviations, arrows, exclamation points, and anything else that throws down onto the page how you're feeling, one weasel by one weasel. Whenever you slow down and can't think of what to write next, write down "Is that all?" That usually brings a whole new set of thoughts that need to be gotten out.

Sometimes, if you have a set of colored pens or markers, you can grab the color that goes with the thought and write away, big and bold. If one page isn't enough, cover 3 or 10. Keep going until everything is out, and you feel your energy palpably shift. You'll probably have quite the mess in front of you!

You can stop there, or you can work with what you've got now that you can see clearly right in front of you what used to be the tangled mess in your brain. You can categorize what you've written by topic or issue, or by "Things I have to do," "Things I'm worried about," "Things that piss me off," "Things I have to buy or fix," "Things that aren't mine to worry about!" Once you have the words, you can organize them into webs or maps, showing the relationships and complexities of the various topics, and the timelines of what must be done before you can do the next things. You can put either the starting point or the ending point in the middle, and add elements either forwards or backwards. An example is that I might want such and such done, but before that happens, x, y, and z must happen. But before x, y, and z can happen, k, l, and m must be accomplished. And so on. This little frenzied fit can actually end up as an Action Plan and Flow-Chart, outlining who needs to be responsible for each piece, but most importantly, what the next possible step might be for you.

"What's the next step?" "And the next step after that?" are the most helpful questions to find answers to when our brains are rioting. Then you can ask "And who should be doing that step?" That's my first aid for chaos. It sounds easy, and sometimes it is. Your mileage may vary.

Brain dumps are also both entertaining and enlightening to look at years from now. You will understand so much more of what kinds of things bother you the most, and what kinds of situations make you feel helpless. You can discover your best ways of dealing with feeling overwhelmed, and perhaps most importantly, you will develop such compassion for your younger self, remembering how hard it was for you at times, and how hard you worked.

Praying in Colors and Doodles

When we have friends and colleagues who experience illness or other difficult setbacks, we often send a heartfelt email saying "Sending prayers and good wishes", and leave it at that. Often there is nothing practical that we can do to help, and sometimes we even dislike hearing about these situations because it can heighten the uncomfortable feelings of impotence and helplessness we may already be feeling in other parts of our lives.

Whether you are someone who believes in the power of prayer, or someone who has serious doubts as to whether it makes any difference, "praying" in colors and doodles is a helpful activity. At the minimum, it helps you to feel calmer as you list the persons for whom you wish well and play with colors on the page. You feel at least that you are sending the good wishes that you'd promised. My teacher Dr. Clarissa Pinkola Estés defines prayer as "Good thought aimed well," and I think that's as good an explanation as any. We just do not know the effect of good thoughts, nor do we know if there is such a thing as telepathy, especially between people who care deeply for one another. And, ultimately we do not know what powers there may be in the universe who can answer calls for help. We would probably be worrying about the suffering person anyway; sending good thoughts and asking for help from anyone and anything that can help is more positive than grumbling about how awful everything is for everybody.

So, get out your colored pens or pencils, and think of where you want to aim your good thoughts. Doodle some shapes such as circles, banners, triangles, or spirals, and print the names and situations you care about inside or around your doodles. Continue to embellish, add curlicues, lines, arrows or whatever shape your pen seems to take on its own. You can doodle a simple tree, and put the names on each of the branches. You can doodle a ladder and write your names on each rung. Doodle a house plan and put each concern into a new room. As you do so, imagine the person or situation in their best health or in the solution to their situations. Imagine, and draw, golden light, or light of any color, shining on them. Imagine happiness coming out from them, and portray that in some way, perhaps by squiggly lines coming out from their names. You can do whatever you feel like doing. Try to just keep your intentions positive toward them and try to imagine them in their best solutions.

Sometimes, you may think of some practical action to take, and if so, note that somewhere so that you will do it. Perhaps you may find that you really care deeply about people suffering in a particular situation, and decide to volunteer or donate money to organizations that are alleviating that particular problem in our world. By this "prayer doodling" you're giving your imagination some time to roam and to think new thoughts, or wander outside of the box of how difficult situations are usually addressed. When you come to a close, look at your page of colors, names, and doodles, and feel good that at the very least, you are sending positive energy into this broken world while adding color to your journal.

Hurricanes to Hope

Venting is a time honored way of using a journal, and for some people who have kept journals, they are disappointed that when they go to reread their old ones, they read all this venom, anger, and sadness even as they remember those times to have overall been okay enough. The evidence they see in their journals doesn't reflect the whole truth of those times, and they wonder about the value of keeping all that negative stuff. They're rightfully concerned that if their heirs were to read those journals, they would think that all their mother could do was complain about her life. Bonfires ensue, as they then ceremonially burn all their old journals.

Having been at a bonfire or two, I see the point in that. At the same time, I wish those journal keepers would have known how to use that anger and venom as fuel in the creation of a better life. Heirs who would read those kinds of processes could well marvel at the creativity and resilience of their ancestor.

More recently, people vent more in public on social media than they do in their private notebooks, spreading the venom around where it stays for years, even after their deaths. I suggest a more useful way to express your anger and outrage. First of all, go ahead and vent. Like a brain dump, get it all out. When you feel you don't have anything more to write, ask yourself "Is that all?" Keep going until you're fully spent. Remember to use initials or code names if you're expressing venom towards real people.

Make a deal with yourself that you will allow yourself your full outrage, but that after the written hurricane you will take each piece of venom and articulate what you WANT to see happen in your world, whether personal or public. Come up with ideas, even "crazy" ones, and let your imagination go outside the box to create the world you want to see. Most of your wants will not be under your control to make happen, but sometimes, some of them will. Anger is like fire — a wildfire can destroy whole towns, but fires in our furnaces keep all of us from freezing each winter. Now that you know how strongly you feel about certain things, how will you direct this powerful energy?

Following Cycles

We all live our lives in cycles. There are the months and the years; there are menstrual cycles; there are production cycles in the workplace; there's project cycles of planning, execution, testing, release; there is the school year; there is the lunar cycle, and the seasonal heavenly cycle of solstices and equinoxes.

I have often incorporated different calendars into my journals. Usually glued into the backs of the journals, I might have a general one that is roughly a copy of my online calendar, one specific for work projects, and a third one specific for lunar cycles. Everyone's desires for what you want to track or follow will be different, so this practice is primarily an invitation to think about what and how you want to track various things in your life, as well as how fancy, color-coded, or artistic you want to make it.

Currently, I handcraft my journals in an 8 ½ by 11-inch size, one for each month. I used to divide them into calendar months, but currently I'm dividing by lunar months, starting each new journal on the new moon. I don't paste in calendars in the back, though I might paste in charts for longer projects, and just move those charts into the next journal as needed. I do write in a 2 page per week calendar in each journal, roughly interspersed with the rest of the pages, each at about ¼ of the way through the month, that is, through the journal. I use those weekly calendars to record the events of my life, the way many have done in those old-fashioned 5-Year diaries that have about three lines for each day. With two 8 ½ by 11-in. pages for one week, though, I have plenty of space. My other pages in the journal are for reflections, the kinds of depth dimension practices I'm writing about in this chapter, or pasting in ephemera such as brochures and programs for events I offered or attended.

Here are some of the questions to reflect upon when looking at cycles, especially at the beginning and end of cycles. What is changing? How is that reflected in my emotions about this change? What is my intention now? Am I depleted at the end of this, like the garden when all the fruits and vegetables have been harvested? Do I have enough energy to give to what is next? Am I getting enough rest? What needs to be composted, what needs to be thrown out? What is of value that can be given away? What beliefs and behaviors of mine are standing in the way now? Is everything supposed to always get bigger and better, and more productive? What relationships must go? What new allyships need to be forged? What is depleting me? What is energizing me? What is needed, now?

For example, here are some reflections for the Thanksgiving holiday. In your journal you can, of course, list some of the things you sincerely feel thankful for in your life. Even if it's a hard day, you can be thankful for the fact that you're not living in a refugee camp as too many of our brothers, sisters, and children are right now. Knowing how the holidays go for many of us, though, perhaps at the end of the day you can list the things in your life that you'd LIKE to be thankful for, but don't FEEL any gratitude for at the moment, such as the mother who criticized everything you cooked today, the cousin who broke your Tiffany lampshade when he punted a football in the living room, or the daughter who sulked throughout the meal and wouldn't pull out her earbuds. If you're feeling artsy, you can draw a basket in your journal, write out your "I'd LIKE to be thankful for's" on little pieces of paper, then glue these choice people and events as though they are falling into the basket. Draw alongside the basket a lid for it. Then the page can represent the challenges that are inescapably a part of your life, but by metaphorically putting them into the basket and closing the lid on it, these people and events do not need to obsess your thoughts, nor hijack the happiness that you do have.

Here are some questions I've asked myself for the past couple of Novembers, my most unfavorite month. I often think of November as just like February, only worse. In February, it's often miserable out, but there's only about a year until it'll get warmer; in November, you know it's going to be at least three years before the weather gets better. Does the upcoming winter speak to you of death? Of rest? Of hibernation? Of loss of color in the world? Of increased activity due to the school year? What's your soul's response to November? Write about it, or image it with color. Does black and white say it all? But if you add red to the black and white you have the three colors of alchemical transformation, and now other metaphorical possibilities open up.

For the Solstice or for Christmas, reflect on why virtually every spiritual tradition in the world has some sort of celebration at or near the Solstice, the time where darkness fills our days longer than at any other time of the year. At least it's this way in the northern hemisphere! Our southern neighbors are getting ready for the day of the longest sunshine and are planning beach parties. Imagine what it was like for humans thousands of years ago witnessing the daylight shrinking and shrinking, the weather getting colder and colder, and then the glorious realization that Life was coming back! The sun came back to warm the earth and its peoples, getting ready to receive the seed and save us, once again, from starvation and darkness. How are you waiting for light in your own life? With light as a metaphor for enlightenment and for the Divine, how are you waiting on the Great Mystery at this time in your life? How might you be waiting for God? What or who lights up your life?

These days, I follow the New Moon and the Full Moon each month. I reflect on the metaphors of darkness and light, of not being able to see in the dark, and of a light in the dark. At the New Moon I ask what I want to grow in my life, and make an affirmation out of that desire, recognizing that it's more like a hope than a plan, because I'm in the dark and can't see what's really going on. At the Full Moon, I notice what I see, what's going on in my life these days. I ask what I now want to let go of, what needs to recede, what I want to lessen, and create an affirmation for that. These are simple practices, but they help me to be in tune with what's going on both around me in the heavens, and what is going on within me. It's like a check-in with myself about every two weeks. It's the New Moon when I start a new journal each month, taking advantage of that new, creative energy, allowing me to collect all the goodness that might be coming. I "collect" both psychologically and spiritually, as well as physically as I begin to fill my journal with new thoughts, ideas, images and hopes. As the moon reaches its fullness, it's then time to start to bring that particular journal to a close, letting go of what's not working and clearing out space to let something else grow in my life.

Following cycles is a great way to notice how your inner energy and ideas fit, or don't fit, with the metaphors as well as the physical seasons outside and around you. As you know more about these fluctuating energies, it allows you to go with the flow a bit more often than fighting what's happening all around you, kicking and screaming as you're dragged into whatever cycle is next. Life, I find, has a bit more ease, and I learn to respond a bit more graciously to all that which surrounds me.

The Times of My Life

This is another way to become aware of cycles, predominantly your own inner cycles. I first learned this with Dr. Clarissa Pinkola Estés, though I've also seen it suggested in other places. I invite you to create a timeline of your life, with three "threads" of events. These threads are braided into each of our lives, and it's helpful to become conscious of them and their interconnectedness.

Have your timeline stretch across two or four pages in your journal, and divide in 3-5 year increments. On the top of the timeline, write in the major events of your life so far. Include events such as where and when you were born, major moves, high school graduation, first job and/or further education, significant relationships and marriage, travel, the death of grandparents or parents, and whatever else. These are types of events that you would share with a good friend when telling them about your life.

On the other side of the timeline, write in the major events of your physical body so far. Starting with your birth, note if it was particularly complex or traumatic. Record major illnesses or accidents. Very importantly, write in the pleasurable bodily events, too: experiences of the warmth of the sun, being sheltered by a tree or a forest, the pleasure of swimming, pleasurable sexual experience. Include the birth of children, chronic conditions, things like that.

On this same side of the timeline, but in a separate stream or color, write down whatever you would call the spiritual or soulful events of your life: baptism or confirmation, "Sunday school" or other religious instruction, a moving experience in nature, feelings of essential "rightness" in the world, feelings of God's presence, however you might describe that. Include times of trial and doubt, times and places you perhaps searched for life's meaning, moments of despair, even when or if you left your religious heritage or decided that you were an atheist or an agnostic.

You will probably have the top half of your pages covered with the events of your life. As you begin to reflect on all of this, be sure to NOT write in the bottom half of your pages. Use a next page in your journal, or a separate page that you can later glue in. You can write in point form or in a stream of consciousness technique.

Begin to notice where a lot of things happen in your life. Are there clusters of events and insights? Or are there long stretches of nothing much going on? What connections do you notice, if any? Have some of the eventful times of your body coincided with soul growth or a sense of personal identity? Have you moved a lot in your life, or traveled to visit other cultures? Are there any patterns in how those events correlate with your physical, bodily experience? Where have been the barren parts of your life so far? What about the "biggies" like first sexual experience, birth of a child, menopause? What about the times when your parents had a serious illness, or if they have died? Who nurtured you as a child? A parent? Or a little patch of woods? Or by the nuns at your elementary school?

What other questions or connections can you think of? Can you summarize any personal insights that this has brought? Be sure to include color, images, or symbols on your page.

If you enjoy this work, something very rewarding to do would be to create a timeline of the events of each of your parents' lives on separate timelines that you draw underneath your own timelines. Just fill them out to the best of your limited knowledge. Include what you know about their bodily life and soul life in their general events streams. Please don't rush out to share this exercise with your parents if they are still alive, though. Glean your own insights first; you may not ever want to share your thoughts on this. When I first did a variation of this exercise with a group with many participants, we became aware of many generational patterns we had not seen before. Even if you have no "aha!" experience with this, just thinking about your parents' childhoods and young adulthood can create a little more understanding and empathy.

Re-reading Your Journal: Putting the Year to Bed

This process also works if you have journals from a variety of years. You just gather them all together and work through them, re-reading them and making any notes you want (on today's page of your journal) of insights, comments, or dreams that have particularly impressed themselves on you. If you had done this review the previous year, go back to read your comments on the previous year as well.

Instead of, or in addition to, I suggest drawing a circle on your page and dividing it into four quadrants. I title the page "Keeping the Treasure" plus the year, and decorate with a color for each quadrant. Label the quadrants "Griefs and Letting Go," "Gratitudes," "Surprises and New Learnings," and "Successes." Then as I go through my calendar from the past year, I fill in the quadrants with what I remember. I add to the page throughout the next few days as different memories come up. You can do this exercise whether you have time to reread the whole year's journaling or not.

I have found that by doing this intentional remembering, I honor what I have gone through and what I have learned. It's a way to be conscious, to be really *alive* to this life, to not get swept up into the overculture's distractions which transform almost all of us from incredibly diverse human beings into perpetually dissatisfied consumers. I become aware of patterns and ongoing challenges, as well as remember so many good things that, because they were not earth-shattering in their impacts, are so easily forgotten. I also accumulate the information that allows me to make changes that will be effective and long-lasting.

For years I would write in my journals, then put them into boxes and never read them again. Then one Christmas, at a very low time in my life, I house-sat for a friend for 10 days. Pulled out of my daily life and routines, I decided to read through my journals — at that time, about 7 or 8 years' worth. Since I had had many struggles during those years, I steeled myself for a difficult, depressing read, but something in me compelled me to take on the project anyway.

I was blown away with what I discovered! Yes, there was plenty of venting and complaining (some of it very justified), but I also discovered a young woman who was trying so hard to do the right things in confusing life challenges, a young woman who was much stronger than my self-perception at the time. I was witnessing the life and struggles of a young woman who was myself. I was able to say "Yes, those truly were hard years. And, I survived them!" I still remember the wonder and gratitude I felt when I discovered what I had written and forgotten.

More recently in my life, I do my re-reads every year or so. Thankfully, my life is much happier than in my early adult years, so I'm not usually blown away or surprised much by anything I read in the journals. Yet I get such a sense of owning my life and developing much compassion for myself and my struggles. There's just enough distance between now, when I'm reading, and then, when I wrote, to allow me to see myself as if I were someone else, as if it were someone else's story. For many of us who are women, we are able to have more compassion for someone else than for ourselves, and this little trick has taught me how to extend my compassion towards my own dear self as well.

Variation:

Those of us who are getting older sometimes wonder what we should do with our "personal archives," as I call my boxes of journals, old calendars and appointment books. Very few of us will have libraries bidding to purchase and house our archives after our deaths, and I don't want my things to become a burden for my son after my death.

One very helpful thing you can do is to set aside a few weeks to re-read all your old journals, and as you read, make photocopies of particularly informative or interesting pages. Make notes of the wisdom you've gleaned through life. Honor your big struggles and show how you overcame them, or how you just muddled through them and barely survived to tell the story.

Think of what might be interesting or helpful to your children or descendants, even if they're not interested at this point in time. You can choose to frame it as an autobiography of the events of your life, or to frame it as the lessons you've learned or the wisdom you've accumulated. Include enough life details so that the reader can understand your struggles, can understand *how* the lessons or the wisdom were found. Just imagine how grateful your descendants would be to read one volume about your life, rather than plow through 40 years of diary-keeping! You would then be free to either destroy all the individual journals, or to arrange for their storage.

Before destroying anything, though, think about whether your life was lived at a particularly interesting time in history or if you lived through some unique events. Oftentimes there are universities that would love to do research on individuals' lives, and your diaries might be a treasure trove for them.

More Journal Prompts

Questions to Ponder in Writing

- What am I noticing now?
- What surprises me these days?
- What is new or different?
- What do I remember?
- What do I want to remember?
- What have I forgotten?
- Have I been forgotten? Have I forgotten myself?
- What isn't being said?
- What do I want to know more about?
- What, or who, do I disagree with? Why?
- When am I happiest? At busy-ness? At rest? With whom?
- What am I wanting right now?
- What energizes me?
- Are there any vampires in my life? Are there things or people that drain me of energy, of my life's blood?
- Where does my anger live?
- If I could ask for anything, what would I ask for, and from whom would I ask it?

- If I could do anything, what would I do? Could I do that in my life as it is? If not, how would my life have to change to be able to make it happen?
- What matters? What's the matter?
- What doesn't matter?
- What if … ?
- What am I wanting to let go of?
- Who's showing up in my journal these days?
- Who's showing up in my dreams?
- Where does my mind go when I'm not thinking about anything in particular?
- Do I have any real regrets?
- What delights me?
- What do I hate? Why?
- What questions am I asking these days? Which are urgent? Which are important, even if they're not at all urgent?
- What is my favorite animal? How am I like that particular animal?
- Am I wearing the colors and the types of clothes that delight me? If not, why not?
- If I were suddenly gifted $1,000, no strings attached, what would I do with it? What about $10,000? What if it were a million dollars? How much would become a problem, if any? How much would be a burden?
- Where is my life going well? Where is it being troublesome?
- What was the hardest thing I've done lately? What was the hardest thing I've ever done?
- Am I feeling okay in my body? What tension am I holding? Where? Why?
- Am I content? Why? Why not?
- What am I hoping for lately? What dreams are coming to my awareness?
- Is this all there is?
- Who or what am I giving my life energy to? Why?
- Take a few moments to ponder my cup of life … Is it overflowing? Is it empty? Or is it somewhere in between?

- If I could go anywhere, where would I go? Why? With whom?
- If I could give a gift to anyone, what would it be?
- If a genie gave me three wishes, what would I wish for? (Asking for unlimited wishes is not allowed!)
- If I could have lived anytime in history, or anyplace, what would I choose? Why?
- What am I worried about these days? What am I sad about?
- What am I grieving?
- Do I need more rest?
- Do I need more dancing?
- What kind of adventure do I need? What kind of adventure would I love?
- What would be the one thing, if I were to do it on a regular basis, that would make the biggest difference in my life? I asked myself this question for the first time about 25 years ago, and the answer that came to me was to write in my journal regularly. I'd already been writing sporadically for many years, but the nudge was to write regularly. I made a sincere attempt to do so, and I succeeded. And yes, it has made a huge positive difference in my life!
- Do I need more depth dimension practices in my life?
- How am I feeling about depth dimension practices?
- What else should I be asking?

Note: Many of these questions could be interesting conversation starters or dinner table conversations as well.

Mining Our Collections

If you have a collection of words that intrigue you, or a collection of quotes, pick three of them at random and then write in response to the three of them. Are there any connections among them? Does one make you think of one thing, then your brain boomerangs back with the second, and the third has you throw up your hands in frustration? Can you tell a story if you arrange the quotes or words in a certain way? If you add a few more words or quotations, can you make sense out of them then? Do their meanings cancel each other out? Or, use the words or quotations as a silly kind of oracle: ask yourself a question, then pick an answer randomly from your collections. How does your mind make sense of what you got? As you write in response, marvel at how your brain is a meaning-making organ, at how we can so often make some sense out of random pairings or collections of things, ideas, or events, and at how our brain can see patterns and even generate patterns when there is no intrinsic pattern.

Be Surprised by Etymologies

Etymologies are the language origins of words. They often reveal surprising depths to the meanings of words, and generate questions by how they show up in different contexts. For instance, the Latin word *pater* means father. When used by a Christian in referring to "The Pater", another name for the prayer "the Our Father", it usually has a good and sacred connotation. It has a completely other sense when a feminist is describing "the patriarchy".

The Latin root for "seed" is *semen*. From that we get words such as seminal, seminary, and of course, semen. What does that imply as to which gender is expected to study in a seminary? Might women want to start an ovulary, instead, from *ovulum*, little egg?

Mater is Latin for mother. It's the root of "matter", "material", and "matrix", also of "maternal", "matriculate", and "matrimony". Now the term "Mother Earth" takes on a further depth of meaning. What matters most to you in this life? How do you treat the material of this world, and the material of your body? How do you get to the heart of the matter?

Psyche is "soul" in Greek. It also means "butterfly". When Dr. Estés offered one of her series of training workshops, the subtitle was "Psychology in the Truest Sense of the Word". The trainings were about our soul lives, but also about our psychological processes and woundings. Yet the word "soul" is very rarely used in the academic or professional work of psychologists. Why is that?

Look at your collection of words, and use a good dictionary to look up their etymologies. You won't always hit gold, but you will often enough to give you lots to ponder. Of course, you could simply plunk into google "Etymology of _____," but if you do that then you're exposed to the temptation of all of the internet. When doing this as a depth dimension practice, I suggest using a good print dictionary. Many years ago, the *Book of the Month Club* offered the complete Oxford English Dictionary as one of its new membership bonuses — the complete 20-some volumes in two volumes, printed so small that it came with its own magnifying glass that was necessary to read it, on pages as thin as that of old bibles. The OED is the best dictionary in the English language for the origins of words, and tracks how the words have been used throughout history. It's been a favorite of mine for a very long time. However, there are many print dictionaries that have decent etymologies, and are often found at library sales for a dollar or two. It doesn't need to be the latest edition, at all. Find a dictionary and keep it where you do your depth dimension practices. Enjoy!

Clarus is Latin for "clear", also implying light, or radiance. How do you find clarity in your life? Ask yourself often, "What am I not seeing?" "What isn't clear?" "What is being hidden from me?" "How can I bring a little more light into this situation?"

Make Up the Words that OUGHT to be Words

How about *seriosity*? A seriosity is something that happens that is concerning or inconvenient, but isn't so tragic that you can't joke about it just a little bit. To describe a seriosity that is even more serious, you can use a grave *seriosity*. It's not known whether it should be spelled *seriosity* or seriousity.

Aggranoying is the most descriptive word that I find good reason to use often. It's a cross between aggravating and annoying.

Overwealmth is my favorite word that I've made up. It describes that situation when something good happens or you've been given something significant, but there are conditions that make the new wealth so much of a burden that you're overwhelmed. I first used it when I was working at a sexual assault center and we received a large grant from the government. We badly needed the money, but we had to use the grant, along with providing full documentation for how we used it, within a very short time. How to responsibly use a significant amount of money when we had not planned for it, and didn't have time to tender bids or create new programs, was actually a significant challenge. We couldn't hold over the money to spend in the future, and all projects had to be completed by the time limit. Overwealmth, for sure.

Associative Writing

Learning to write this way comes in very handy when you want to analyze your dreams, and it is revealing and somewhat entertaining when you apply it to just about everything else.

When you look at a word or an image, what thoughts, images, or memories come up? What does it remind you of? Write down all your associations. Do you feel your body respond? Do you have any bodily sensations when you think of that word or image? Write that down too.

Reflect on the fact that all day (and all night, too, in our dreams) our brains are making these kinds of connections with almost all of what we see and hear. These kinds of associations help us to understand our emotions and moods much better, and help us to be aware of the dozens and hundreds of ideas coming into our minds every day. There's always material in us, as a resource for creativity or fodder for reflection. We are rich beyond measure! – Or is that cluttered beyond measure?

Gifts

What has been the best gift you've ever received? You define "best". I'm thinking of "what made me the happiest?" or "what has had the most lasting impact?" or perhaps "what has been the most surprising or unusual?" Think about not just this year, but at any time in your life. And, of course, it doesn't need to be limited to just one gift.

Write about this. Who was the giver of this fine gift? What has become of the gift?

The first part of my last name, "charis", is the Greek word for gift. It also means grace and blessing, and is the word used in theology for divine grace, that is, the free, unconditional giving of the divine's own self into creation.

Now think beyond your best gift. As I wrote earlier, Gratitude Journals are a good way for us humans to compensate for the "negativity bias", the tendency we have to remember the bad stuff and to forget the good stuff. In difficult situations, ask yourself "What could be right, or good, about what's happening right now? What good might come of this? How can what's going on help me get what I want or need? Is there anything I can be grateful for here?"

In the face of fear, in the face of the constant bad news cycle, it's important to remember that babies are born, people make love, friends and families share meals and smiles. There are gifts, graces and blessings all around us, even as there is bad news and despair. Remember this, and know that it is not being a Pollyanna, but a courageous person, to CHOOSE where you will place your attention and invest your energy. Where you invest your energy is how you live your life. Many of us unreflectively have the feeling that we're the ones giving all day long, and that we're receiving very little in exchange. But it is possible to reverse thinking that we feel hurt and disappointed by others most of the time. Focus on what you're receiving in every moment: air, warmth, food (at least for most of us who are able to be reading this book at this time.) People listen to us; our ideas are sought out by family members and colleagues. Most of us already possess what it is we need not only to survive but to thrive. As far as feeling disappointed by other people most of the time, consider for a moment any pain, trouble, or inconveniences we may have caused anyone today. What about yesterday? Last week? Life is hard, and disappointing, but almost all of us have at least some choice in just about every moment. Claim it, and exercise that choice.

"Maybe, Maybe Not"

There is a story claimed to originate in many cultures that speaks to the uncertainty in life. In the Chinese version I heard years ago, the story goes something like this: a man and his son live alone out in the country. Someone tries to steal their herd of mares, but the thief is stopped before he can take the horses away. Nevertheless, the horses are freed and run off. All the man's neighbors sympathize with him saying how awful this is. "Maybe, maybe not" is his cryptic answer. The next day his son, looking for the scattered horses, brings home not only the escaped mares, but also a beautiful strong wild stallion that the mares attracted. All the neighbors congratulate the man on his good fortune. "Maybe, maybe not" is his only answer. Then when the son tries to ride the wild stallion, he's bucked off and breaks his leg. The neighbors duly sympathize, and are met with another "Maybe, maybe not." The next week the soldiers of the kingdom ride through the area looking to draft any young men to fight in the unending wars of the king. They don't take the man's son, though, because he is of no use to them with a broken leg.

The point is, of course, that we cannot foresee the consequences of every event that happens in our lives, that "good" events don't always turn out to stay good, and that "bad" events may shift into something good. Even though we don't know what the consequences of our desires may be, we expend much energy into trying to make certain things happen. Write about times when the consequences of an event in your life turned out to be quite different than you had expected. How did you feel? How does it make you feel towards future events? Does the uncertainty in life frighten you? Or is there also a sense of exhilaration in finding out how things turn out?

Uncertainty is our basic condition, and everyone else is in this situation as well. How have you made peace with this uncertainty? How does it feel to know that while we each are able to do things to influence the future, none of us can ensure a desired future? Ponder in your journal the following three aphorisms:

- ◆ Uncertainty abounds.
- ◆ All is impermanent.
- ◆ This, too, shall pass.

Crosswords, like Crosswalks, Take Us Across

Make a crossword (a crossword puzzle without the clues) of a set of words that mean something special to you. Here's one possibility:

What do you call your soul time? I often call it "soulwork" or "exploring life's depth dimensions." Do you do soulwork? Do you "encourage" (*cor* being "heart" in Latin), or bring heart to your own life and to others? The author Bill Plotkin uses the term "Soulcraft". Is the soul enlarged or deepened by "working" on it, or by "crafting" it? What other words can describe being with what is both deepest within you as well as most transcendent when you are **with** the Magnitude all around you? Do you live an ensouled life? Make a crossword or other design with these words.

A Soul by Any Other Name

So many of us are in so many different situations regarding "soul", the sacred, "God", religion, and our spiritual heritages. I myself have struggled with this and worked through so much regarding this depth dimension of life. Ponder some of these D & R's of life, and express your thoughts in words, colors, or images. Whatever you call yourself, whether Buddhist, Christian, agnostic, atheist, or anything in between, try to clarify some language for yourself for this aspect of life.

On the bad days, when life is flat and I can't believe that there could be any "God" when so many people throughout history have and are suffering so much, and the brightest I can feel is some gratitude that I've not grown up in a refugee camp orphaned and schooled in the hatred of my enemies. On even those bad days, I feel, or hope, that there's more to life than just surviving, that there are some deeper realities, even if they are purely human possibilities and potentials.

Those deeper things, and my personal allegiance to wanting to develop knowledge and experience of that, is what I mean when I talk about "soul".

Yet some of us have strong negative reactions to the word "soul", or just have no idea what the word can really mean in this mysterious crazy world of ours where it seems that the traditional home of these ideas, that is, religion, has gone crazy with power, abuse of the innocent, and fighting it out with whatever other group it can label as "other" and "wrong".

Nevertheless, it is of great value both personally and for the world for each of us to explore and claim what is really "real", what is really "deep", and what is really worth living for. So I invite you to brainstorm a list of words that express these ideas that are meaningful for you. If you don't like the word "soul", how about D & R's, "the depths", "spirit", "essence", "the source", or "my heart"? If you already have a language and a spiritual home in these really "reals", write it down and translate some of those words into the language that you would use with your atheist friends or with very little children. Play with words and language until you become comfortable saying what you, yourself, really believe, what you yourself can put your life behind. Of course, this might take more than 20 minutes!

To Offer a Blessing

Use your journal to brainstorm this, and to construct your draft. Start with thanks that you know about and care about the person or the situation, and then hold in your mind's eye who or what situation it is that you want to bless.

What do you wish for the person or situation? How do you want things to be? Be somewhat general, as we don't really know the specific details of others' deepest needs. Ask for help, from wherever it may come. Ask that the person or situation find what would be of the greatest help, soon, in ways that are immediately recognizable to them and in ways that they can put to good use right away. Ask that they or the situation be surrounded with love, and smooth ease in moving towards strength and wholeness. Use your own words, fill it with your intentions. When it is phrased to your liking, decide what you will do with this blessing. Sometimes it's most appropriate for it to just stay in your journal. Other times you may want to send a copy of it or say it to the person themselves. If it's a situation, you might be able to send your blessing to the committee in charge of the situation, suggesting that they read it at the beginning of a decision-making meeting. Finally, do what is within your power, within your reach, to bring about what you have wished for in the blessing.

What is Prayer?

Ponder this in your journal. Is prayer asking for something? If you don't believe in the traditional idea of God, can you still pray? Is prayer "presence with"? Is it giving thanks? Giving thanks to whom? Is prayer asking for forgiveness? How do you pray with another person? Do you need words? Is wonder, awe, a form of prayer? Or is prayer just good intention?

Do beings other than human persons pray? Can your dog pray? When your cat is sitting there looking regal, is she deep in contemplation? Do grasses pray by growing? Do waves pray? Is prayer fulfilling your natural purpose?

Is prayer a matter of addition or subtraction? One of my most sincere prayers is "Please remove from me anything that is not myself" which I learned from Dr. Estés as our group was examining how many expectations, projections, and demands are placed on us by others, by parents, by the culture, by the powers that be that benefit from our blindnesses and silences and self-censorships that they themselves have created and enforced within us. That would be a prayer of subtraction. Or is prayer multiplication? Is prayer the multiplication of care, of love, of compassion, justice, and freedom? What is prayer?

The Reverse Bucket List

We all know that a Bucket List is the list of what you'd like to do while you're still alive, before you "kick the bucket." Things like "going to the south of France," "motorcycling across the country," and "visiting my cousins in the old country" figure big on them.

A reverse bucket list is the list of the peak experiences that you've already accomplished, survived, or lived through. Make yourself a list of the biggies in your life, and then write out some thoughts in response to these questions:

Which have brought you such joy? Which have brought you a helluva lot of aggravation before they brought you joy?

Which would you like to tell others about, or leave as a legacy, with lessons learned and how you felt before, during, and after?

- Whch have been dreams and aspirations that you have made true in your life? How did you plan for them, make them priorities, watch for the right moment to act on them? How much did you just luck out?
- What new experience in them scared you, challenged you, or surprised you?

- ◆ Which experiences were life defining?
- ◆ Which would you never, ever do again?

Looking back at what you've already experienced can prompt dreaming forward, too. What do you still hope to do in your life, in new situations, with new health issues, different resources, perhaps different people? How can you now spark living with gratitude and with anticipation of your next adventure?

Image-nation

What comes to you when you ponder the words image, imagination, mage, magi, archimage, magic, imagine, magus, imago? Today, when I wrote "imagine", I thought of "migraine".

What about you? What world do you make of your images? Is imagination "real"? Are there Three Magi who might visit your soul with gifts? Play with the words and see where they take you.

Love More, Do Less

List 3 ways – or 13 ways – that you can love more and do less in your everyday life. Now do them! Or *don't* do them, as the case may be!

When You Show Your Soul Brightly

What or who shows up? What or who shows up within yourself when you show your soul brightly? Around or outside of you? Do you have new or different images in your mind? Do different people tend to show up in your life then?

How is it exactly that you show your soul brightly? Do you smile more? Do you silently bless all whom you look out on? Does it happen only when you're well rested or feeling happy? Can you do it with other people around?

The Four Elements, the Four Directions

Earth, air, fire, and water have been associated with the four directions from time immemorial. Each direction, and each element, also has particular qualities associated with them, though the exact associations tend to differ among different cultures. Sometimes the four elements are associated with the different seasons, sometimes with the different stages of life. Before going to look up any of these associations, do you have personal associations with any of the directions?

When you think of south, for instance, what images, ideas, memories, or sensations come up for you? I live in Canada, often depicted as the Great White North, yet I live in southern Canada and southern Alberta, only an hour away from the U.S. border. In my city, I live in North Lethbridge. So where am I? When we talk about our border to the south, it's with the United States. When I lived in the U.S., south of the border was Mexico. Each of those places brings up different memories of times in my life, and qualities that are evoked by the word "south".

Write about your own associations to each element and each direction. Then go ahead and research some more traditional associations. How do yours line up with the more cultural ones?

Then tell a story about the associations. Start out in "fairy tale mode" by beginning, "Once upon a time, a woman came from the … " See if your story evokes any more memories or other associations. Incorporate the smell of fire, the feel of water, the scent on a breeze, and the feel of walking on hard-packed dirt.

Write Your Own Psalm

In the Hebrew and Christian bibles, the book of psalms contains the ancient lyrics for songs directed to God. We ordinarily just read them now rather than sing them. They are filled with emotions ranging from love to murderous anger, and everything in between. Many people are surprised to discover that such rage and violence can even be included in a sacred book, but it's all there! Whenever you are feeling strong emotions, write your own psalm. Or you can take one and modify it to your own situation. Whatever your deepest longing is, whatever your frustrations and angers, betrayals, love and joy are, give expression to it by presenting it to the Mystery we call God.

Soul Tribes

Halloween, Oct. 31, is celebrated in many cultures, but primarily among the Hispanic, as the Day of the Dead where we honor our people who have gone before us into death. It is the day before All Saints' Day in the calendar of the Christian Churches, Nov. 1, and Nov. 2 is All Souls' Day. The Catholic Church also has the concept of "the Communion of Saints", of which we are all a part whether or not any of us have been officially canonized as a "saint". These celebrations and ideas prompt the question "Who makes up *your* Soul Tribe? Who are the people who have helped you make your soul shine in the world? Who are the ones who encourage you to be your best? Whom can you imagine standing with and saying, "These are my people!" And you may have several different Soul Tribes, ones who have taught you valuable soul lessons who are no longer in your life, others who you can always count on to bring you back to core values. Your family may or may not be part of one of your Soul Tribes, though your sister may make it into many of your tribes. And your chosen family may be the closest of all. List these people's names or initials, or include them in a circle or web. You can image them in various colors. Just acknowledge the people around you, living and dead, who have had a part to play in who you are now.

Thinking of Death

Write about death. Or do you definitely **not** want to write about death? Whom have you been close to who has died? What was that whole process like for you? Does death feel natural to you, or does it just seem wrong, wrong, wrong? Do you imagine death as letting go into the whole life/death/life cycle that we see in nature all around us? Does death frighten you?

If you had your preferences, how would you like to die? Are there any situations that you would definitely not want to experience as you die? Remember to write up a Living Will so that your family and then the health care people can follow your wishes as much as possible. Would you like to be buried, or cremated? There are now more options regarding burials and returning to the earth than in previous years, and you may want to investigate what is available to you in your area. Have you had this conversation with your spouse or family?

What do you think happens after death? Do you believe in an afterlife, or do you think we just blink out of all existence? Do you have hopes around the afterlife? Do you have any thoughts about reincarnation? Personally, I know that none of us knows for certain what happens after death, and I have hopes, but no sure beliefs. People who have near death experiences share their mostly very positive and loving experiences, and those reports are often very encouraging for others. I don't know if there is an afterlife. If not, I hope that as I die that I feel that I've used my life in ways that have contributed to happiness and healing, and that my remains can fertilize a tree somewhere or shade a park bench welcoming rest and contemplation. And if there is something after death, what an adventure that will be! I hope that we are able to continue to love, help, and mentor the living, either until whatever happens next, or for eternity.

Our Place in the World

Your journal is the safest and most useful place to work through many difficult social issues, especially the big issues such as racism, sexism, oppressions, colonialisms, poverty, climate change. None of us can escape being implicated in these issues, just because we're a human being on the planet at this time. While there are times that we might prefer to just not think about these things, I strongly encourage each of us to grapple with these issues. The consequences of these issues kill people, and if we're lucky enough to not be at immediate risk, then we are in a situation of being able to potentially do something to mitigate the sometimes deadly consequences. But we can't if we don't look at these issues, learn about them, and learn how we are embedded in them. There are many excellent books available that educate good-hearted persons about what they don't see, have never learned about these things, and how we stand in relation to those systems. Don't expect your friends who are "other" than you to educate you. It's very costly to try to do so for the person who has suffered under these evils. I encourage you to do your homework, get educated, work through books that encourage reflections on these topics, use your journal to examine all of this in depth. And then engage in deep, rich, vulnerable conversations. It's the least we can do as people who want to be responsible to bring in a world where all can have a home and feel at home.

I hope that you use a journal that works for you and that you love. Let it reflect who you are, and it will reflect back to you who you are becoming. Let it become a container for the treasure that is you, and a tool for becoming who it is you want to be in this life. Expect that your needs and preferences will change as the years go by, and enjoy playing with various prompts that intrigue you. Journals are valuable in the moment, and they are valuable when you go back to read the various chapters of your life. Enjoy!

4 Image

It's a truism to say that we are deeply influenced by the images in which we are immersed. We are so bombarded by advertising, by images on the internet, by TV commercials, that we often don't consciously notice them anymore, yet they are still stimulating our nervous systems with their bright colors and influencing our moods and ideas with their messages. When we used to have TV, my spouse often claimed that he didn't even notice the commercials and certainly wasn't influenced by advertising, yet I noticed he would buy the brands that had been advertised. I asked him why, and he said that he didn't know; he'd heard somewhere that they were good products. I could be wrong, but it sure seemed to me that he was being unconsciously influenced by the commercials.

Many years ago when I was living in a convent, there were about six months where I had not left the grounds of the convent, with no television or magazines available, pre-Internet. While I loved the peace, I eventually needed something from a store, so a couple of us took a trip to the mall. I became so overstimulated with all the bright colors, all the "stuff", all the advertising, that I became sick very fast: I developed both a raging headache and a nauseous stomach. Reflecting on that experience, I was astonished at how I had been bombarded with that same kind of stimulation throughout all my previous life, but never noticed it until I had "fasted" from that kind of consumption for several months. And then there are many of us in our culture who take in a steady and almost exclusive diet of certain categories of images, such as news junkies, horror movie aficionados, or fans of violent computer games. I don't even need to mention the pornography industry, which also has its consequences in how young women are now often expected to look and to perform in intimate relationships.

I don't believe that the images around us determine our moods or behaviors.

Most of us still have plenty of choice regardless of our media diets, but what we take in certainly influences us deeply. At the very least, we get an inaccurate view of reality. People still fall in love, play with their children, and treat their business colleagues with decency, but you'd not know that from the daily news, for example. I'm hoping in this chapter to help us become much more aware of what images we take in and to examine how that influences us, especially in our moods and our attitudes toward the world, and our place in it. I'm not suggesting that we avoid all ugliness or shocking imagery; sometimes particular images, though disturbing, can help us really see what's going on, and can potentially change the world. I'm thinking here of the 1972 Time Magazine cover of the young Vietnamese girl screaming and running naked after a napalm attack. It helped countless people safe at home understand a little better the consequences of war.

I also want to help us remember that we can produce our own imagery, and to offer several ideas as to how you can do that whether you consider yourself artistic or not. Color is powerful, and we feel a sense of power when we cover a complete page with red paint, or yellow paint. Does reading that bring up an image for you? What does a fire-engine red page remind you of? How does it make you feel? How many words would it take to describe all of that? You can express so much in just one color, imagine what you could express if you developed a few simple skills in drawing or in creating a collage filled with symbols! Once we become sensitized to the power of images, we can then choose what we want to take in as well as choose what we want to put out into the world for others.

It's important to realize that in a consumer, capitalistic culture almost all the images in advertising are intended to make us dissatisfied. It's how they create the desire in us to buy whatever it is that the advertising is selling, whether a product or a political idea. Even when the advertising is humorous or poignant, or made to stir our anger, its point is to destabilize us, to make us unhappy, and to think that there is something wrong with either ourselves or with the world. Advertising reminds us of things we may have never thought about before: are your lips too thin? There's a product for that! The formula is: See what bad shape you're in! We have something that can solve that! Just come and get it — for a price.

What's interesting about that, in a book that is dealing with a reflective and somewhat spiritual stance towards our lives, is that the formula in advertising is also the model that traditional Christian evangelists use. When preaching the need for conversion, the outline for the sermon goes 1) look at yourself; see what a miserable place you're in, how alone, how messed up (you are pitiful and in need); 2) Jesus knows us in that place; in fact, he willingly accepted death to atone for our sins; Jesus has saved us from the consequences of our sins, forever (there is a solution to your need); 3) all you have to do is repent; turn towards God and accept Jesus as your Lord and Savior (here's how to get that solution). In Christian evangelism there is no explicit monetary cost to this solution/salvation. Yet, the existence of the churches relies on people feeling grateful for this salvation and freely contributing money so that the churches can continue in their evangelical work. And then there are a few famous televangelists who solicit so much money from their viewers that they've made a personal empire from their preaching, building huge businesses with myriad offerings. Historically, every time that religion gives rise to empire building, corruption soon follows. Thus, religion does not fulfill its intentions to create communal space where humans can contemplate more than the day-to-day survival of their physical bodies.

Except for the immoral preachers, I don't want to criticize these evangelists. I've personally witnessed many who are sincerely moral, offering to people the best that they've known for personal healing, meaning, and plan of life. Rather, the question I'm posing is how is it that we humans motivate others to part with their resources, primarily cold, hard cash? The method is some means of exchange; I offer you a product and you pay me for it, whether I pick the price or you give me what you think it's worth. But if you're not aware that you need what I have to offer you, how will I persuade you to part with your money? This is where the exchange can become manipulative, where sellers create false needs that their products can fill. Most consumerism is based on this kind of creation of false need, or is based on appealing to our feelings of envy or need for status. And they do this with very carefully researched images. Companies hire the very smartest of behavioral psychologists to help them figure out how to use our genuine human needs to convince us that their products will fill those needs.

Sometimes, they do. Grocery stores are essential services because we need to eat, and the stores provide the food. Yet there is so much more available to us than the simple fulfillment of human needs, and it's how the companies entice us to purchase items that are not needed and how they use images to manipulate what we perceive to be our needs that I'm so interested in. So how do we become conscious of all of this and then reclaim our freedom from any manipulation? I think the best way to do that is to become aware of what's become almost invisible and then examine how we want to respond. When we are inundated with images everywhere we look, it's hard to remember that we can choose what we want to pay attention to in our lives. What we pay attention to becomes our experience of life, and the experiences of our lives ARE our lives. So, be aware of what you invite into the cathedral of your mind by noticing where we place our attention, or let in through the back doors of passive indifference to images that are designed to seep in to influence us.

Besides becoming aware of the images around us, I want to offer practices to learn the power of symbols and archetypes so that we are inspired to use these images in our own lives. Very simply put, symbols are ideas or images that are like doors to greater meaning rather than simply a one to one correspondence with an object. For example, what do you think of when you think of a fire? A fire can evoke danger and destruction, but if we're not in immediate danger of being burnt, a fire can also remind us of warmth on a cold night, of singing with friends around a campfire, of the transformation of materials from one state to another, of smelting metals, of anger, of passion, and so on. And so the symbol of fire holds many meanings, even opposite meanings.

Archetypes are the big brothers and sisters of single symbols, holding not only a wealth of meanings, but whole patterns of human relating. The archetype of the father, for instance, communicates to us cultural ideas of fathering a baby, of guidance and teaching of youth, of protection and provisioning of families and of the society. It can also communicate how the archetype can shift over time through an abuse or twisting of the idea, so that father can also communicate the idea of patriarchy, of control of the family and by extension, how "the fathers" control society, of how some fathers abuse spouses and children, of the power to decide others' life or death. And of course, both symbols and archetypes are colored by the personal experiences of each person. The ambiguity of symbols and archetypes are what opens our minds and spirits to the plethora of meanings, evoking both personal and cultural, or even universal meanings. The context of how symbols and archetypes are used are clues as to how the communicator intends the symbol to be used, but the one using the symbol can also use its ambiguity to invite more reflection and a co-creation of meaning.

I also offer practices that can develop skills so that you not only appreciate artwork and images, but can use them yourself. Just as almost all of us have learned to write emails as part of our daily lives, whether we have a talent for writing or not, all of us can learn to use images to communicate, whether or not we feel we have any talent for art. I use art not as a means to bowl over viewers with exquisite beauty — I don't have those skills — but as a means to teach us about ourselves as we notice what we like or are drawn to, to discern what is important to us and what we want to share with others. It's not about a finished product necessarily, but about the pleasure in the process. I invite you to let yourself know how you're feeling at certain points of collecting or creating images, and ask where else you might be feeling that in your life, or have felt that in the past. I invite you to notice what comes up, how you feel when working or playing with images. What ideas or other images arise? Are these connected to recent memories, or are there old meanings that you've been carrying without being aware of them? Art, and images, allow us to SEE it, not just THINK it. We often forget our thoughts far too easily and quickly, and therefore often redo the same old, same old. Art, and images, are a means to bring more creativity, reflection, and intentionality into our daily lives in memorable and even transformative ways.

Getting Acquainted with Images

Start Noticing the Images around You

As you go through your day, notice the images around you. You can write a reminder in your calendar at the beginning of your day to pay attention throughout that day, or post reminders to yourself throughout your home or workplace. You can also pick the genre of image, whether it's the images on billboards, the ads on your social media feed, trade journals, magazines, newspapers, business magazines, TV programs or Netflix, or commercials on TV or Netflix. Perhaps pick a day to concentrate on each genre. Just notice. If you want, you could photograph some of the images.

When you have a quiet moment in the day, write in your journal your thoughts about the images that you noticed. You can describe them briefly, or include copies of the photos to paste into your journal. Ask yourself some or all of the following questions and record your answers:

- What feelings come up as I look at the image?
- What is the image promoting as an ideal or normal? What does it say about the way things "ought" to be? What kind of "oughts" are there in my life now?

- How might this image be understood by someone very different from me, whether a very wealthy person, a person living in poverty, a person who is Black, Indigenous, or a Person of Color, an LGBTQIA2+ person, or a 1950's traditional American wife?
- How does the image reflect who I am? Am I the kind of person who is "supposed" to benefit from the image?

Your comments can be simple or as complex as you want. For instance, when I lived in Toronto in the 1980's I started to notice how images of women were used to sell just about everything. Yet they were the images of only a few types of women, women who were thin, beautiful, young, shaved, groomed, and white. If not white, they were portrayed as "exotic." Mothers, workers, or fat women were more often portrayed in ways meant to be grotesquely ridiculous, if they were portrayed at all.

Notice ad campaigns, including ones from years ago that you might remember, such as the Marlboro Man, or the Virginia Slim commercials. "You've come a long way, baby" used the gains of the movement for female equality in the workplace as the justification for having a cigarette of our own. Do the portrayals of romance reflect anything that you've ever lived in your own life? Are their fantasies entertaining, or are they teaching you how you "ought" to desire certain kinds of romance?

Repeat this exercise several times, until you develop the habit of noticing what images are fed to you in a day. Where do you find unusual images? Where are you surprised by an image? Do you see different types of images in different areas of your city, or in different media outlets targeted to different groups of people?

Collect Images

When you find images that you're attracted to, collect them. Take photos of them, or photocopy them. Tear them out of magazines and newspapers. It doesn't matter if they are from feature stories or from advertising. Print out images that you like from the internet, or save images from wall calendars or desk calendars.

Sale books from big bookstores often include the works of various artists, or themed photos. As I spoke about in the last chapter, "Quiet books" often have quotes interspersed with beautiful photographs. Used bookstores are treasure troves of art or photography books, and often sell old art calendars as well. You can tear out any of these images and glue them into your own journals.

Print out photos of images you like. Figure out how to store all the images you collect. You can start with putting them in an envelope pasted into the back of your journal, or a file folder. Or find a box that you store in a convenient spot, and throw them in. Keep your art books together on a particular shelf.

Anytime you feel like it, glue an image into your journal to inspire you or to brighten up a blank page. Or just gaze at the images that you like, and ask some or all of the following questions:

- Why did I make the effort to keep this?
- What do I particularly like about this image? Is it the colors? The textures? The subject or topic of the image? The humor? The emotion?
- How does this image make me feel?
- Where is it that I find images that I like? Are they all around me, or do I have to make a special effort to find them?
- How does this image grow my soul? Does it enrich me, or invite me to think in expanded ways, or in ways I haven't thought of before?

What to do with Collected Images

Of course, the only real answer is to do anything you want with them! Here are some ideas:

Separate out images that you can "use up" from the images that you want to save, by using them in collages or pasting them in your journal. You can make photocopies of an original image to "use up."

Separate out your collected images from your own created images.

I sometimes separate out images by size or orientation. For instance, I have four file folders, one for larger images (ones that take up more than ½ of an 8 ½ x 11 in. page), a second for vertical images that would fit onto a journal page, a third for horizontal images, and a fourth for small images (less than 2 x 3 inches). This way I can easily find the perfectly sized image for the blank space I might have on my journal page, or find images for collage.

You can categorize images in a variety of ways if you want to. You could separate out images with quotes on them from images with no words; images of people from landscapes or things; images of women from men and children;

archival images from contemporary images; images of things from abstract images; images of everyday from highly symbolic images. I would only do this fine categorizing if I wanted to be able to find particular images quickly when working or playing with them, such as in collage or illustrating text in your journal. There is the practice of *Soul Collage* as described by Seena B. Frost where you choose particular images to collage from cards you assigned with different meanings, and so finding the image you need in a categorized file might be more desirable than rummaging through a six-inch-high pile of papers.

You can create blank books of images that please you for perusing whenever you want to surround yourself with the beauty you already know exists. These books can be themed, highly organized, and become works of art, or they can just be pages covered with pretty pictures, like an old-fashioned scrapbook. An activity for children that is sometimes really fun for adults is to have a simple spiral notebook plus some catalogs or magazines, then cut out images and paste them into the notebook. Children often make alphabet books, plant books, or animal books, where there will be a page of images of things that begin with the letter "A", etc., or pages of animals that are from Africa on one page, North America on another. An inexpensive way to create notebooks for this kind of collecting is to take two or three magazines of the same size, and glue them together to make a "book" about 1 inch thick. Glue the back cover of one magazine to the front cover of the next. Use white paint or gesso to cover the parts of the pages that you don't want to keep, and then paste new images onto the white backgrounds. If you do this, make at least two "Magazine Books" to work on at the same time, so that a page from one "Magazine Book" can dry while you're working on the other "Book." Also remember that these books are fragile and probably will not last for years and years and years. But they are highly useful for giving this practice a try, with little financial or emotional commitment.

Inspiration Notebooks: You can keep blank notebooks of ideas or images, or copies of different kinds of patterns. These are especially useful as sources for artwork that you might want to create yourself. I have a notebook of patterns I like that I have come across from a variety of places, from books to the shape of a garden gate on my walks. I may then copy them in my journal or use a piece of one for an artwork. That notebook also has lots of doodles in it that I've copied from various places. I have another notebook where I collect images of women that look to be very easy to draw, especially dreamy or symbolic images that often have just a few suggestive lines. I sometimes practice my drawing skills by trying to reproduce the images exactly; of course I cannot use them as is for my own artwork, but can take ideas from several different patterns and images and put them together in a new way.

Meditating on Visual Images: Visio Divina

I previously gave you a few questions to ask yourself as you gaze at images that please you, but this practice goes a bit deeper. It is the visual counterpart of Lectio Divina (Divine Reading), called Visio Divina (Divine Looking). Here you want to not just notice some pleasant image, but to spend some time with an image that has enough depth that it will reveal itself to you as you devote yourself to it. Traditionally, this practice has been done with icons from the Eastern Orthodox Church, but icons are now available from a variety of painters, and other works of art that have depth and meaning are also good options. It's okay to choose an image that you may not understand, but do not choose an image or artwork that disturbs you, or that has elements of the horrific in it.

Before you start, set your intention that this will be an intentional time of taking in this offering from an artist looking to communicate something with their viewer. Dedicate whatever time you have to greater self-awareness, greater depth, being open to a blessing through the artwork. Find a comfortable place to gaze at your art. First, look at the image slowly, and note what catches your eye. Gaze softly and kindly, with both focus and then taking in the image as a whole. What is the painting about, if anything? What other kinds of images have you seen that are like this? Is there anything about this particular image that attracts you, or that intrigues you in some way? Is there anything that you don't like, or that you wish were not in the image? If you are gazing at an icon, remember that icons are created especially as an aid to prayer, an aid to some kind of communion with Greater, or the Divine in whatever way you may consider that Holy Mystery, and that you are somehow praying together with all of the people who have ever prayed with that particular icon throughout history. Note that icons, some other images, and nature have all been considered "windows to God." How is this image that kind of window? Notice the color, the shapes, and the imagery, noticing both the surface 'story' as well as what they might mean symbolically.

Ask yourself if there is anything about the image that reflects your life. Does it remind you of any questions that are important to you or that you might be pondering at this time of your life? Is there any kind of personal message that you can take from this painting? What if you yourself were part of the painting, included as part of the imagery? What might that feel like? Do any insights come? What is the feeling tone of the image? Does that feeling tone say anything about your own inner world? As you gaze, what is it that you think, feel, or remember? What we see often tells us as much about ourselves, our past, present, and possible futures, as it tells us the intent of the artist.

A friend of mine had painted a whole series of paintings that were suggestive of two humans wrestling with each other. There were all kinds of fighting poses, with many variations of the bodies touching and grasping each other. I asked him why he had painted a series of men fighting with each other. He looked at me with surprise and responded that he hadn't thought of them as fighting, but as embracing each other and dancing with each other. I was amazed that my interpretation had been so far off from the artist's intentions, but as I sat with that, I realized that at that time I was working very intently with issues of violence against women, and violence in general, especially men's violence. My days were filled with those kinds of images, and when presented with these new images, I unconsciously interpreted them to suit my frame of mind. It was a huge lesson for me in how we see things; that we almost never come to something as a tabula rasa, a clean slate. We see things first from how we are, and often need to remind ourselves that there may be other ways to interpret the scene before us. I've never forgotten that lesson, but wonder whether I would have internalized it so deeply had I not had such a shock when I found out the artist's primary intention.

After musing about how the image might relate to your own life or have a message for you, it's traditional to have an inner dialogue with God about the artwork. If that doesn't fit for you, imagine having a dialogue with the artist or with a wise person about it. Ask if the message you're taking from the image is all there is for you. Ask if there is another way to interpret the image, perhaps in a completely opposite way. Whose face or faces might you place onto or into the image? Ask for insights that you haven't yet thought of.

And then finally, just sit with the image without thinking about anything in particular. Take it into you, let it work its way into your mind and heart. Be open to anything new that might arise in you. You may find yourself accessing deeper parts of yourself, being worked on by the colors and symbolism in the painting. Art has often been used to expand our consciousness, so give yourself the opportunity to be stretched and surprised.

When you feel finished with it, you may want to write in your journal notes for yourself about this experience. Don't be surprised, though, if it's hard to describe exactly in words what you gained. Some things can be expressed in an image that are difficult or impossible to express in words. Perhaps you can simply list some single words that will remind you of the experience.

Prepared Sets of Images:
Oracle Cards, Tarot Cards, Inspiration Cards

There are hundreds of decks of affirmation cards that you can purchase which pair images with inspirational messages or meanings. They are easily gotten from the online retail site amazon. Usually the images are exquisite, and often are themed with a particular style (baroque, funky, art nouveau) or with a particular set of images (cats, wild animals, urban themes). All the cards in the set are created by the same artist, so you get to understand a person's style. There are all sorts of ways to use the cards for inspiration or for a message to ponder, often beginning with choosing at random a card for the day and placing it somewhere where you will see it often throughout the day. Many oracle decks offer ideas for "spreads": patterns of choosing a few cards at random, placing them in suggested patterns in relation to each other, and then letting the images and meanings of the cards interact with each other to bring insight and new ideas to a situation you hold in your mind as you pick and lay down the cards.

Tarot Cards: People may approach the cards with strong feelings of great curiosity, or fear, or deep-seated feelings that they are somehow connected with evil and should be avoided at all cost. Personally, I find the Tarot to be a rich symbol system that speaks of the journey through life, from innocence and unknowing to maturity, wisdom, and universality. Tarot decks are also the precursors to our decks of playing cards. They've been around for hundreds of years and there is a rich lore in the literature around them. Each of the Major Arcana cards portrays the archetypes of people or events that most people come across in their lives. I don't believe that Tarot cards, or any cards, can "tell your future", though by projecting our life situation into the images, we can often receive insight and new ideas as to how to handle our challenges and mysteries, or ideas for interpreting situations that we're in at that moment. A helpful way to look at the cards is to ask a question, and look at the cards that come up as a snapshot, in the moment, of a possible way of action. Do you like that action and the probable results? If so, continue on in your plans. If not, choose to do something else. The strength of the cards is in their ambiguity. The images can mean many different things to different people. There are hundreds of decks, interpreting the archetypes of the cards in a great variety of ways. Some have a very positive and sunshiny feel; others feel darker, sometimes in a deep, mysterious way. One can make a life's study of the Tarot, its images and patterns, suggestions and possibilities.

Explore Nature in New Ways

Find photographs of the images taken by the Hubble Telescope to get a view of the vastness and wonder of deep space. These are easy to find on the internet; however, remember that you don't want to get distracted from your depth dimension practice by the other attractions of the internet. There are books with collections of these photographs, and a trip to the library to check these and other books of photography would be a wonderful field trip over a lunch hour or free afternoon.

We see a different perspective when gazing at nature either macroscopically or microscopically. There are collections of photographs that highlight the design of how plants grow, of their symmetry and their individual variations on the patterns of their species. Cross-sections of plants, fruits, and flowers often look like colorful and highly complex mandalas, easily leading one into wonder and meditation.

At other times I've been taken with photographs of people's faces, or collections of ordinary people in daily life. They expand my world, reminding me that my own daily life may have similarities with people's lives all over the world, but also that my way of life is only one of literally millions of ways of living.

Field Trips and Explorations

Go to places that fill your eyes and heart with images and colors that feed you. After I had lived in Toronto for several years, I took the train to visit a friend who lived a few hours away in a small city. I had been out of the big city very little over the previous five or six years, and as the train pulled out of Toronto my eyes were filled with the green of late spring in the country. My eyes began drinking in the green as my mouth would drink in a large glass of water on a thirsty day. I had no idea how starved I had been for green fields, collections of trees, rivers and streams. It literally felt as if a hunger I had not realized I had was now being satisfied.

Fortunately, most of us have access to the outdoors, if only in parks or while driving to a different city. Really look at the scenes that are different from your daily round. Besides local parks, lakes, rivers or even the neighborhood creek, one could travel to more exotic locations. But if you do, don't spend all your time seeing what's around you only from the point of view of your camera. Let yourself be there, unmediated. Notice if different landscapes speak to your spirit in different ways. Does the desert feel like the rainforest? Does farmland feel like the ocean? Which ones cause you to feel gloriously alive? Which ones make you want to go home?

Other field trips that are nourishing, plus a bit of eye candy, are explorations of museums, especially big ones that you can't fully take in on just one day; temporary art exhibits; flower gardens and tours of private gardens; shows of crafts and hand-made art items; sometimes even fashion shows. You could simply take a walk in a part of your city or town that you haven't walked through before, noticing design elements of the houses and figuring out the history of that section of town. If you live in a very big city, you could go on themed walks where you "collect" photos of doorways, roof decorations, graffiti, or manhole covers. Try taking your photos in black and white in order to really notice the forms and patterns, and not be distracted by color.

It's true that the world is full of images that are ugly, cruel, or despairing. And it's also often the case that once you see what you see, you can never "unsee" it. Yet that's not all of reality. It's important to have deep knowledge and confidence that beauty is possible, that out of death life grows, and to really see that we each can highlight or create images that nourish, calm, console, excite, and inspire.

Simple Ways to Add Color and Pattern to Your Own Journals

Minimal Recommended Supplies (and Why)

In Chapter 2 I gave you some ideas for art supplies that you may want to have on hand. My focus in this book is on accessibility and ease, so my suggestions tend to be inexpensive, easy to use, and readily available. Here I want to offer some pros and cons of the ways to get color onto your page, especially for beginners. Once you have more experience, go where your interest pulls you; you will then have the motivation to learn the ins and outs of whatever medium you want to experiment with.

I've suggested getting a set of colored pencils and markers. They are useful for lettering and coloring, and most households have a set or two sitting around. Try them out to see if you want a dedicated set for yourself to keep in the bag where you have your supplies. I also suggest some sort of watercolor supplies: they are easy to transport, easy to use and clean up, and don't take a lot of space. Even with no artistic skill, you can make pretty backgrounds that can express many emotions from dreaminess to boldness. All you have to do is move the color around. There are three main types of watercolor media: pans of dry watercolor (the palettes that have perhaps 12 colors in them, where you need a wet brush to pick up the color), watercolor pencils, and watercolor crayons.

With a watercolor palette, it's really helpful to buy a brush or two, such as a small round (pointed) brush and a flat brush about ¾ of an inch wide. The brush that comes with the watercolor palettes is often not of very good quality, and it's difficult to lay down a lot of color with only a small brush. Before you play with the colors, put a few drops of water on each cake of color to soften the watercolor. Another way is to carry a small water spritzer bottle (old eyeglass cleaner containers are great to recycle) and spray the whole palette. Wet the watercolor when you first start to set up so that they have a few minutes to soften by the time you're ready to use them. Have two cups of clean water and a few paper towels beside you. Dip the brush into the water, then into your chosen color. With the brush filled with color, smush the color into the lid of the palette (or have a white plastic or glass plate to use as a mixing tray). If you aren't planning to mix any other colors into your first color, you can just take the filled brush and set it to your paper. This is the trick to getting strong, bold color: soften the watercolor pigment so that you can pick up lots of color. More pigment brings deeper color; more water lightens the color. When you want to change color, rinse the brush by swishing vigorously in one of your cups of water. Stroke onto a towel to ensure you've cleaned out the color, then dip the brush into the clean water cup and choose the next color. When you've picked up the second color, you can apply it straight to your paper, or you can mix it into the little pile of the first color that you smushed onto the lid of the palette or onto a plate. This way you can create an almost infinite number of custom colors by mixing in this manner. It can be fun and relaxing to just stroke lines of color onto a page, one color after another, mixing some, or letting some run into the adjoining color. Play with different amounts of water on your brush, and see how the water affects the colors. When done, rinse out your brushes and lay them flat to dry. Rinse out your water cups, and you're done.

Using these watercolor palettes gives you lots of options and much to play with. However, you do need a work surface that is relatively flat and that doesn't move. It's not easy to use this on a commute or even a longer train ride. And the water cups can spill. To get around the water cups, you could purchase water brushes, special brushes whose handle can hold water that you can squeeze out to wet the brush and clean it.

The two other watercolor options are the pencils and crayons. They look just like regular dry pencils and crayons, but are formulated to dissolve their pigment when you apply a wet brush to what you've drawn. As you apply the color to paper, stroke your wet brush over them, producing a very similar look to that of a regular watercolor palette. Though they cost a bit more than the traditional pan palette, they are well worth it because of their versatility. You can use them while a passenger in a car; they're easy to carry to a coffee shop and use while you're enjoying your drink. You can also use them dry, and wait until later to activate the colors with the wet brush. The tips of the watercolor pencils and crayons can be dipped in water and applied to the paper that way, as well.

There are three other types of paint available: poster paint, acrylic paint, and oil paints. I do not recommend oil paints for this type of depth dimension practice because they take a very long time to dry and cannot be cleaned up with water. Poster paints are better than nothing, but tend to be very flat and do not mix well. I do recommend two of the types of acrylic paint available: what's called craft paint in small bottles, and artists' acrylic paint in bottles or tubes. There is a little more mess with acrylic paints than with watercolors, and some colors will stain clothing if you don't wash it out immediately. But the depth of color is much deeper and more dramatic than with watercolor. As well, spilling water on a page painted with acrylic will not ruin the color (as acrylic is a type of plastic), while watercolor will dissolve with an onrush of water. Craft paints can be purchased in dollar stores and craft stores, and are quite inexpensive. While they are perfectly serviceable, the colors tend to be opaque and matte, meaning there's no shine to the colors. Artists' acrylics come in liquid form (bottles) or in a more buttery texture (tubes), and you can get student grade or professional grade. The generic brand name paints from craft stores like Michaels are a good student grade, and are great for this type of work. Interestingly, the highest quality of acrylic paints, the Golden brand, are luminous and quite beautiful, but tend to be a bit sticky when dry. This means that if you use them to paint in a journal where pages touch each other, they may stick together, and thus ruin your pages as you try to pull them apart. There are ways to get around this by using wax paper inserts or waxing the pages after you're done, but it's easier for this depth dimension work to use either the craft paints or the student grade acrylics, and save the Golden paints for canvases or artwork that you intend to hang on the wall.

An easy way to use acrylics in your journal is to simply pour a few dime sized dollops in the middle of your page, then use the edge of an old credit card to swirl the paint over the page. This can make a background that you can journal on in pen, or a general background for collage or image-making. Brushes and tools used for acrylics are easily cleaned with soap and water.

There is a seemingly endless array of art supplies and techniques, and you could spend a lot of time and money trying to figure out the best things to get started with. Wandering through a good art supply store or even a craft store is very entertaining, and even the online options are eye candy. However, they are not needed for depth dimension practices. Acquire a couple of ways to spread some color on your pages, and go from there. Some teachers suggest getting either or both of oil pastels or soft pastels. They look somewhat like crayons, but are usually square rather than round. They are nice for a variety of effects, but I don't recommend them because they tend to either leave a funny feeling (residue) on your fingers afterward or else become powdery and make a mess. Start simply and build slowly and as you want. This is exactly how I started on my artistic journey: I started playing with color in my journal, then wanted more. I now paint on canvases regularly and have a large body of work. As time goes by, you can add to your skills and to your supplies if you want more. In summary, I recommend a set of colored markers, a set of watercolor pencils, and either a watercolor palette with 8 or 12 colors or a small set of watercolor crayons. With the addition of water, a brush, a small jar of water, plus a couple of paper towels you have a moveable feast, and easily have enough to explore creatively and reflectively with color.

Coloring Books for Adults

These coloring books have become so popular because they serve a real need we have — to do something calming and beautiful, and have a result that is pleasing. You can purchase the coloring books from online to your local drug store. You could also google "coloring pages" and print out some beautiful pages. I find that florals, mandalas, and geometric designs are the best for allowing your brain to wander into productive and informative spaces that often inspire some writing.

Using regular colored pencils or watercolor pencils works very well; some markers work well, too. Watercolors or watercolor crayons are finicky to use with some of the smaller areas of the design. After you're finished, you can glue the finished page into your journal, or cut out areas of the designs and glue them in. They will offer a pop of design and color every time you open your book.

Invisible Writing

Sometimes you just need to rant a bit, either in anger or when whining about something. When you want to write, but know that you don't want to keep the writing to refer to later, write with a watercolor pencil. When you're done, dissolve the pigment with a wet brush, and you will end up with a lightly tinted page of color. You can glue onto this background of color an image that reflects how you've been feeling, or else write or sketch something else over the colored background, this time in pen or permanent marker. It can become a symbol of how we can transform negative things in our lives to something useful and even beautiful.

Swaths of Color

In the quiet corners of the day, invite your soul to come forward. Reflect on the recent past. Have you been getting the soul nourishment that you need? What have been some surprises? No need to write anything, but filling some pages of your journal with color provides the right headspace for reflection and psychic ease. These pages of color can be left as is, or can serve as a background for future writing, image-making, or collage.

If you're using the acrylic paint, place a few drops of liquid paint, or a dime-sized dollop of paint from a tube onto the page. Swirl around the page or part of the page. Add another color in another area of the page. Notice how the colors mix. Is it pleasing, or does it dull the colors into mud? (If you want to learn more on avoiding that, research "color theory"). You can paint stripes, or just swirl the paint around, enjoying the sensation of movement and how the paint responds. Since acrylic cleans off with water, you can use your fingers, and remember the feel of fingerpainting as most of us did as children. Just enjoy the color. Notice how it makes you feel. Notice your response to different colors.

If you use watercolor, notice how the wet watercolor takes on a life of its own. Watercolor is harder to control than acrylic, which can be both its beauty and its frustration. There are two main ways of using watercolor, wet on wet or wet on dry. Both give great effects, just different. Wet on wet is wetting the paper first, then painting with your wet brush filled with wet watercolor. Wet on dry is painting with your slightly damp brush onto dry paper. You get much more blending and movement using wet on wet. Try wetting your journal page first, either with painting the page with clean water or by spraying water on the page. Drop your color in, and watch it follow the water around it. If you want that effect, but want to contain the paint inside of a shape, paint the shape onto your dry page with clean water, then add the color. The paint moves freely in the wet section of the paper, but does not move onto the dry part of the paper.

You can do a wash on the page in one color, going from a deep, darker shade right through to a very light pastel hue. This is called *ombre*, different shades of a color blended together. To do this, start with a horizontal line across the top of your page with your brush filled with juicy pigment. Try to finish the line in just one stroke. Then dip your pen in water quickly, just in and out, and paint another line right underneath the first, without adding more watercolor pigment. You should have a lighter shade of your original color. Continue doing this, dipping the brush briefly into water with each stroke, until your color runs out. It takes a little practice before you can produce strokes that have a balanced and even gradient of color — but the practice is enjoyable, and even your first tries have beauty in them.

Another easy way to play with the watercolor is to paint horizontal lines of different colors, one underneath the other. Or you can choose just two or three colors and repeat them in a pattern. You can decide whether to do it wet on wet or wet on dry. The two variations will come out quite different. The unpredictability of it all invites quite a meditation on how our lives so often go: we may make exquisite plans, and while things sometimes go along with those plans, so often "life intrudes," and all you can do is cooperate with what's happening! Whether you do this wet on wet or wet on dry, you will have some blending of colors happening. How do you like that blending? Which colors blend beautifully together, and which make muddy colors? How does that blending remind you of how you and your friends mix and blend with each other? Do some friends make beauty, just by being next to each other? Do other friends need a third person between them before their blending could be called beautiful? Is that a problem? Or is there a type of strength in that, as well?

When you have a page of either one-hued ombre or lines of different colors, those lines can be guide lines for copying out a poem in a beautiful way. Be sure to wait until the page is completely dry before writing your words onto the page. You could also do this by writing out a poem or quote first, then painting the watercolor afterwards. If you choose to do it that way, be sure your pen or marker has permanent ink. Otherwise, your poem will simply dissolve in the wet watercolor, tinting everything with the color of the ink.

If you have stencils (or make simple ones out of cardboard or file folders; very simple shapes of repeated circles, squares or triangles work well), after your first layer of paint dries paint a darker shade through the stencils on top of that bottom layer. It needn't be perfect or even particularly neat, especially if you plan to use the page as a background for your writing. It just adds visual interest, and slightly obscures your writing. This can help you to write even more truthfully or riskily, as your words won't be immediately legible. You will know what you've written, and if you pay close attention, you can reread your writing, but it won't sit there, "staring out at you, naked on the page" as I often phrase it. This is a little trick to use when you may want to try out some new ideas in writing, but are a little hesitant to be *too* honest, or *too* blatant, even to yourself.

This paint play can be incredibly relaxing, and is a fine activity when you're listening to music or to podcasts. Since you don't necessarily need privacy for this, it's also a good activity to do while your children or friends are around. Invite them to join you. I've noticed that sharing a pleasant simple activity together like this tends to invite deeper conversation and more intimate sharing. There's something about not having to look each other in the eye which, along with the relaxation that occurs, invites people to share what's on their hearts.

I've been a member of a group of women who met once a month to share whatever we had been reading lately. We started out several years ago as a more traditional book group, discussing one book that we had all read. But after a while, it was hard to find books that we all wanted to read, as we were all different with quite specific tastes in literature! Yet we still enjoyed each other's company. As a traditional book group, we had taken one or two months of the year to just "show and tell" about our favorite books. Those months had been very enjoyable, so we decided to have a book "show and tell" every month. I decided to bring watercolor paper, a few watercolor sets and brushes, some plastic cups for water, and plenty of paper towels, and most of us just played with the color while we chatted. It was surprisingly enjoyable, and I recommend it as an easy-going, non-stressful, not very messy activity with lots of different kinds of groups. It might even make holiday times with extended families more peaceful!

This is now how I do much of my journaling: colorful backgrounds with lots of writing on top of the painted backgrounds. I still have many days of more artistic or more complex endeavors, but writing has always been my primary journaling technique. I keep a few pages of the type of paper I make my journals out of close to where I paint on canvas. Whenever I have extra paint that I haven't used up, I use it on the blank sheets. Other times I intentionally paint on the individual sheets of paper. I then mix the paper I'd already filled with color with white sheets when I am ready to create my journals. I don't plan what colors to use beforehand, and enjoy the randomness of whatever color greets me on the next page. When I use darker colors of paint, it is sometimes harder to read what I write over it. But even those pages serve a great purpose as it helps me feel more comfortable in letting friends page through my colorful journals; they notice the background color, but don't take the time or effort to read my journal entries, keeping my writing relatively private while satisfying their curiosity as to how I use all that color. Of course, we all differ in how private we want to keep our journals. Be sure to respect your own desires in this and decline requests to share if you are not comfortable doing so.

After you play with your paints like this, laying down swaths of color, take stock. Did you enjoy it, or was it a chore? Did the freedom of not having to draw a picture help you feel more freedom in slinging the paint around? What kinds of conditions do you need to feel comfortable in trying something new? Did you enjoy doing this during spare moments throughout your day, or did you enjoy it more when you had an hour or so to devote to it. If you hadn't done this painting, what else would you have done during that time? Was it worth it to miss that, in order to paint a bit? Are there any new questions on soul life that have been sparked within you? I often find that as my mind wanders while I paint, I get new ideas or insights. I love the relaxed, dreamy feeling in my mind as I play with color.

Illustrate a Quote, Poem, Letter or Your Own Thoughts

As you feel more comfortable with a brush in your hand, consider making cards of your favorite quotes or poems to give to friends and family. If you enjoy calligraphy, you can use brush lettering rather than only pen and ink. You can get as fancy or as formal as you want, even though simple is often just as effective. This is a good way to share some of your favorite poems or quotations with people in a meaningful way, and is a sincere form of service when you have the exact quote that you know a friend needs during a particular life challenge. It's also a good way to play with paints and inks when you don't have any privacy yet still find that your fingers "itch" for brushes and color.

You can paint a background leaving a blank space for the words, or simply write your quote over the background. Write out the text beforehand on a piece of scrap so that you can plan where you will start your text, etc. You can measure it very carefully, or "eyeball" it. You can use calligraphy or your own handwriting. There are almost endless options here. Don't make it stressful, and infuse your love and care for the person you intend to receive it while you're writing it out.

If the poem or quote is not your own, remember to be respectful by copying out the words carefully and giving attribution to the author, even when you're just sharing with a good friend. If you are using someone else's words or photographs, be mindful of copyright laws and do not sell them without getting proper permissions ahead of time.

One Word Reminders

Paint two facing pages in your journal (or onto other paper) in the most lovely, relaxing, juicy, joyful colors you can think of. On the first page, think through and write down all the things that make your days wonderful, or worth living, or that "get you through the day". I'm thinking here of things like a relaxing cup of tea, 15 minutes of inspirational reading, meditation, the quiet in the car on the way home from work, or the sunshine hitting my work table in the morning. What are the little things in the day that sustain and nurture you, that help you live a life worth living, that make *you* happy?

On the second page, choose one word from your list, a word that calls to you, that jumps out at you, or that shimmers for you in some way. Write that one word very large on your page with either your black pen or with paint. If you're so inclined, make the lettering special, perhaps adding new colors within the letters themselves.

Now, resolve that to the best of your ability, you will bring whatever action or quality that word refers to into every day of your life. At least until another word shimmers!

There's Always the Unexpected

Today didn't start out, or continue, as I had planned. Unexpected things came up all day. How do the surprises happen in your life? List a few times when you were visited by the unexpected (which might be either a serendipitous event, or a time when your plans just fell apart). Cover your words with colors that reflect emotionally the outcomes of those "unexpecteds." Pick colors totally unique to yourself. I might pick blue because it reflects pleasant, peaceful, and expansive moments; you might use blue for the sadder consequences of unexpected events. I love purple and black for regal, mature, responsible moments but my friend is depressed by those colors.

You can also take the time to think through and record in words or image a time in your life where a series of unexpected things happened that changed your life: your job was terminated and you ended up moving across the country and meeting your new love along with your new job; you tried to semi-retire and found yourself unexpectedly pregnant with an entirely surprising second half of life (my own story). Do you look at interruptions and unexpected events primarily with dread, or with curiosity?

Repeated Shapes

Let's go into right-brain play. If words come, of course record them, but I invite you to start with a blank page, then pick a shape such as squares, triangles, circles, or hexagons, and draw that shape repeatedly on the page. Paint them different colors. You can place the shapes next to each other, or overlapping, or keep them all separate. They can be a variety of sizes, or all quite uniform. Notice if you want the shapes to be exact or identical; do you use a compass or cup to draw your circles, or do you free-hand them? Do you nest the shapes within each other? Do you enjoy free-styling the shapes?

Let it become pleasurable to draw these repeating shapes. If you want, you can record a list by writing each item into a different shape. Or you can fill the shapes with different symbols or letters, practicing a variety of fancy lettering styles. You can draw a checkerboard for squares; by placing a diagonal line in each square you now have a page of triangles. Your checkerboard need not be exact; in fact, curve your lines for a sense of movement and enjoy the wonkiness. Your squares can be big or small; some may be rectangles with curved sides. You could divide up some of those squares into triangles, making peaked roofs for the houses and towers suggested by the squares underneath.

This is a great stress reliever, as long as drawing the shapes does not stress you! You could do this while watching TV or movies with your family; you can do this while chatting with friends. I think you will be surprised at how such a simple idea can be so pleasing to look at once you fill them with color. The artist Paul Klee painted a whole series of what he called "Magic Squares," all shapes, all sizes. Imagine how your shapes might be magical.

Drawing the Web of Your Life

Let this practice be a contemplative reflection on the richness of your life, or an assessment of what you might want to cull from your life at this time. Open to a two-page spread in your journal (that is, two face-to-face pages that you will use as one page). You may already have a colored background, but if not, lay down a single color. Then with a pen or marker, write your name in a small circle or square in the middle of the page. Draw some lines radiating out from there, and place words that symbolize the different areas of your life in shapes that you create at the end of the radiating lines. You may have three main areas; you may have ten. Mine include "Soul", "Family", "Work", "Friends", "Poetry Circle", "Writing", and "Chronic Illness".

Draw more lines radiating out from each of those nodes, create some shapes, and write the names of the people who are included in each area of your life. You can go on to include tasks or major responsibilities in each area, or include any other category that makes sense to you. Notice where certain people or tasks are connected to two or more categories.

Once you have more or less filled the page, pick three colors to correspond with "things/people you're **enthusiastic** about", "things/people you feel **neutral** about", and "things/people you just **tolerate**, or actively **dislike**". Go ahead and paint over the appropriate shapes according to how you feel. Paint right over the color of the background. When you're finished, take a good look at your page. Is there one color that dominates? Which one? Does that invite any considerations for you about either being very grateful for your life or for thinking about how to make some changes? Is there a mix of colors?

Do particular colors dominate certain areas of your life? Do certain people come up several times in the same color, or are they in different colors depending on the area of life in which you work with them? Just notice. Does anything else draw itself to your attention? Remember that you don't have to do anything about any of this right now. In some areas of your life you may have more choices than in others. (For instance, you can't really give back your children even if they're in the "just tolerate" color! Fortunately, because they're always growing, they're always changing, and perhaps it's just a matter of waiting things out.) This is all just information, but information that may guide your future decisions.

Repeat this exercise every few years. It is fascinating to see how things change (or don't change, for that matter) as the years go by. This, too, can offer data for reflection as to how you are aligning what you want in your life with what you do in your life and with how you spend your time in your life. What choices do you have? What might you want to do now?

Very Simple Drawing and Doodling

Do not underestimate the simple power of repeated lines, small shapes, and doodling. You can add these in the margins of your written entries, or make it a habit to leave ¼ to ½ of most of your written pages blank. You may find an image you've collected that you want to glue in, or want to add a sweep of color later. In my journals I often use different types of lettering to express different emotions, with generous amounts of circled and underlined words in a variety of colors. I'll doodle faces in the margins with a variety of expressions and hair styles (like sticking straight out!) to add to the expressiveness of my words.

Often before writing, especially if I don't know exactly what I want to say or how I want to start, or simply to center myself beforehand, I will draw an ever-expanding spiral with the lines as close together as my pen or marker allows. The concentration and the slowing down of doing this helps me make the break from the emotions of whatever I was doing before, and I can come into this new space with more openness and clarity.

A similar technique that yields a slightly different "feel" from the ever-expanding line is to sketch a small shape, say a triangle, or heart. I then draw a slightly bigger triangle or heart around that, and then another and another, filling whatever space I have available to me. You can leave that as is, or go back in with markers or pencils to bring color to each layer of shape. Sometimes the type of color seems to make a big difference to me. Alternating black and white expresses quite a different feel than coloring a rainbow, for instance. Is it a pastel day, or a red and purple day? What about repeating different colors that are meaningful to you in some way? I often will use the alchemical colors of black, red, and white when I'm seeking to transform a feeling or situation. If you're feeling political or patriotic, you could use the colors of your national flag, or you could use the colors of a sports team. All of these very little additions add to the complexity of self-expression, and they make a difference.

Perhaps you already have a vocabulary in your doodles. Use these to enhance your writing, or simply doodle across the whole page. Learn some simple patterns to embellish a page, such as zigzags or staggering the length of lines that surround a section of your page. Repeating the pattern is relaxing and expressive, as well as getting your hand muscles practiced in expressing what your brain intends. Alternate lines and dots around a section, then add three or four more layers in different colors to create borders. How are you using these borders and boundaries, to separate, to highlight, or to balance the page? Just as you're drawing these repeated kinds of borders on your page, notice that in daily life it often takes a repetition of setting your boundaries before other people will respect those boundaries. Practice some simple shapes such as leaves or simple flowers to add to these lines and patterns. What kinds of little things will embellish your life to make it more striking, more pleasurable? What do you love? Learn to draw it or symbolize it, and include it on page after page in your journal.

But How Do I Draw a _____?

Google is your friend here. Google "how to draw _____", and you will bring up step by step instructions from graphic to classical. Remember not to use the internet very much while doing your depth dimension practices though, because it's so easy to fall down rabbit holes and only come up for air long after the amount of time you intended to devote to this has gone by!

Perhaps purchase a book that teaches children how to draw simple objects, and keep it in your bag of supplies. Ed Emberly is an artist with several of these kinds of books. All of his objects are based on simple shapes and are able to be completed by anybody who can draw a rectangle and circle! As you gain experience, remember that the outline of everything we see is a collection of simple shapes put together in different variations. When you begin to see those basic shapes, you can represent almost anything in your journals. Stylized shapes can suggest many images: an oval drawn on top of a rectangle can represent a person. A small slanted rectangle next to a horizontal rectangle, plus four lines for legs and a curved one for a tail can represent a dog. Add some ears. Make the rectangles a little rounder, and you have a cat. Remember that the point of depth dimension practices is not perfection, but expression and reflection. You may find yourself with some new hobbies, as well.

I'd like to finish this section with some suggestions as to how to draw a simple face, which then empowers you to express all kinds of emotions and all kinds of people. Draw an oval, or egg shape with the smaller end at the bottom. Sketch in or imagine a horizontal line halfway between the top and the bottom of your oval shape, and draw in the eyes on that horizontal line in a roughly almond shape. That's the most important piece in making a face look life-like, as inexperienced artists almost always draw the eyes far too high on the face. Then halfway again from the horizontal eye-line to the bottom of the chin, draw in the nose. You can suggest a nose with a shallow curve that looks like a small smile, then add parentheses (the nostrils) around it. Place the "parentheses" a tiny bit above the shallow curve, as the shallow curve is the bottom of the nose. Halfway again between the nose and the chin, draw in some lips.

Ears are elongated "c's" starting at the level of the eyes or just below, and extending to about where the bottom of the nose is placed. Lots of individual variation works well, so don't try for perfection. Then add the hair, starting the hair line just a little down from the top of the oval. If you have your person with bangs or fringe, bring the bangs down to the eyebrows just above the eyes. Remember that the neck is actually quite wide on humans, coming down vertically in line with the ears. Now, you most probably have a recognizably human face, and you can play with the shapes of the features, especially the shapes of the eyebrows, in order to express the whole gamut of emotions. Alternately, you can omit all the facial features, or draw in just eyes, to allow the viewer to project whatever emotion they want onto your simple sketch.

Mandalas

Circle designs can be as fancy or as informal as you desire. Try just free-hand designs starting at a center point as simple as a small circle. If you imagine the finished image as a clock, now draw in a design such as a tear shape, triangle, or elongated oval at 12:00, 3:00, 6:00, and 9:00. A little farther out, draw some more shapes or lines in a symmetrical pattern until you've filled your space or exhausted your imagination. You can color in the shapes, or draw in the shapes and lines in different colors from the beginning. Yet black and white images are quite striking as well.

I find that when coming to my journal I sometimes have no idea what I'm going to do. Drawing a simple mandala free-hand, or mindfully drawing a spiral or something with repeated lines is an easy go-to for getting into a state of relaxation and reflection. While starting with those simple shapes, I often find what it is that I've been worrying about on the back-burners of my brain. Then I can address those concerns either explicitly in writing, or in a more abstract way with image or color.

You could also keep a compass and 6-inch ruler in with your supplies, and draw more exact mandalas. The beauty of the endless variety possible is inspiring, and the construction of the symmetrical shapes calms and balances the mind. Another option is to keep your shapes in a mandala large enough to write words in. You could use these mandalas to help in decision making or examining an issue by writing in the various aspects of the issue, or the pros and cons, or inside and outside considerations. The extra creativity involved in doing more than simply writing from left to right and from top to bottom seems to loosen our previous ways of looking at things, helping us to find options we would not have thought of otherwise.

Watercolor Effects

Beyond simple swaths of color, here are four easy ways to add different effects or patterns:

- **Salt:** After applying the watercolor paint, while your paper is still wet, sprinkle salt on the paper. When the paper is completely dry, brush off the salt. The salt absorbs some of the color, and will leave dotted white patterns on your colored page. Using kosher salt leaves bigger splotches than table salt, as kosher salt has much larger granules.
- **Resist:** Before painting the blank page, use a white crayon (a regular kid's crayon, not a watercolor crayon) or even a white candle to draw patterns on the page. Simple lines, a checkerboard pattern, or random circles are fine. Then paint over the page, and your designs will remain the color of the blank page. The wax works as a resist, not allowing your paint to be absorbed there. You could also write out words with the white crayon, leaving a vaguely written background, or if you have stencils, you could copy the pattern onto the blank page

with the resist. It results in beautiful effects that are very simple to create.

+ **Plastic wrap:** After applying the watercolor paint, scrunch up a piece of saran wrap or any kind of plastic wrap, and blot onto the wet paint. It will pick up just enough of the watercolor paint to leave an almost marbled effect. Or scrunch the plastic wrap onto the painted surface and leave until the paint is completely dry. Remove the plastic wrap. You will have a whole mix of random designs. You could also blot the paint with scrunched up tissue or paper towel. This picks up quite a bit more paint.

+ **Bubble wrap:** Instead of applying paint to the paper, apply paint to a section of bubble wrap. Don't try to cover all the indentations or valleys in the bubble wrap, just apply paint to the raised bubbles. Use the bubble wrap as a type of stamp and cover your page with random circles. They won't be perfect circles, as the bubble wrap will stamp with wherever the paint lands. This imperfection is surprisingly inviting to then cover with writing or other images.

Collage

Go through your stash of images that you've collected from magazines, books, and other ephemera. You may want to start collecting words from headlines and keep in a plastic sandwich bag. Collect words that intrigue you or that reflect your values and things you like. You can also collect papers such as wrapping paper, background patterns, or plain colored paper that you can purchase or make yourself from scrap papers and paint.

Sit with your collections and pick a small pile of what attracts you that day. Don't think too hard about what to choose. Let your fingers find whatever they want. Arrange the papers and images on a page of your journal, or on another backdrop, in a way that pleases you. You can put them together very randomly, with parts of images covering other images, or you can put them together separated with thin white spaces, as though in a mosaic. Instead of using scissors to cut the papers and images to the size you need, tear them for a different effect. Try a variety of arrangements. If you can't decide how to place your pieces in an artistic manner, place them in the way you'd expect a 5-year-old to place them:

anywhere on the page! Once you have an arrangement that pleases you well enough, glue the papers down with a glue stick. You can also use matte medium or white glue with a brush. When applying the glue, be generous, and make sure that the glue extends to the very edge of the paper. I keep an old catalog in my art space to place my papers face-down and then apply the glue by extending it off the edges of the papers onto the background of the catalog. Keep your glue brush in water when you're not using it, and be sure to wash it out thoroughly when you're done. Remember to sign your work.

After you finish your collage, sit with it for 3 - 5 minutes, and see what you can see. Sit in silence, and ask your inner wisdom to reveal to you anything that might be useful for you. Are there any connections among the images? What are the colors like? What emotions come up as you look at the whole? What is the "feel" of the whole? Does it remind you of anything — an event from your life, a person, or a dream? Have you felt like this before? When? What happened? Make some notes about this in your journal or on the back of the page. You may wish to write about it more deeply at another time.

Now you have a lot of choices. You basically have a very textured page, and you can decide whether to highlight some of the images, or to cover them lightly or heavily with paint. You can leave the collage and call the page done! For me, if the individual images are not important, I like to paint the page with dilute white paint or gesso. That way the colors are all toned down, but still show through a little bit. You could then use the page as if it were a blank page background and do whatever you would ordinarily do in your journal on top of this highly textured background. I like to write out a poem or quote on top of a collage.

Sometimes it takes risk and experimentation to find ways to express our soul, and then discernment on if and how to bring that out into the world as gift. Trying new things in a journal is a way to rehearse risk and experimentation without fear of ruining anything. More often than not it becomes a new happy discovery which helps us overcome our natural fears of experimentation in other arenas of life. Collage is a wonderful analogy of taking the random pieces and events of our lives and bringing some beauty and meaning out of placing them all together and looking at them in a different way. It can help us rehearse how to live our lives with more openness and curiosity. Your soul loves this kind of play and expression!

Contemplative Photography

Now that all of us who have a smart phone have a high-quality camera in the palms of our hands, we can amass photos with almost no cost. Instead of just photographing people or events, try taking a walk and photographing whatever catches your eye, whether it's a ladybug or the cracks in the sidewalk, the shadows of the branches of trees on the white, white snow or the chickadee as the lone sign of life on a gray winter afternoon. You can print out the day's finds on plain copier paper, cut them out, and make a collage. Whatever you might ultimately do with them, take some time to look through them contemplatively and ask yourself the kinds of questions I recommended in the Meditating on Visual Images section or in the Collage section above. Do you tend to take the same kinds of photos over and over again? If so, why? Is it that you find a particular beauty or meaning in that subject, or are you having difficulty in moving to something new? Do your photos say more about your subjects or do they say more about you? How do your photographs reflect the person that you are?

Collect your photos with a variety of challenges you give yourself. You can photograph images only in black and white. You could collect photographs that you take when you're feeling sad, or when you're feeling angry. You could take a photo of the same tree on the same date every month for a year, and assemble a hand-crafted book with the photos. Take photos of a familiar place over a period of time, such as a garden or the plants in your yard, and share them with a young child. Through their eyes, see growth take place from a perspective you may have lost through distraction or familiarity.

Become Fluent in Symbolic Languages

Find a book on symbols and peruse it reflectively. Of course, you can look online, but don't get distracted. Make notes, or copy out some sketches of different symbols. You can start with categories of symbols if you're afraid of becoming overwhelmed. Look for symbols for the elements, for example, or of the seasons. Look for symbols of the months of the year, or symbols for different kinds of archetypes. Look both for the meanings of the symbols, and for how the symbols are designed.

Play with what you learn. I have a small blank book filled with copies of different symbols and glyphs that I've discovered over the years. Design a tattoo for yourself, whether or not you actually get it inked. Design your own sign or sigil. Come up with a symbol for your family, or design a family crest. Experiment with how you can communicate complicated ideas in simple images. Rather than communicating only a one-to-one correspondence, design images that are multivalent, having many meanings.

Reflect on what kinds of symbols you are attracted to. Think of how you might duplicate those designs in various ways in your life. You can easily start with drawing them on t-shirts with permanent markers or fabric markers. Embroidery is a classic form for recording important images and symbols onto household items and small items like handkerchiefs. Mark a cross and a circle onto the top of the bread dough before baking. Experiment with how you can make more of your daily activities a little more symbolic, a little more meaningful.

Explore the large topic of Sacred Geometry and numbers. Find out what attracts you, and ask yourself why. Develop the ability to see beneath the surface meanings of things, and begin to wonder at the hidden depths of just about everything in your daily life. Question if those meanings are intrinsically embedded in those items or routines, or if it is our human gifts of perception and imagination that "find" those meanings. Think about what human beings can imagine and create. Think about what you imagine and might be able to create. Ask if it even matters whether the connections we discover among things are "really" there, or if we "just" project them. Ask yourself what "real" means, and how much it matters to material reality in a universe that contains far more than can be known by Newtonian physics. Fall down some rabbit holes and find things that you would never have dreamt of. Don't believe everything that you think, but think about more than you believe. Have fun!

Using Image to Create More of the Kind of Life You Want to Live

Imagine what your inner self looks like when you're in situations that are not ideal for you. Make some sort of representation of that in image or color. Imagine what your inner self looks like when you're happy, at peace, and contentedly going with the flow. Make that into an image in some way. You can draw images of actual situations, or just use color to hint at it.

As an example, for many of us as kids, Saturdays were days to sleep in and maybe get together with some friends. For a day or two, our lives could be not so busy — we could drift — even get bored. For many of us now, Saturdays are way too filled with errands and getting caught up with all that we didn't get done during the week, if we're even fortunate enough to have the whole day off regular work.

Do you ever get to sleep in? What does your inner self look like when you do? Mine looks like a deep slow smile. What does your inner self look like when you have to get up to the alarm, again, throwing yourself into the day sleep deprived and more than a little grumpy? My inner self is red angry, with a very grumpy face with eyes half closed.

With sketching or with just splashes of color, make into an image what you look like in those two different situations. Or imagine a different situation. Now, think seriously about how you'd like to be living those situations which make up your life. What little things, or big things, are under your control so that you can move just a little bit closer to that? What "family policy" changes can you make? What can you let go of? We often think that we just "have to" keep doing what we're doing, but most of us have more power to change things than we think.

Am I Seeing What Is Really There/Here?

Just now I'm looking at a billowy pile of gray clouds across a gray sky. There's the merest hint of the color lavender in one small area. Is that color really there? Or is it reflecting off the window in some way? Is it an illusion sparked by my window's curtains? Am I imagining it? If I'm imagining it, is it real? Represent what you see outside into your journal. Add those things you're not sure are there, but you think you see. Now it's real, because it's now in your journal, and it's there.

This practice works not only for colors in clouds, but in interpretations of voice tones, in "visions" we have, in figuring out peoples' motivations, and in what supports or harms our own health. Remember when eggs and butter were "bad", but now they're "good" for you? Remember when you weren't supposed to have any fats, but you could eat all the sugars you wanted? Loosen up your iron grip on what you assume is "real", and "true".

What do you see in your ordinary days that may or may not be real? What of those things feed your soul? For those that do, make an image of it somehow in your journal, and make it real, at least in one sense of the term "real." If it dampens your soul, let it be gone. Don't reinforce its existence any more.

On the other side of "what's real?" is the phenomenon of not seeing what is obviously in front of you. A good example is floaters in your eyes. As we age, the gel-like substance in our eyes sometimes hardens and breaks off, causing you to see spots or shadows. When you focus on them, they shift and you can't see them. In my experience, what I find fascinating is that when the floater first breaks off, it's very visible to me, and I keep wanting to blink to get it out of my eye. I'm very aware of it and it is annoying. Yet, in a matter of weeks, I no longer see it. It's still there, but my brain has gotten used to it, knowing that it is not part of what is "out there" in my line of visions, so it doesn't register with me. So this is a case where something is real, is material, is there right in my eye, but I don't see it anymore. Stretching this reality to metaphor, what things in our lives have we gotten so used to that we don't see them anymore? Might it be the look of sadness in our partner's eyes? Or the people experiencing poverty who are hanging out near the back of the grocery store? What about smog, so visible when we land in a new sooty city, yet we become used to it in a matter of days? Can you draw an image that makes visible the things that we just don't see anymore, because we've gotten used to them? This can also be a joyful process of discovery. Before my son was born, I cared for my 5-year-old nephew for two weeks. He had an eye for iridescent bugs and shiny pebbles. The world became so much more wondrous to me when we would go for walks around the neighborhood that I thought I knew so well. He'd bring my attention to all the iridescence and shine I hadn't noticed before.

Draw or color some inner and outer landscapes that include that which we no longer see, as well as landscapes that include what we think *ought* to be visible, but isn't. At least not yet. Think about how we can help other people see both the truth, and the wondrous possibilities that *could* come into being.

When we're going back and forth between what I would call consensual reality and our inner seeing, keep yourself grounded. Have one foot firmly planted in the consensual world of perception. This is not only a way to safeguard your mental health, but also a good way to remember how it is that most of the people around us see the world. When we can see the mundane through their eyes, we can more effectively figure out how to help them bridge into seeing *possibilities*, into seeing what *could be*.

What Do I Want to Remember About Today?

As you're going through your days, practice a dual vision at times. Be completely embedded in living your life, but at the same time notice whatever it is that you want to hold as memories. If it's appropriate, take a photograph that symbolizes that to you, or keep a reminder to put into your journal, like a colored napkin from a restaurant lunch with friends, or some pinches of dirt from your hike carried home in a tiny plastic bag.

Remember that it's natural for all of us to have a negativity bias. We much more easily remember the bad times in our lives rather than the good things. That bias gives the difficult times more power over our inner selves and distorts our memories of how things actually were and are. So we must be proactive about at least balancing our memories in order to remember our lives with any accuracy. Include those memories into your journal not only with words, but with photos, sketches, and small artifacts that you can glue or tape into your journal. Look back at your days with soft eyes and love in your heart, and then decide what it is you want to remember about your days.

This is a good time to remind you that most of the practices that were included in the "Word" section of this book can be adapted to include images and color. Also remember that the more senses we use in recording our thoughts, memories, and ideas, the more we develop a habit of awareness of more in life, and therefore experiencing a richer life. Recording, reflecting, and envisioning our lives helps us not only to experience richer lives, but empowers us to be full participants in them. We create our little piece of the world with more beauty, more love, and more justice. Our lives are rarely defined by just one or two heroic actions we take, but are far more defined by how we live our daily lives. Noticing where we have choices and then making those choices creates possibilities for tomorrow, and for the future that our children, and the children seven generations from now will inherit. Live this moment, now, in all the depths that it holds, and it opens up more possibilities for the love and justice that will make a world that nurtures all of us.

Boxing Up Holiday Stresses

Start out with one of your beautiful backgrounds. In point form or in simple sketches write out all the stresses, common, chronic, and specific to the season, that you are or will be dealing with in the coming month. Just brainstorm everything. It's not only the number of stresses that you have, but the intensity of them that you want to note in some way. You can make your writing or your image bigger or darker for the stresses that are more intense. Once they're down on paper like this, you'll know what you're dealing with, and don't have to feel that overwhelming dread of the unknown.

Now take a look at them and thoughtfully acknowledge them. Take some time to get in touch with what's most important in your life, what motivates you to keep going. Try to represent by an image those priorities in your journal on a facing page, even if only in colors you love. Hold on to that feeling of knowing what's most important, and now go back to your stress list.

Be as proactive as possible in preventing illness, depression, and burn-out. As you read your list, think of the natural categories into which they go. Some might be everyday stresses that are aggravating, but that are basically under control. Others might be worries about people or situations that are completely out of your control. Others might be chores and errands that are related specifically to the season. Perhaps a pile of them are related to physical conditions that you need to be careful about when stresses pile up. You'll intuitively know what categories make sense to your situation. On the next page of your journal, draw some boxes, as many as you have categories, and label them. Now rewrite or draw your stresses into the appropriate categories. Are there any boxes that you can give to someone else to handle? Are there any stresses that you can just drop? Cross those out and make a note to delegate what you can or to manage other peoples' expectations as to what you will be doing. Boxed up like that, your image is reinforcing to your psyche that these stresses can be handled, that no one particular stress needs to take over your entire life, nor ruin an entire season. Make the boxes and your items in them as beautiful as you can, to remind yourself that, as much as is in your control, you are creating a beautiful holiday season and by extension, a beautiful life.

Blind Contour Drawing

This practice is an exercise in focusing your attention, examining something so deeply that even if it is a familiar sight, you might begin to see it anew, noticing many new details. Choose something to draw, something small that is on your desk or on the wall in front of you, like a stapler or a painting. It could be your own face in a mirror, or your children flopped on the couch watching a video. Place your hand with your pen or pencil on your page, and then without taking your pen off the page, and without looking down at your page, draw whatever it is you have chosen. Go slowly, and try to represent using your fingers what it is that your eyes are seeing. When done, look at your drawing, which will probably be rather surprising, with lines that are wonky and shapes that are wildly distorted. Ask yourself if you noticed anything new or different about your subject by looking at it so closely. Ask yourself if your drawing reveals anything new or different about your subject. Think about how accurately we are or are not able to represent (re-present) what we notice, and ponder how accurately we see the situations around us most of the time, when we are not focusing so intently.

When we describe a situation to ourselves in our memory, or describe a situation to someone else, how much have you paid attention to what is really there, or to what is really going on. Or are you relying only on your surface attention?

Creating Your Own Images, Imagining Transformations

As you begin to feel more comfortable in creating your own drawings, whether in stick figures or doodles, in blobs of colors, or with more realistic skill, begin to "show" your thoughts and feelings rather than just "telling" them in words. The next few practices include suggestions on how to do this. Many of us know that we don't like where we are or what we're doing, but rarely take the time and effort to figure out where we want to be or what we want to be doing exactly. By taking that time to envision a preferred future, and then to embody that vision in some sort of representational way, we are taking a first step to making that preferred future actually happen. As you know better, and can see a picture of what you want or where you want to go, you will naturally move into that direction whenever you see a choice in front of you that will take you closer to your preferred future.

It's like trying new clothes on to see if they fit or if they make you feel more "you"; draw your future, or draw your transformation, and see if it fits. If it doesn't, draw something else. Remember too that you do not need advanced skills in sketching to do this. Simply laying down colors, with perhaps a note or label to help you remember what you saw in your imagination, is often enough to make the image "real" in your psyche, and help you to move forward toward it. You can glue in images that resonate with you in response to any of these exercises instead of drawing, as well. Just help yourself to see in image where you want to go, who you want to be, or how you want to transform. Be curious and watch your images transform. Include as many details as you can.

Who's Moving Through My Life These Days?

Using your file of collected images, tarot or oracle cards, or lists of archetypes that you have compiled, shuffle through them to find whatever images or ideas resonate with you today. Once you have a few, put the rest away, and sit with your chosen images or ideas. Ask them "Who is moving through my life these days?" Do your chosen images remind you of any people who have literally been moving through your life? Do they inspire ideas of who or how you would like to be in your life these days? Do any remind you of any particular challenges that are either in your life presently or that you intuit may be coming up soon?

Once you have a few ideas moving around inside, see if you can represent them in an image outside of yourself onto the pages of your journal. Represent in sketch or in colors the archetypes coming up for you, imagining them in ways that are helpful to you or in ways that you would like to be. It is very important that if there is anything coming up that is scary, deeply negative, or trying to control you, that you represent those things in a transformed way or in a way that cannot harm you. Represent them behind bars, or in a box, or somehow contained. Or create an image of yourself with allies and protectors around you.

As you are playing with pencil and color, tell yourself a little story as to how these images and ideas can help you find treasure in your daily life. If they are there in your imagination, imagine how they can show you something that will teach you, or help you, or delight you in some way. Draw or image the scene where you find the treasure or the teaching. When you are finished, send a heart-felt thank you, or even a thank you note, to yourself, your imagination, and your imagined characters for showing you a little more of what's going on in your own psyche.

What Does Your Soul Look Like?

"Soul" is a word that is hard to define or even to describe, yet whenever you use it, you know the person in front of you has some idea of what you're talking about. Yet, are we thinking of the same thing, the same idea, the same concept? It's very hard to put into words. So don't. So draw a picture instead, or use a bunch of colors.

Does your idea of soul shift if, instead of thinking of a soul as within your body or mind, you think of your body within your soul? Now what would that look like?

A Human Being

When someone asks you how you're doing, is the first thing out of your mouth "Oh, I'm busy"? We live in a culture that fetishizes "doing" and "accomplishing" and "producing". What is your whole relationship to "doing"? Are you a human being or a human doing? What comes up when or if you invest time in not doing? Is this a soul issue for you?

Represent yourself in an image as a human BE-ing, not a human DO-ing. When you're finished, ask yourself what's different between that image and a photo of you. What do you like in the image you made? Is there some way to incorporate that into your daily life?

Metaphors for Inner Transformations

Think about bees, about how they collect pollen from the flowers, something very ordinary in their lives. They mix the pollen with their blood, sweat and tears (well, literally their saliva, I mean). They sit with it for a long time, fanning it, and slowly, wonderfully, that ordinary substance mixed with the bodies (saliva) and work (fanning) transforms into ambrosia, the food of the gods. Sweet, natural, honey!

Something like our lives, is it not? We take our ordinary selves, then through blood, sweat and tears, and a long time of sitting, tending, fanning our small hopes into some enthusiasm, we make ourselves something sweet with which to nourish and delight the world. Can you represent this transformation in your journal? Draw one bee to remind you of this, and then represent in color, images, or words how this might be happening in your life. Or draw a page of honeycomb, a page of golden hexagons.

Using another example, think of the common metaphor that the waste in our lives and the detritus of all our broken dreams can become the compost that will allow new things to grow in the future. Draw, paint, collage, or otherwise represent that which is waste in your own life, and then represent some of the new growth that may become possible. What do you want to grow out of the experiences of your life?

What needs to be composted now in your life? Remember that for the compost to be formed, there needs to be a lot of microorganisms (that is, helpers), and a lot of heat (perhaps passion?) generated to do the alchemizing of the waste into something new. And it needs time. Otherwise, you'll just have a pile of rotting waste. Who are your helpers? What's the heat that will do the alchemizing? How will you ensure that your life isn't just filled with a pile of rotting waste?

Other metaphors can provide a template and a vision for when we need to transform some things in our lives. Think of a squirrel hiding nuts from a tree and one of those seeds grabbing hold in the ground, growing, growing into a home and nourishment for birds and other animals. Or think of a bear going into hibernation where the sperm unites with her eggs and in spring the mother bear awakens with new life — hungry, demanding new cubs. Or gardening. Or the cycle of rain: to earth to river to sea to sky and then to the earth again, bringing its water to plants to seeds to animals and then to earth again in urine, cycling back to sea and sky and raindrop. How can we recognize those processes as metaphors that bring us encouragement as well as a path to follow?

132

To Respond with Love and Imagination

We live with tragedies broadcast to us many times daily through every media outlet. If it's not the latest statistics of people who have died from the coronavirus pandemic, it's Australia burning, or the latest mass shooting or riot in the center of the city. What is a sensitive and loving soul to do? Most of the people I know go on to Facebook with commentary and emotion. Perhaps it helps them process their emotions; perhaps it just fans more inflammatory comments. I suggest you use your journal to process the tragedies from the daily news feed, to figure out how to deal with these ongoing assaults. While I do call these litanies of serious problems assaults to our senses and hearts, I know very well that hearing about a tragedy is far, far less traumatizing than living through the tragedy itself. I mean no lack of sensitivity to those who are suffering; however, I want to draw attention to how the news can affect those of us who hear of one tragedy after another, from all over the world, with little or limited ability to offer helps and healings to all of those who are affected by those tragedies.

One thing that I have found helpful is to think seriously about what is mine to do in this hurtful and hurting world. Where do my skills and interests meet the needs around us? Where can my life's efforts make some meaningful difference over time in alleviating suffering? Once I have identified the two or three areas or issues that I want to devote myself to, I educate myself and develop skills to respond effectively within my reach.

While I do care about sick babies in developing world countries, I'm not likely to be able to fly halfway around the world to make a life helping out there. I can donate money, but my actual physical and psychological help needs to be offered here, within my circle of influence. It takes time and energy to discern this, but when you do, and then actually dedicate yourself in practical ways, you are much more able to respond to the myriad tragedies with an honest knowing that you are already doing what you can, within your power, to help. Doing that helps the anguish that comes from being aware of so much need. Just being informed of what's going on in the world does not help those who are victims of tragedies and injustices, but actively doing your part to help does. You are then free to limit your intake of the news, even limit it drastically. We don't need to be bombarded with more, more, more when we are already doing what we can, including working towards larger political responses that are just and helpful.

As you think about the things you care about, the harms you wish you could help, sit in silence in front of your blank page. If you want, you can briefly and simply represent the suffering in an image. But more importantly, think of your own skills, resources, and abilities. What are your own responses to these issues? What can you yourself bring to alleviate the suffering, to even eliminate the problem? Imagine yourself responding. What does it look like, what would you do? Represent that on your page. Again, stick figures or simply blobs of color are enough to represent your thoughts.

I once painted an image of myself with the body of a large rock, or small mountain. I was holding a tablet on which I was writing. It reflected back to me how I wanted to respond: sitting solidly, literally grounded, listening, loving, responding, speaking and writing words that both tell the godawful truths and words that may strengthen and heal.

This is a practice to be done over and over, every time you are overcome with the horror of a tragedy and have a huge desire to be of help. If no image comes to mind, try drawing an image of a weeping willow tree. Its branches are sensitive to the winds around it, bending and thrashing around, but its wide trunk and deep roots keep it stable and rooted in the nourishing earth. Strong storms will not bring this weeping willow down. Bend, but do not break. Now become that tree.

Beyond Image into the Third Dimension

These practices "work" through several processes, including that unexpected one we often call serendipity. Doing these practices engages both the rational parts of the brain as well as your image-processing areas of the brain. They engage your senses and your motor skills as you create the image in front of you. Perhaps most importantly, they invite you to project yourself into a new image, creating a vision that tends to make something that seemed closed and fixed into something that now feels dynamic and open to change. It helps us believe that something else just might be possible, and invites us to consider it and think of the details of how that might come to pass. It doesn't matter how "good", that is, how skilled or representational your images might be. Artistic talent is totally optional, and no one but you ever need to see what it is you've created.

On the other hand, these practices might invite you into spending the time to develop your artistic skills. That's what happened to me, and now I enjoy writing, painting, and creating poetry, along with my previously developed skills in sewing.

If you're so inclined, explore how this two-dimensional image-making can extend into creating your own personal talismans, items that you craft that can hold meaning, intention, and vision. I know people who have made small healing dolls, tiny treasure boxes, prayer beads, quilts, hand-painted clothing and bags, and a variety of other three-dimensional creations that are so much more meaningful than something you would buy in a specialty store. I invite you to move into any of these directions where we can take our ideas, hopes, passions and dreams and bring them into the realities of our lives in new ways, teaching us how to create a world where we are all welcomed and can find home.

5 Dream And Story

Why Pay Attention to Dreams and Stories?

Paying attention to the dreams, images, and stories that arise spontaneously in our lives is a very powerful practice. They are the portals into what's going on within us, just below our conscious minds. They let us know what is unresolved, what we're worried about, what we hope for, and what stands in our way. They give us clues as to the path to take, and let us know what and who to be cautious about before we even think to attend to those things. They bring new ideas as we're visited by beings and archetypes that exist in our community psyche. As we consciously collaborate with what arises spontaneously, we are able to bring more of our dreams into reality, and are assisted by the deep mythic imagination that brings images and ideas that can show the next step, the next possibility. Discovering how to work effectively with dreams and narrative has been both exciting and wondrous, as well as tremendously useful in my life. Yes, it takes patience and perseverance to learn their ways of communication, and moments of scintillating illumination are sometimes interspersed with long periods of mediocrity, even boredom. Most of us know only too well our daily worries and what we need to do next, and our dreams are always insisting we pay attention to those things. Yet when we least expect it, they break into the daily grind with sparks of newness and delightful synchronicities. And that's when we're invited through their doorway into possibility and creation. It's worth the patience and the work.

In this chapter, I'm going to be talking about the dreams we have at night and how to begin to analyze them to find out what they're saying about our lives and to plumb them for whatever inspiration they might hold for us. But I'm also going to be talking about how we humans use stories to organize ideas and experience into meaning. Just as birds make nests and beavers make dams, humans make meaning. It's the way our minds work. This is the basis for our dreams at night where we take the experiences of our days, mix them all up with our concerns and desires, and come up with some crazy story that we often remember on awakening. Fundamentally, this is how all story works, and so I'll be talking about becoming aware of not only night dreams, but daydreams, the stories we tell ourselves about why and how things happen, our dreams of what we hope will happen in our lives, the narratives we share to let people know about us and our lives, and our family stories. While night dreams arise spontaneously, we can also create stories that we want to live into, and so I will also look at guided visualizations, or guided meditations. Whether spontaneous or consciously created, our stories are how we experience and create our lives.

Anyone who writes fiction knows that there are many ways to tell a story. When something happens, witnesses can often agree on the sequence of events, yet almost each person has their own understanding of how exactly things happened, or why things happened in the way that they did. Ask any criminal court judge about the conflicting stories of eye witnesses to a crime! These differences in the how and the why of a story often tell us as much about the person telling the story as they tell us about the truth of the facts of the story.

And what is the truth? The facts? According to whom? We usually mean the facts as if the event had been recorded on video from all angles, so that anyone looking at the video would agree on what happened. But even then, we might interpret what we see in very different ways. We often tell stories and even hear stories that reinforce our presuppositions about the people involved, not aware of those presuppositions until something happens to shake up the narrative. For instance, when you were a child, you may have been punished for breaking a mirror that shattered when your older brother dropped it. That is the sequence of events. But how do you tell the story? Did your older brother blame you for breaking that mirror because you ran into him as he was carrying it? Or did he blame you because he thought your parents wouldn't punish the spoiled little five-year-old brat he thought you were then? Did you feel unjustly accused when you lost your balance in the slippery entryway, falling against your brother who was "too clumsy" to hold onto the mirror? Or did you think he purposely got you in trouble because he resented you from the time you were born? Or did he not blame you at all, but was late to his job as an ambulance driver, and rushed off before disposing of the broken mirror? He didn't know your parents would blame you for the mess when they came home before he could finish cleaning up the broken glass.

Our stories are so often filled with our projections. We take what we fear or what we dislike, and attribute those qualities to the characters or events of the narrative. At the same time, we take what we love or who we love, and include them as our heroes in the stories. Or we take what we want to have happen, and lo and behold, that's what is happening in our stories. Some of this is deliberate, but so much of this projection, both negative and positive, seems to just arise naturally in how we tell the stories of who we are and of what happens to us. Our projections, like our shadow, are important to become aware of because they hold locked energy that could otherwise be used to shift our lives in ways much more amenable to healing, happiness, and creativity.

The strangeness of night dreams often serves to shake up our narratives about how things are going in our everyday lives, and this can help remind us to shake up, that is, question other stories we tell. Shaking things up can open new ways of understanding our daily lives and what might be possible in them. But first, we need to know what some of the stories are that we're constantly telling ourselves, both our night dreams, our daydreams, and stories we tell each other. I'll explain some techniques for remembering our dreams and recording them, and how to catch some of the other stories going on within us as well.

The gift of night dreams is that they can bring new material, and are not controllable most of the time. They are free to tell us things we've never consciously thought before, free to shake us up. They are free to tell us when we're off track, free to tell us what we'd perhaps wish we didn't know.

Not all night dreams are a story, though. Sometimes we awaken with just a feeling, or just one image. Or we remember that we dreamed about our first lover, but can't remember anything else about the dream. These dreams can still have much in them that is revelatory, even when there is no plot and few details. When that happens, I suggest that you associate to the image or feeling as I described in Associative Writing in the chapter on Words. For instance, let's say that you dreamed of a tree, but that's all that you remember. Ask yourself what you think, feel, or remember about that tree. When you first awakened, did anything come up as you first identified the image from the dream? Did you have a strong feeling of some kind? Where else in your life do you feel that way, or did you feel that way in the past? Was it like a Christmas tree, or like a spreading oak tree in a field? Did it remind you of a tree that you pass every day in your comings and goings? Did it remind you of a Christmas with your grandparents from when you were a child? Did it make you think of the description of Yggdrasil, the mythical world tree of the Norse? Did it make you feel protected? From whatever your associations are, you can pick up clues as to what has come up for you lately. You can then ask where that image can be useful to you in your life now, or in whatever some of your concerns might be. Play with the image and your associations to it, and see whether there are clues in there for an answer to a question, to the solving of a conundrum, or simply a reminder of how various and wondrous is the world that we live in.

How Stories Work

There are four aspects that make a set of words or descriptions a story. First there is a setting, and characters in that setting. Secondly, something starts to happen, as in mounting action. Thirdly, something happens that is a problem, or that is unexpected. It makes a listener pay attention and wonder what happens next, and is called the crisis even though it need not be dangerous or terribly problematic. The last aspect of story is the resolution of the crisis. These aspects of stories, that is, setting and characters, mounting action, crisis, and resolution, don't need to be revealed in that particular order, yet all of them need to be in the story for us to feel satisfied.

These are the four aspects of dreams as well. When you want to work with a story, it's helpful to identify each of those aspects. Sometimes all four aspects aren't in the dream, or seem not to be at first glance. That's what gives dreams some of their unfamiliarity and their mystique. It's like an invitation for us to complete the story that's only half there by employing our conscious mind to finish it. It's also a reminder that our dreams can well give guidance and options, but don't often tell us right out what our best choice should be. Our conscious will and our awake life ideas are as important as the dream in actually creating our daily lives.

Another thing to keep in mind when thinking about story is the difference between literalism and symbolism, or fundamentalism and metaphor. This can become rather complex at times, as one of the first things that people ask when they hear a new story is whether or not it's a true story. Years ago, I was puzzled when a storyteller answered this question with, "Well, of course it's true, but I don't know whether it ever happened or not!" Something can be symbolically true even when the events never happened in the way that is told in the story, as in when a story tells us that if you lie often to your neighbors then they probably won't believe you when you do tell the truth. Was there really a shepherd boy who lived at a certain time and place who liked to joke with his neighbors by getting them all excited when he cried "Wolf!"? Were there actually villagers in the spring of such and such a year who came together to protect their sheep from the dangerous wolf, who were frustrated and angry to find out that there was no wolf? And when this happened several times, did the villagers then start to ignore the calls for help from the boy, assuming that he was again lying? And because the villagers didn't come to help, did the real wolf that eventually came eat up the shepherd boy, too? We don't know, and it really doesn't matter. The story tells the truth whether it happened or not. Dreams, too, tell us truths even though the events of the dreams may never have happened in awake life.

As we look at stories in our lives, whether dreams, daydreams, the stories we tell to others, our family stories, or the hopes that we have for the future, it will be helpful to ask these kinds of questions of our stories. We will find that our stories, too, are often very rich, holding clues as to how we see the world and how we organize our beliefs and events into meaning that can offer the possibilities of a deeper and richer awareness of our lives.

Remembering and Recording Our Dream and Stories

I will describe these tips primarily in how they apply to our dreams. These techniques, though, can be used to record all our stories in the same ways. In reality, you have to start somewhere, and it's our dreams that catch our interest and hold enough mystery to give us the motivation to begin this process. It's actually a fair amount of work to record and to analyze our dreams, but once learned and become a habit, extending the skills you learn to other kinds of stories is relatively simple.

Many people say they don't dream, or else that they remember a dream only very rarely. It's more accurate to say that they just don't remember their dreams, because the psychologists assure us that we each have 5 to 7 dreams a night. That's about 42 dreams a week, or over 2000 dreams in a year. That's more data than any of us can effectively analyze on a regular basis, but it highlights the fact that there's a lot more going on in our daily lives than we are commonly aware of. Even getting a hint of what's going on in our nightlife is interesting and enriching.

To start remembering some of these dreams, first set a firm intention that you will remember them. Get in touch with your desire to remember them, your curiosity to know more about yourself, and your willingness to do the work to discover this. Figure out how you will record your dreams. Some people think that voice recording their dreams on their phones would be easiest, but in fact doing so introduces another layer of work as you then need to find the time to transcribe your voice recording into writing. Oftentimes the recordings are difficult to understand or contain lots of repetition, because we're still half asleep when we're making the recording. Or they have long pauses where we're falling back asleep, and then we have difficulty remembering what we already said or didn't say about the dream. At least that's what happened when I tried this "shortcut"!

Dedicate a notebook just for collecting your dreams, and keep it and a writing instrument right next to your bed or even next to your pillow so that you can reach them before getting out of bed in the morning. Make sure your writing instrument is clipped to your journal page so it's easy to find, or you can tape your pen to a string that in turn is taped to the spine of your dream journal. Open the journal to the next blank page, date it, and write "I will remember my dreams" at the top of the page.

If at all possible, do not wake up with an alarm clock. The jarring noise of the alarm scatters any dream that we might be in, and pulls us into a completely different brain state that is the opposite of the dreamy, gentle state that facilitates dream recollection. Dreams scatter as soon as we begin moving, so it's important to remind yourself of the dream before you get up to go to the bathroom or get ready for the day. If you need to ensure that you are up by a certain time, try an alarm that uses a brightening light to awaken you as it mimics a more natural way of waking to a new day. Also, because you want to awaken gently and leisurely, try to manage your intake of liquids the night before so that you don't have to run to the bathroom the instant you awaken.

As you come to consciousness in the morning, before you roll over or move in any way, ask yourself if you had a dream. Often you will remember something from the night, and you should repeat what you remember of the dream to yourself a few times before moving to grab your dream journal. Before sitting up, write at least a few words of what you remember so that the dream doesn't scatter as you sit up to write more. Write down as much of the dream as you can remember, as soon after the dream as you can manage. Write it in the present tense, as if you're still right in the middle of the dream. Keep plenty of space between your lines, perhaps writing on every other line in a lined notebook. Keep enough space between the lines so that you can later add comments above your words. You can record the dream in story form, point form, or in fragments, but try to get down every detail that you remember. If you dreamed of a car, do you remember if it was a blue car or a red car? What feeling do you wake up with? How did you feel in the dream? Is it the same feeling, or different? Who was with you in the dream? What did you do? Often our recollection of dreams is hazy, or there is much in them that doesn't make sense. Just record what you can. You could draw a picture, even with just stick figures. I often use the phrase "It was something like ..."

While a dedicated dream journal makes sense for most people, adapt your practice to your own needs. For instance, during the night I move from bed to recliner chair and back to bed again all night looking for a comfortable position that allows me to fall asleep. When I awaken in the middle of the night, I often remember a dream or a fragment, and I've found that it's really useful to catch those then, as I rarely remember them in the morning. So I record my dreams by having three clipboards of the same sized paper, along with a pen attached to each clipboard so that I can find the pen without even opening my eyes. I have one clipboard right by my bed, the other on the table next to my recliner, and the third in the bathroom in a magazine rack directly in front of the toilet. Because I share my bed with my spouse, I don't want to unnecessarily wake him up by writing my dreams down in the middle of the night, so when I awaken with a dream, I hold myself still for a minute or two while I tell myself the dream a few times. Then I go to the bathroom and while sitting there, grab that clipboard and write the dream or write a few notes. We have some nightlights in the hallway that offer just enough light so as to write, but after so long of recording dreams in the middle of the night, I can record a dream with my eyes still closed. My finger holds the place where I last started a new line, and I just pull it down an inch or so when starting the next line, orienting my pen by where the finger on my other hand is placed. If you turn on a brighter light, that will usually cause your dream to scatter. Other people have used a pen that has a light in it to record their dreams. They are sometimes difficult to find, so others have just taken a flashlight in the shape of a pen and taped a pen refill to the flashlight. Also, by not turning on a brighter light, it's much easier to return to sleep after recording your dream.

In the morning, collect your dreams or look in your journal, make sure what you've written is legible enough, and be sure to add the date. If there's more about the dream that I remember, I'll add it then. If I am traveling, I make a note of where it is that I spent the night. Then I give the dream a title. Don't think about the title too much; it doesn't need to be witty. In fact, the simpler and more descriptive the better, so that in the future you'll be able to easily recollect the dream just by reading the title. Coming up with a title is the first way of summarizing what might be an important fact about the dream, and is a first clue in analyzing the dream. Once the data is collected and dated, you can go about analyzing the dream later. Because I collect my dreams on separate pieces of paper, I am careful to store them together and in order by date. I have a regular journal, and I keep my dreams in a pocket at the back of it.

If you use a journal to record your dreams, leave a few pages between dreams if you go for a couple of days before analyzing them. You want to leave some space not only between the lines of the dream to make comments, but also afterwards to add more details or to summarize what wisdom you might take from the dream. Yes, it's hard to estimate how many pages to leave blank between dreams, and it's really frustrating to go back to a dream you had a week ago and not have enough space to write down all your thoughts as you go back to mine the dream. On the other hand, it's also frustrating to have lots of blank pages in a finished dream journal either because you didn't get around to working with them or because you just didn't write very much in response to them. I have a system I've developed over the years to record, track, and work with my dreams that enables me to go back to find any dream and where I may have commented on the dream whether that's on the dream report itself or in my regular journal either at the time of the dream or quite a long time later. While I'll explain that system here, please know that if you're new at working with your dreams, it's perfectly adequate, and simplest, to just record your dreams upon waking in a dedicated dream journal such as a simple spiral notebook, leaving a page or two blank between dreams.

Cat's Fancy Dancy Dream Recording System

Please remember that you don't need to adopt my system at all in order to work very effectively with your dreams. But if you're someone who has been working with your dreams for a while and are frustrated by trying to find old dreams or where it is that you wrote about them, this system might just be what you're needing.

There are three parts to my dream recording system: the dream reports written on separate sheets of paper that I store chronologically in a pocket at the back of my regular journal; my regular journal in which I often work on and comment on the dream; and a separate "Dream Title Journal" that I also keep in the pocket at the back of my regular journal.

The "Dream Title Journal" is a very thin notebook in which I write down the dates and titles of all my dreams. It's arranged chronologically, and I start a new notebook at the beginning of each year. I create my own notebook out of plain paper folded into a pamphlet style book, bound with a simple 3-holed pamphlet stitch. I make it with 8 sheets of paper, each twice as wide as the finished size of the notebook I want, so that I have a cover plus 28 pages. This gives me two pages for each month for recording the dream titles, with a little extra room if I want to list dreams according to themes, or to list recurrent dreams.

Here's how it all works:

Whenever I have a dream, reenter a dream, go on a dream journey (intentional daytime dreaming), or notice a daydream (spontaneous daytime dreaming), I write up a report on a separate sheet of paper. I write down everything I remember about the dream or journey, either in story form or in bullet points. I always write the date in the upper right-hand corner of the report, and in the upper left-hand corner, I write a title for the dream.

Before I put the dream report away in the back pocket of my current journal, I log it chronologically in my Dream Title Journal by writing in the date and the title. I keep the Dream Title Journal tucked into the back cover of my current journal. If the dream is also related to a category that I'm keeping track of, I immediately log it onto the page for that category as well as listing it chronologically. For instance, I have had a whole series of dreams where I'm moving into a new house. In each year's Dream Title Journal, I have a page in the back dedicated to "New House Dreams" where I list the date and title of each new dream I have about moving into a new house. I have another list of recurrent dreams I have about teaching others in various situations, and a third list that includes all the dreams I have that include a particular person.

Whenever I work with a particular dream, that is, expand or amplify it in my journal or associate to any of its nouns or verbs, I write those notes in my regular journal. Usually, it is the same day that I have the dream, but if it isn't, I write down the date that I write about it in my Dream Title Journal right after the title of the dream. The Dream Title Journal will then have the date of the dream, the title of the dream, and then every date that I write in my journal about that dream.

The value in doing this is that I can easily find a dream that I've had in the past, along with everything else I have written about the dream in my regular journal. Each day, as I'm recording the dream in my Dream Title Journal, I also notice if it's a recurring dream and then log it onto the appropriate page where I'm keeping track of that category. I know I could get quite more detailed with a computerized database, but I have no need for that level of complexity. I record the dream by hand in order to catch the details without having to move to the computer, and then list them in a way that I can find the dream later. This comes in handy when something happens in awake life that seems to relate to a dream that I had previously, and I want to compare the awake life results with the contents of the original dream. I might remember that I had the dream in the spring, and then I review the dream titles from March, April, and May of that year to find the exact date, then go to the journal I had at that time to find the original copy of it in the back pocket, and look up the date in my regular journal to see what I wrote about the dream as I had worked with it. If I'd worked on it on other dates, then the Dream Title Journal lists those dates as well. A few months ago, someone had asked me if I had had any dreams since the beginning of the Covid 19 pandemic about a person we both knew. I knew I had, and it only took me a few minutes to find the 18 dreams that included that person.

Substances and Situations that Interfere with Dreaming and Dream Recollection

Many things can get in the way of remembering your dreams. If after sincere preparation and attempts to remember your dreams, you still are not catching any, look to your life and what you may be ingesting to see if any modifications can be of help. The use of marijuana in any form suppresses dream memory, unfortunately, and sometimes it's a matter of having to choose between your use of cannabis or your desire to work with your dreams. Any medication you take may interfere either with restful sleep or with dream memory, especially sleeping pills or anti-anxiety meds. Alcohol, of course, also inhibits dream memory.

Any kind of sleep disturbance can inhibit dream memory, such as wildly fluctuating schedules, irregular sleep or insomnia, deep fatigue, unrefreshing sleep as accompanies fibromyalgia and some other health conditions, being awakened by pain, or ongoing anxiety. Also, what you do during the daytime, but especially in the few hours before you go to bed, can interfere with sleep and dreaming. I don't know of any research study on this, but I wonder how watching the nightly world news just before turning over to fall asleep affects our dreams. I have found that watching a movie in the evening, or even reading an absorbing novel or mystery, influences my dreaming for the night. I dream about whatever story I've just seen or read over and over all night. I am very sensitive to the images in the news if I see them just before going to bed, so I consume my news early in the day. Heated discussion or argument can definitely influence your dreams as your psyche attempts to resolve the feelings stirred up by the conflict. Some of these factors are unavoidable or uncontrollable, but we often have more choices on modifying our lives than we at first think we do. Just be aware that many things that we take in may influence our ability to dream or our recollection of dreams.

Analyzing a Dream for its Meaning(s)

I describe working with dreams "analyzing" them rather than "interpreting" them, because I think it's unrealistic and perhaps even impossible to expect to come up with one meaning which then explains the dream completely. This is also why the various "Dream Dictionaries" are of such limited help to people. Spending just a little bit of time thinking about what the images and symbols of your dream mean to you will give you more information than looking up your dream images in any dictionary. You and I both might have a dream about a dog. The dream dictionary might say that dreaming of a dog means loyalty and unconditional love. Well, maybe. But if you have been deathly frightened of dogs since you were a small child, your dream dog may be referring more to someone or something in your life that you perceive as very dangerous to you. And perhaps my dream dog is the memory of the highly charged emotion I had the night before when I watched a movie where the beloved family dog sacrifices its life to save the life of the young son in the family. Some of the dream dictionaries give several possibilities as to the meanings of various symbols, and that might be helpful in jogging some of your own memories and associations around the dream image. So they can be suggestive, but they won't give you "THE" meaning of your dream.

For me the word "analyze" speaks to looking at something from a variety of perspectives, with a variety of possibilities for meaning. When I analyze my dreams, I play with the images and the actions in a variety of ways, generating many possibilities for meaning. In response, I almost always have an intuitive "nope" to some possibilities, and a felt "aha!" to other possibilities. Always go with the "aha's!" That's where the treasure is. Sometimes, though, you might get a whole lot of "uh … maybe's." When that's the case, I ask for a further dream to clarify what meaning it might have for me, or I wait for more information throughout the next few days that might give me some clues.

I say "ask" for a dream. Whom do you ask for a dream? Well, it depends on where you think dreams come from. Are they from God, or a Higher Power? Or are they from our deepest selves, the unconscious or the subconscious? A correct answer might be any or all of those. A simple way that holds onto the varieties of ideas of where dreams originate is to say "they come from Dreammaker", and that's how I prefer to refer to a dream's origins. Who or what is Dreammaker? Dreammaker can be understood as the function within us that puts images together and presents them to us for our guidance, our insight, and even for our entertainment.

Associating to the Nouns in Your Dream

You've got your dream report in front of you. You've given your dream a title. Now, notice if your dream is a story, or simply a string of images. Does it have a setting and characters, mounting action, a crisis, and a resolution? If so, it might be telling you about the likely outcome of a plan of action you might be thinking of taking. Remember that that is different from telling you what will happen in the future. Dreams are like a snapshot of a moment in time. Time moves on, and the picture changes. So anytime you feel that a dream is telling you what will happen in the future, know that a better way of thinking about it is that it is telling you that if things stay exactly the way they were in the dream, then it is *likely*, though not for certain, that it will have the following outcome. You always have a choice in your awake time to change the conditions, and then you will have changed the outcome that the dream has suggested is possible.

But what if you don't know how the story in your dream relates to your own awake life? Or if your dream isn't a complete story but is rather only a few images with maybe an action? While I have learned many ways over the years to work with dreams, I wish to here acknowledge the Jungian psychoanalyst Dr. Clarissa Pinkola Estés for her teachings which I summarize in this section. I have found this dream teaching to be the single most helpful way to analyze dreams: simple, yet deep and effective. This teaching can be found in her audio "The Beginner's Guide to Dream Interpretation" published by Sounds True (2003) and was elaborated in Dr. Estés' in person trainings.

Go through your dream and circle every noun in your dream report. A noun is a person, place, thing, or idea. Starting then at the beginning, take each noun and associate to it by asking yourself, "When I think of x, what do I think, feel, or remember?" Another good question to ask yourself is "What is an x, and what do you use an x for?" Write whatever you come up with onto the dream report directly above the noun. Go through and do that with all the nouns in your dream. If you have dozens of nouns, pick the ones that seem to carry the meaning of the dream, plus any other of the nouns that seem to call out for your attention. You could also color certain emotionally charged nouns red or orange, with others colored green or blue. Just take your watercolors and run them over your dream report as the colors seem to fit the narrative.

Now go back to read your dream, but this time instead of reading the original nouns of the dream report, read whatever words you wrote down that you associated to those nouns. Think about the general situation in your awake life, and the kinds of things you've been concerned about, thinking about, or have to make a decision about. See if your new reading of the dream report has anything to say about any of those concerns. Read your dream report with your associated meanings out loud. There's something about hearing it aloud that jogs even more associations. Much of the time, these simple actions are enough to let you draw some insights about your dream.

Let me give an example. Last night I had a dream I titled "Taking my skirt for a walk." Here's the dream report:

"I have a handmade heavy tweed skirt that I made for myself. It's kind of like a kilt. There's some heavy hardware on it. The waist has a self-belt, with leather buckles as a closure. There are other heavy pieces of metal on it, like a pin and another closure. I'm in the suburban city where I grew up, walking around from the back of my childhood home around the side of the house where the bedrooms are, but instead of a window into my bedroom, there is a door there that I think leads into a garage. Instead of a screen door in front of the door, there is a cloth curtain hanging down over the door. In the dream I remember that many doors have cloth curtains like that to allow someone to easily move through the doorway, and I wonder how it holds up during the harsh winters of Chicago. I walk past the cloth curtain and the bedrooms to the sidewalk, turn right, and go for a walk holding my skirt up in front of me. It doesn't look like the street in front of my childhood home, but more like an older neighborhood with lots of trees along the streets, much prettier than the neighborhood I grew up in, and with older homes. I'm feeling pretty happy, and proud of the skirt I had handmade for myself."

When I awoke, the dream felt like a big "huh???" to me. Taking a skirt for a walk didn't make any sense to me, and it all seemed rather nonsensical. But then I began associating to the nouns in the dream, and here's how my thought process went: A skirt is a piece of clothing, something I wear in front of other people to be presentable, to not be naked. Clothes are often reflective of the personality of the person, and show others how the person is presenting themselves in the world. This dream skirt was made by me, not anyone else, and I like it. It is fashioned like the clothing some of my ancestors probably wore. This skirt is heavy, with lots of buckles and hardware. Buckles and hardware remind me of something like gates that safeguard who can enter and leave someplace. They also remind me of jewelry, which I love.

My family home was an unhappy place for me, where I felt imprisoned. In my waking life I actually tried one time to escape the house through my bedroom window. But in the dream, there's no bedroom window but a door to a garage. A garage stores stuff. Besides cars, the way we get around in life, the garage stores lots of things we don't use right now, but stuff that might come in handy or that we will need sometime in the future. I'm remembering a previous dream I have had where I had received a legacy from someone who loved me. It was a large garage, filled with all kinds of resources from which I or others could make all sorts of new and delightful things. I felt I had been left a huge treasure!

The cloth curtain might indicate that at the right time, in the summertime, it would be easy to go into that garage to see what is there and take something out. There's also the phrase "pull back the curtain", meaning to reveal something that's been hidden. When I was a child, my father seemed to be all powerful, and I felt that he believed that I existed for his service and pleasure. But now, in my adult life, I've pulled the curtain back, and see him for the troubled, unhappy man that he was.

In the dream I go the right way on the sidewalk, holding my handmade skirt ahead of me. I'm walking in "my" neighborhood, a place I truly would like to live in, with old brick spacious homes and lots of flowering trees.

Once I've made these associations, I go back and read aloud my dream, speaking the associations rather than the nouns in the original dream report:

"I hold onto the person I am now, a person different from whom I might have been, someone whose life I have created myself, and I really like who I am. I'm in touch with my ancestors, and I have the power to control who will come into my life and who I will keep out. I have the adornments and jewelry that suit my tastes now. I walk out of the history of my family of origin, but if I want to look back, there might be lots of things stored in my memory that have to do with the ways I get around in my life. There might be resources there that I can make something new with. If I pull the curtain away, I can see things as they were and as they are, and seeing these things is a treasure for me now. I walk away from the house, and it's the right thing that I've done. I now walk in a neighborhood, a way of life, that is life-giving, pleasant, and spacious, the way I've always wanted to live."

From a dream that at first seemed to be meaningless, I've found a true affirmation of how I've created the life I live now, and what a good life it is. There's more that I can ponder about the dream, such as why my dream came up with a skirt rather than a blouse or a pair of pants, as I almost never wear skirts these days. I can also ponder what memories might still be available to me in that garage that used to be my bedroom, especially what treasures my past might hold alongside the difficult memories. But for now, I'm done. I'm appreciative of the dream and blown away by its creativity. I also like it that it is an affirmation that I'm happy in my life these days; that I'm finally living the life I've longed for.

I would never have uncovered these insights, though, had I not asked myself "What is it that I think, feel, and remember?" when I looked at each of the main components of my dream.

Associating to the Verbs in Your Dream

If you don't come up with any insights about your dream after associating with the main components like this, you could look at each of the verbs that you wrote down in your dream report and associate to those. Verbs are action words; they are anything that you or another is doing. In my dream above, I have/own something,

I left my childhood home, I walked around the childhood home, I held the skirt in front of me (like a banner?), I walked the right way, I walked in a neighborhood, and I loved it. Just now in writing this, when I wrote "held the skirt in front of me", I thought of holding a banner in front of me such as how a knight in a medieval pageant might have held his standard in front of him, indicating his identity and allegiance. That insight reinforces the previous meaning I had discovered about the dream being about who I am now and what my values are.

Considering Other People's Associations and Cultural Meanings

If after adding those associations you still have not had any "aha's!" about your dream, you could expand your associations to how other people, how your culture, or how other cultures might associate to the components of your dream. You could ask people in your family or your friends how, if it were their dream, they might associate to those nouns or verbs.

Remember that there is no authority "out there" who can tell you definitively what your dream means. The dreamer is the only one who can say what their dream is about. At the same time, though, none of us lives in a vacuum. We each have friends and family whom we hold within ourselves in some real way, and all of us live within and have come out of a cultural context. All of these will reverberate at times throughout our dreams.

When telling your dream to another person, let them know that you're not expecting them to know what your dream means, but that you are asking them what they would imagine the dream was about if it were their own dream. In fact, whenever you talk about a dream with the person who is the dreamer, it's a very good idea to start your comments with "If it were my dream, …" This is a reminder to us that we are projecting our own insights onto another person's dream, and that we're not privy to some secret meaning that even the dreamer can't fathom without us! Yet as long as we can keep our humility about what we have to offer, our projections can be helpful. "If it were my dream… " expresses that reminder well. Be sure to hold your ideas lightly, and don't take it personally if the dreamer rejects your ideas. We're just offering possibilities, possibilities in addition to what the dreamer can come up with themselves. One other important point is to remember that if you are ever asked to help analyze someone else's dream, or if someone confides their inner life to you, do not ever douse their enthusiasms or hopes. They may be feeling new insights or possibilities, and we should be careful to not discourage or disregard. We never know exactly what is going on in another. Be truthful, but remember that you are the authority in only your own life.

Not everyone has people in their lives with whom they feel comfortable sharing their dreams. For those people, and as an added resource for those who do have "dreamy friends", you can consult "other people" in the form of those who write on the topics in your dream. Try looking for your noun or action in Wikipedia. You can also just put it in the search bar and try your luck. You could search for "the symbolic meaning of x" or "the spiritual meaning of x". It's common to come up with a lot of ideas that don't apply to your dream or your life at all, yet sometimes you'll find something that just fits. Dream analysis is much more art than cryptography, so pay attention whenever your inner self tingles or you feel an "aha!" Look for more resonances in your feelings than spending most of your time weaving new intellectual ideas and connections. Although that's a lot of fun, too!

Is Everyone and Everything in My Dream Just Part of Me?

This is one of those "trick" questions that is partially true, and partially false, and, on the other hand, fully accurate. I used to disparage this way of analyzing dreams because it both seemed too simple as well as often feeling judgmental of the dreamer, that is, judgmental of myself. *Whaddya mean, my father in that dream is part of myself? I've spent my entire adult life trying to exorcize myself of his influence and now you're saying I'm acting just like him?!?* That's why I included the "just" in the title of this section. Any truth of this technique of working with dreams is a whole lot more complicated than any "just"; and, it's easy to twist this technique into a way of blaming ourselves for things in our dreams that are reflecting situations that we really don't like in our awake life.

To use this way of analyzing your dreams you would ask yourself where each person or thing in the dream is an aspect of yourself, or where this person or thing from the dream is in your life right now. So you would underline all the nouns as you did previously, and then write them down in list form, leaving a space or two between the nouns to record your answers. Then you would ask yourself, using some of the nouns from my own dream that I included above, "How is this skirt an aspect of myself?" "How is this house an aspect of myself?" "How is this curtain an aspect of myself?" Or "Where in my life is a skirt like this?" "Where in my life right now is a house like this?"

Make some notations on your list about what comes to you. If nothing comes up, ask yourself the further question "What does an *x* do?" or "What is an *x*?" For instance, I would answer for the skirt "A skirt is part of my clothing. It covers my nakedness and is there for everyone to see." Or for the garage I would answer "A garage keeps things safe from weather or from being stolen. A garage holds cars, which are the vehicles that let me go around town doing my business." Then go back and read your dream slowly, adding your notes about the nouns into your reading of the dream whether your notes are about aspects of yourself or simply a description of what the noun is or does. It is often awkward to simply substitute the notes for the nouns, because your notes don't necessarily have a one-to-one correspondence to the nouns, so go slowly and just get the feel of how deep and complex your dream might be. Often insights will arise and give you indications of what's happening in your awake life that you might not be conscious of.

Where this technique might not be helpful is if you too quickly conclude that a person or thing in your dream IS you; that you are that kind of person, or that you yourself are a "bear" or a "steamroller". While dreams may bring us insights that aren't very comfortable to admit, dreams usually give us insights or messages that we are able to take in and consider without wanting to immediately reject them. Dreams don't come to insult us or ridicule us.

Let me give an example of a non-helpful way to use this technique. Say you dream that your father (with whom you've had a difficult and frightening relationship) is currently insulting and criticizing a young store clerk. In the dream the clerk desperately wants to get away from him but your father corners the clerk with no one else seeing what's going on. Your father continues to verbally abuse the clerk, but quietly enough to not attract any attention from anyone else in the store. The clerk feels trapped and is afraid that your father might hurt her further. She feels more and more desperate and frightened, and wonders if anyone would even hear her if she calls for help.

In trying to understand this dream, if you were to simply ask, "How is my father an aspect of myself?" you might answer "I've grown up to be my father. When I speak with others in what I consider constructive criticism, I must be frightening to them and must be trapping them. I need to face how I am abusing other people." But if you were to ask "How is my critical father showing up in my life?" you might instead notice that your boss, who in many ways is an accomplished, admirable woman who is a mentor to you, also has a critical streak.

On some days she is mean and unfair in how she speaks to you, and won't tolerate any protest or explanation from you. This job is important to you as a stepping stone in your career and you have been very fortunate in getting this competitive position. There are no comparable positions in your location. You have been minimizing your boss's impact on you, but now this dream calls you to take notice that your boss treats you in ways similar to how your father treated you.

These are very different insights that can come from the same dream, and it's important to notice which insight feels helpful, which insight triggers an inner "Aha!" The first insight may make you feel defeated and depressed, but if there's a part of you that says, "Oh, wait a minute — there's something to this …," then that invites further exploration and action. But if it just leaves you feeling confused and depressed with no inner recognition or nothing helpful to your life, then drop that insight for now, with perhaps a request to Dreammaker that if there's something helpful to that interpretation of the dream, that you will receive more dreams about it that feel truthful and bring a sense of recognition in you.

The second insight comes from a slight nuance to the idea that all parts of the dream are a part of yourself. By asking how that part of the dream may be showing up in your life, you invite a variety of ways of looking at your dream. In this case, it brought up an insight that then invites you to ask more questions. If the insight is true, then what would you like to do with the new realization that your current boss is treating you in ways that your father treated you? You're not a child anymore, and have more options for responding to that situation now. Will you bide your time before taking action, observing the situation until it's clearer? Will you speak to your boss, bringing up your perception that her criticisms are unfair and unhelpful? Will you quietly look for another job? Will you respond to her criticism differently now? Will you quit your job?

Much of the time when you're analyzing your own dreams you will come up with many possibilities for what your dream may be saying. This is especially true if you have asked others for their insights or if you have consulted books or the internet for meanings for the meanings of the symbols in your dream. How do you know what the "right" interpretation is? Go with your gut. What *feels* right? What feels helpful? Which interpretation opens up possibilities for next steps? As I've said before, no one else but you can say for sure what your dreams mean. However, sometimes we're still left in the dark, hopefully more intrigued than in a muddled confusion. What to do then? Ask Dreammaker for more dreams to clarify the situation.

Also consider that there are many unknowns in life, and that perhaps the dream is not simply from your own psyche referring to your own life. Your dream may not be "your" dream, but may be thoughts and feelings you've picked up from other people translated into the story that you're dreaming. The dream may "belong" to an ancestor, telling secrets and emotions that the ancestor could not express in their own lives. We are learning more and more about intergenerational trauma and about how ideas, patterns, and reactions are passed down through generations. There is research that suggests that these are biological processes initiated in response to extreme external conditions in a past generation that are passed down, influencing how certain genes are turned off or on in the present generation. There is so much that we do not fully understand.

Other physicists suggest that time as we perceive it is an illusion, and that we may be dreaming of events that happen in what we would identify as the future. These ideas are also found in many ancient teachings about dreams, that we are able to dream future events in our own lives or in others' lives, or dream of world events before they happen.

Most of the time, dreams are about your own personal life, but your own personal life does include all that you're aware of around you including political situations and world problems. I've read that when researchers have looked at the dreams of people during or before huge world tragedies such as World War II or the tsunami that killed hundreds of thousands of people in 2004, they have seen many dreams that one could say "prophesied" these events.

Anecdotally, during the covid pandemic I was hearing more and more people dreaming about plagues, death, being imprisoned (quarantined?), even being gagged (face masks?)

Aside from the question of whether those dreams could have been prophetic, another phenomenon could be that the psyches of the people who have these kinds of dreams were playing a "what if?" kind of mind game. In both our awake lives and dream lives, we often wonder what might happen if certain trends that we are seeing in our lives were to continue. They are ideas of a possible, even probable, likelihood of events that are unfolding. We may dream of community events that are frightening, but that also means we may dream of the kind of community we want to live in, seeing it in our dreams before we start to work to make it happen in our awake lives.

When we have dreams that feel prophetic, the first line of analysis is to imagine the dream as a possible outgrowth or conclusion of factors or energies that are presently at play. Do you like the outcome? Then the dream could be seen as a confirmation of the path you're currently on. If the dream fills you with foreboding, then look at the various factors at play and see what you might be able to do to change them before they play out in awake life. Change the conditions and you can help change the outcome. When these prophetic-feeling dreams portend some worldwide or universal tragedy, don't think that the dream is a guarantee that the disaster will occur. Do what is within your power to change that possible outcome, but also be wise to consider what you might or should do if that outcome were in fact to occur. How might you do what you can to mitigate the harm that might come to you or others? Might you get your vehicle checked out and prepared for an emergency? What other practical actions could you take? Having several days' worth of food and supplies in your home is always a good idea. Do what you can to be as ready as possible, within the realm of reason. Live your life in response to both rational analysis in awake life as well as listening to the non-rational information from dreamlife.

I have found that it's not very useful to perseverate on trying to figure out what's really happening, especially in the area of dreams. It's much more generative to ask yourself "How might this be helpful to me in my life now?" Don't be closed to possibilities that seem strange or even "impossible". Be willing to "not know", but stay open to the possibility that your dreams, when united with your awake intellect and common sense, can be a great source of information and guidance.

Asking for a Dream, or Dream Incubation

You can't order yourself to dream about something that you want to dream about, but you can certainly set up the conditions for the possibility that you will dream about a particular topic. First off, come up with a statement or question that as clearly as possible states what it is that you want to dream about, or asks a question that you want an answer to. "I want a dream that gives me more helpful information about my relationship with my boss" or "Please send me a dream that guides me in what I should do next regarding my troubled relationship with my sister."

A skeptical part of you might say "Oh, I'll just dream what I want to have happen. I won't get any new information!" But even if that is what you dream of, look at the background situation and background characters of the dream. Is there anything there that gives you an insight as to what might happen if you do get what you want? Is there any information as to what you need to do next in order to make your preferred outcome more possible? Even if there is no more new information, pay attention to your feelings in the dream and your feelings when you awaken. Are you happy with what is happening? If so, your dream might simply be confirming that yes, this is what you want! But there might be other feelings, perhaps fear, or ambivalence, or even feeling let down. That is helpful information for you, perhaps a reminder that any one desired future situation does not guarantee happiness forever, or a recognition that even getting what we want can bring up a series of new problems or opportunities that we just can't know about right now.

Or your inner critic might say "I'm just making all this stuff up anyway." Of course you're making all this up anyway! Yes, our dreams come from our inner selves and are stories we tell ourselves about ourselves and all that is in our lives. Dreams do, however, tap into more than our conscious ego self. They can remind us of things and situations that we may have noticed but not consciously remembered. They can bring up not only our current lives and concerns, but show how our daily life is influenced by people and ideas from the past that we think we've forgotten. Dreams can take barely formed intuitions we have and weave them into stories that might help us make new associations, helping us live more consciously and deeply. So yes, we're making up our dreams, but our dreams have more resources to tap than just whatever we remember from the day before. Just be open to new information and connections, and have trust that you are much more complex than however you are feeling on a particular day. We hold a plenitude within us, including our immersion in whatever is Greater than our individual selves. Dreams are one of the best ways to access that complexity and those resources.

In order to incubate a dream, it's helpful to collect ideas and objects that resonate with the topic you're asking about. The evening before, spend a little time coming up with your statement of intention or your question. Write it down in your dream journal, and write down the ideas that resonate with your request, that is, whatever you were thinking of when you tried to condense all of your curiosity into one statement. You can just note them in point form, or you can draw them or paste in pictures or photographs that signify them. If you have any objects or photos that symbolize your topic, bring them to your bedside table. For instance, if you're asking for further clarification on a dream you had about being on the back of a galloping horse, if you have a figurine of a horse or a piece of jewelry containing a horse bring it to sit next to you as you dream. Regarding photographs, don't bring photos that may give you completely new ideas to dream about, such as your cousin in the photo rather than the horse standing next to the two of you.

After you've pondered the topic, written a bit, and brought any pictures or objects about the topic to your bedside table, write your intention again, and keep your journal and pen handy. You may want to bring some color onto your page by circling your intention with a marker color that seems to fit, or use watercolors to paint a wash of color over what you've written. Be respectful towards your Dreammaker, whoever or whatever you perceive the Dreammaker to be. Ask in sincerity to be kept safe from harmful ideas or nightmares, and have the intention to use whatever information you might receive in a dream in ways to live with more wisdom and integrity.

If you're not going to bed right then, whenever you are ready to slip under the covers, review what you wrote, especially your statement of request or intention and your request or prayer for protection. Robert Moss, a writer of more than a dozen books on dreams, has an invocation for protection that can work for just about anyone, whoever you may think the Dreammaker is. If you want, phrase it differently to fit you and your beliefs:

> May my doors and gates and paths be open,
> And the doors and gates and paths between the worlds be open.
> May the doors and gates and paths of anyone
> who wishes to do me or anyone I love any harm, be closed.
> May it be so.

If you awaken in the middle of the night, try not to move around right away, but ask yourself if you've had a dream. If so, rehearse it in your mind a few times before moving around or getting out of bed. Try to record as much as you can right away.

All this preparatory thinking and writing, including whatever pictures or objects you set beside you impresses upon your psyche how important this is to you, how much you really do want more information from the deepest within you about that particular topic. If you awaken in the night without a dream, noticing the objects beside you just reinforces your dream request, and makes it more likely that you will dream about it.

If you do awaken in the morning without an answer to your request, don't lose hope. Did you have any dream or fragment at all? Write it down as completely as you can, and then when you do have time to analyze it, be open that it might be commenting, even obliquely, on your dream request. If not, continue to do the same preparation that evening, hoping for a dream for tomorrow. It's not uncommon for a dream incubation to take a couple of days. It's almost as if your psyche is saying, "Really, you want a dream? Now? You ignore me most of the time and now I'm supposed to come up with a dream the moment you want one? Well, wait a bit. I want to see just how serious you are about this. I want to know if you'll use dream wisdom, or if you'll just forget it before you're even dressed!"

Something I find amusing about my own dream life is that if I'm regularly doing the work to record my dreams, even if when I awaken they seem just to be chaotic repeats of the previous day's thoughts or activities, then I regularly remember my dreams. But if I think "Oh, I don't want to take the trouble to write that dream down; it's just about the book I read yesterday," and go on with my day, then it never fails that I will go the next three of four days not remembering any dream at all. I can imagine my psyche saying to me a little petulantly, "That's okay, don't write down the dreams I give you! If you don't care enough to write down the ordinary dreams, then I'm not going to let you remember the really juicy ones that will come tomorrow or the next day! That's okay! Don't pay attention to me!"

When you do get a dream that seems to address your request, do find the time to analyze it within a day or two. Remember that our lives are constantly changing with every interaction as time passes. A dream that gives you a picture of what's going on in your psyche about a particular topic may lose its pertinence after a few days. On the other hand, it may not, and be as fresh in its insight years from now as it was on the day you remembered the dream. But it shows respect to yourself and to Dreammaker to work with your dream and use whatever information comes from it in a timely manner. It builds trust in your deepest self that there is guidance and insight within you, and that you will listen and take it seriously.

If, after several days, you don't remember any dream that addresses your request, look at your daily awake life. Is there anything going on there that has answered your curiosity? Does the topic still grab your attention in the same way? Remember that we can analyze awake life stories (that is, interactions or situations) in similar ways that we can analyze our dream time stories. Has there been anything that has happened over the past few days that reminded you of your dream request? Have any books "leaped" out at you? Has anyone brought up your topic in conversation? Have you overheard any conversations that have reminded you of your dream request? Has anything in a magazine or online grabbed you as connected with this topic? Are there any memories from the past, even from your childhood, that have come up that may be related to your topic?

If even this line of investigation brings up nothing meaningful to you, you have at least three more choices. You could make the topic your current research project, and assemble information from books, the internet, et cetera. Or you could ask your friends and acquaintances, or consult a wise person or counselor for their thoughts, memories, feelings, and associations to your topic. Thirdly, you could reenter the dream in waking life to see if more information might bring insights. I will talk about how to do this in a later section.

But what if you do receive another dream about your topic, yet it seems to reveal no more new information and you're as confused as before? Then I would suggest dealing with these dreams as you would a recurrent dream.

Recurring Dreams and Nightmares

These kinds of "problematic" dreams can be both frustrating and frightening, or sometimes just perplexing. Here is an example of ones which are simply perplexing: I have had recurrent dreams about moving into a new house for several years, with more than 50 of these types of dreams in the past two years alone. For me, the dreams are never identical to each other. Only the subject matter is the same. Most of the time I'm moving into a bigger and better house, more suited to my lifestyle and desires. Sometimes it's a newly built house, sometimes it's old and run down. Most of the time I'm with my little family including my spouse and my son, sometimes I'm just with my spouse, and other times I'm moving alone. Many of the dreams involve my moving back to or on to a university campus where I'm planning to study or teach. None of the dreams are frightening or particularly frustrating, except for my wondering why I keep having them.

Most of the time recurring dreams keep coming simply because your psyche wants you to know something, accept something, or address some issue in your life that you've been ignoring. Your psyche is saying something like "Smarten up! This is really important, and you're just ignoring this!" In that case, the best response is to work with those dreams. Spend some time and sincere effort in analyzing the dreams until you understand what the problem or challenge is.

Notice if there is a change in any aspect of the recurring dream. If so, when did the change happen? Do you remember doing anything different in your awake life near that time that may have shifted the dream a little bit?

Ask for some clarifying dreams when needed. Talk with others about these dreams. When you understand what they might be about, do something in your awake life to acknowledge them. Make a decision. Do something different from what you've been doing in relation to the situation or topic. Do some artwork or procure something that symbolizes the situation or the issue. I often memorialize some shift that happens by getting a special piece of jewelry, or making a talisman for myself. Notice if these awake life actions make the recurrent dream stop, or if they change the dream. Seek to understand the situation and your awake life options better. Responding in these ways almost always resolves these types of dreams.

Sometimes even with all of this, it's not so easy to understand those dreams. I've found it very helpful in those cases to ask two questions of each important noun in the dream "Who are you? And why are you in my dream?" Ask the questions each time you work with your dreams, and record whatever comes up. If nothing comes up, just ask the questions the next time you have the dream or similar dreams. At night, before you go to bed, think of the characters or situation of the recurrent dream, and ask the questions, listening for any thoughts that might bring insight. When you're in the middle of the recurrent dream, if you are aware at all that you are dreaming, then ask the characters or situation in the dream "Who are you? And why are you in my dream?" And, you can reenter the dream and in full consciousness, ask the characters yourself.

Before I speak about how to do that, though, I want to consider nightmares. Nightmares are usually dreams that tell a story without an ending. There are the setting and characters, the rising action, the crisis that usually involves intense feelings of dread, suspense, or terror. In the midst of this crisis, you wake up, upset, often happy to have escaped whatever terrible fate seemed to await you in the dream, but still carrying the intense emotions of the dream. You roll over and try to go back to sleep, yet most of the time you end up awake for hours, sometimes fearful that if you fall asleep, you'll just be in the midst of the nightmare again.

Other nightmares don't have a story, but only a terrifying image. And some don't even have an image, but just emotions, emotions more terrible than many people have ever felt in their awake life. While it's sometimes the case that you can identify something in awake life that causes the nightmare, just as often the nightmare seems to come out of the blue.

In the immediacy of waking up from the nightmare, there are three things that help. Think of how we adults usually treat children who have awakened from nightmares: we invite them to tell us their dream, then we help them to resettle by getting them to the bathroom and bringing them a glass of water or milk, and then telling them a story with pleasant imagery. Use those same elements to calm yourself after a nightmare. If you've woken up your sleeping partner you can tell them the nightmare, but an even better option is to record it in your dream journal right away, while the emotions are strong and you remember as many details of the dream as you can. At least record the dream the next morning if you don't right at the time the nightmare woke you.

If you are concerned that you don't want to reinforce the feelings of the nightmare by writing them down, I suggest writing the dream down on a piece of paper separate from your dream journal, then folding the dream up and putting it in an envelope. You can store the dream in the back pocket of your journal, or glue it in. This symbolizes you containing the dream, putting it in a "box" (the envelope) so that it doesn't leak out and poison any other of your dreams. These little actions or rituals may seem silly and unnecessary, but we humans are symbol-making creatures with bodies. Doing things, such as writing, folding, and putting the paper into an envelope, uses our bodily senses to reinforce a message that we want to communicate strongly to ourselves. We are using symbolic actions to direct our thoughts and emotions to a certain end. It may feel silly, especially if you consider yourself a rational and secular person through and through. So, it feels silly. But it also helps. The Dreammaker within us may not be quite as rational and secular as the fully awake ego is in the light of day!

Once you've told the dream to a person or recorded it, then you want to change the state of your physiology that has been stressed by the panic and terror. Walking around a bit and drinking or eating something will often be enough to shake out the intense feeling, but if the fear or terror has gotten a deep hold of you, then turning on the lights and even taking a shower may be necessary to calm down enough to fall back asleep. Appeal to as many bodily senses as possible in order to move into awake, consensual reality from dream reality. If you shower, use sweet smelling soap or shampoo and use a washcloth to rub your body, becoming ever more aware of yourself and your physical body right here, right now. Say your telephone number out loud, backwards. Doing this pulls you into using the more "left-brain" analytical part of the brain, and helps you orient yourself in awake reality. Then as you return to bed, it helps to consciously turn your attention to something pleasant, whether that's favorite music, the memory of a great conversation, the feeling of being loved, or whatever else that is calming for you.

The next day, work with your nightmare as you would with any dream that feels important. Associate to the nouns and perhaps the verbs. Ask yourself if any events of the day or two before the dream may have contributed to the nightmare. Have you watched or read any frightening story recently (including, perhaps, the nightly news)? Do you get any "aha's" in reviewing the events of the past few days? Do you have any ongoing worries in your life? What about unresolved relationship difficulties? Have you heard stories lately about people in situations like yours who have met tragedy and ruin? What are you scared of? Are there any physical conditions or illnesses that you might be worried about? Are you going through some physical or emotional "rite of passage" in life, such as childbirth, menopause, divorce, lowered testosterone, job loss, or retirement? If you suspect that any of these things might be related to your nightmare, strive to resolve the awake life issues and your nightmare will most probably not return again.

Might the nightmare be about unresolved trauma from your past that has gotten triggered by something in your current life? Sometimes trauma hasn't necessarily been triggered by anything in the present, though. It may be the case that you are now strong enough and have enough supports in your present life to heal unresolved traumas from your past. Just like when we have a cut and our bodies heal, our psyches are resilient and will usually heal the wear and tear and minor wounds of everyday psychological and spiritual life. Yet just as when we're in, say, a car crash where the wounds are quite severe and we need the help of emergency medical treatment, when we have experienced severe trauma, our natural resilience alone may not be able to heal our psyches, and we need the support of others.

One of the interesting things about psychological and spiritual trauma is that one of the ways our psyches protect us when we don't have the support we need to heal is to freeze or flee, to stuff all the hurt away until we're in a space in our lives where we can look at and heal from the hurt without completely falling apart or being re-traumatized. Many times when I worked at the sexual assault center people who came in for help would be so perplexed as to why something that had happened so far in the past was coming up and wreaking havoc in their current lives. They had figured that those past hurts had been so long ago that they shouldn't be bothering them now. I tried to help them realize that instead of this being a terrible tragedy, this was a positive indication that they were most probably now able to look at and to heal the past trauma; that they had gotten themselves into a good enough position, stable enough and with enough supports, that they could now address these issues and become stronger as a result.

Please remember that we are all different, with different responses to different types and levels of trauma, and that this book is not specifically about healing from past traumas. However, if you are plagued by nightmares that continue and seem to not be connected to anything that's presently going on in your life, the nightmares may be pointing to things that happened long ago that have not yet had the chance to heal. If so, reach out for support from a wise person, counselor, or therapist in your area in order to respond to this invitation to address old hurts. You shouldn't have to go through these difficult things alone.

Let's say, though, that you do not suspect that there is unresolved trauma that might be the cause of the nightmare, yet you still don't have any clues as to what the nightmare might be about. Assuming that dreams come in the service of healing and wholeness, your nightmare must be trying to tell you something that would be helpful to you. One thing you can do is to ask Dreammaker, "Please come to me in ways that I can take the message in, in ways not so frightening!"

Consider that the dream may not relate to you or your own personal life. It may be ancestral trauma or fear that is being expressed through you now; it might be a dream related to the condition of the world.

Sometimes we will just never know what a particular dream means for us. If the nightmare has come once, with no residual emotions or nigglings, then it's probably best to let it go. Perhaps it was the pastrami sandwich you had last night that your dear body was struggling mightily to digest!

Yet many times nightmares are recurrent. When this is the case and your regular methods of analyzing them aren't giving you any useful results, then it may be time to reenter your dream and ask questions within the dream itself.

Reentering Dreams

We can reenter dreams while we are awake so that we can collect more information. With more information, we may be able to understand what the dream has to tell us about ourself.

Start by settling into your chair with your supplies close at hand. Set your timer for about 40 minutes. Just as you want to have your dream journal available close to where you wake up in order to record your dreams in the morning, you want to have your supplies within reach so that you don't have to search for or get up to find your supplies when you come out of this "awake" dream. Take several deep relaxing breaths, and scan your body briefly to make sure you are as comfortable and relaxed as possible at this time.

Say your prayer or intention for protection. Ask any of your allies to be with you as you reenter your dream. By allies, here, I mean any people, passed, or "imaginary", who you consider as friends or guardians that care about your safety and wellbeing. Your allies may not be humans, but be a particular animal, plant, tree, or element (earth, air, fire, or water) that you feel an affinity with. By setting an intention for protection and asking a particular ally to be with you as you reenter a dream, you are reminding yourself that you need not be frightened going back to experience a dream, even one that was frightening when you first dreamt it. You are reminding yourself that you are part of a larger community, that there are beings who love you, and that you are not at the mercy of any image or character that your dream presents to you. Try not to go through this step by rote, but really feel into your own community of love and support and affirm that this is where you live and want to be, while at the same time you want to know about this new, perhaps surprising or perhaps frightening figure from your dream.

Reread the dream report of the dream that you wish to reenter. Stay with only the dream report, not anything you have written in analyzing the dream. Then close your eyes and, in alignment with your breath, count backwards from 10 to 1, imagining that you are walking down a circular stairway passing another floor with each breath. Or you might imagine that you are on an elevator descending into the sub-sub-sub-basements of a huge building. When you get to the bottom, go through the door in front of you (in your imagination) whether it is the elevator door or a door at the bottom of the steps. Imagine that you are now within your dream, at the beginning of whatever you remember from the dream. Imagine yourself going through the dream as you remember it, but this time, ask any of the characters or things in the dream that intrigue you, "Who are you, and why are you in my dream?" Take note of any answers you receive, whether they are in words, or feelings, or memories.

If you start to feel fear or panic, similar to when you first experienced the nightmare, state strongly, "Do not frighten me, do not threaten me! I want to understand why you are in my dream. Tell me who you are and why you are here!!" Keep in your mind that you have your allies with you, and nothing bad is going to happen to you. Most of the time, the fear dissipates and the frightening imagery transforms into something that does not trigger any fear or unease, and then you may intuit what it now has to say to you. Sometimes the frightening image, now transformed, becomes a new ally for you, showing you things about your psyche, your current life, or your memories that are useful to resolve or transform in your awake life.

If the fear or panic continues, come back out of the dream into awake reality by opening your eyes, tapping your feet on the floor to become grounded here in this awake reality, and then do whatever you need to do to shift your physiology from fear to a more normal state. Wash your hands while imagining that you are washing the fear or panic away. Drink something or eat something. Say your telephone number out loud, backwards, to engage the more analytical part of the brain rather than remaining in the imaginative part of your consciousness. If needed, take a shower and change your clothing. Stay grounded and centered in this awake reality. Perhaps turn on the television or watch something live on the internet, to help you shake the dream and be fully awake and in your present life. Perhaps call a friend and chat about the ordinary things in life. Depending on what's going on in your awake life and if you're feeling strong and centered in general, you may want to try to reenter the dream again, at a later time, to see if you can get more information as to its meaning. But if you feel at all hesitant, you may want to try this again only in the presence and with the help of a wise counselor or therapist who has experience with dreams.

But assuming that you do not become frightened, continue speaking with the dream characters, being curious and respectful, asking them what they are trying to tell you. You may not feel that you're having a conversation, but just have memories come to mind, have different feelings, or just think of different people or situations from your current life.

You may get an experience of "Aha!" and feel that you now know what the nightmare was all about. Or you may just feel like you've gotten some new ideas or information, but not yet understand the meaning of those ideas. Either way, once you feel a sense of completion, or an ending of any new information, thank the dream characters for meeting again with you, thank the Dreammaker, and then retrace your steps that brought you into the dream. Imagine yourself climbing back up the stairs into awake, consensual reality, or feel yourself riding the elevator up into awake, consensual reality. Go immediately to record whatever you remember from the whole experience. Use art and color as desired to express your experience. Either right then, or later, associate to all the people, places and things that have been added to your original dream experience, and continue to analyze your dream with the content that you've received through the dream reentry. It is almost always the case that you will gain fresh insight into what your psyche is bringing to your attention by giving you the dream or nightmare in the first place.

If you are still feeling as if you are in dream reality, when you are finished, tap your feet, say your telephone number out loud, backwards, and walk around a bit. Be sure you feel alert and "here" before going on with your day or doing anything which requires your full attention.

As you gain more experience with this technique, you will be able to do it in just a few minutes. The reason you use the timer is not that you should stay in the reentered dream that long, but to ensure that if you were to fall asleep, or if you were to completely lose track of time, that you would be awakened by the alarm when it went off. As most of us in this culture are a little to a lot sleep deprived, it's not uncommon to fall asleep after you relax yourself and count down to reenter the dream. If that happens, no worries. Be grateful for the nap you no doubt needed, and try the re-entry at another point in time. And if you happen to have a dream during your nap, be sure to write a dream report! It may very well have some information that you've been asking for!

Reentering a Dream in Order to Complete It

Another reason to reenter a dream is to use your conscious mind to bring a dream to closure. I will do this after I've already reentered a nightmare and collected more information, and after I've worked with the new information in order to analyze what the dream might be trying to bring to my awareness. I will sometimes feel that although I've mostly understood the dream, I'm still left with the uneasiness of a dream that got to its crisis, but was never resolved. So I will go back in with the intention to consciously bring resolution.

To do this, spend a little time imagining various ways that the dream could have continued until the story would have been complete. Pick one of those options, an option that brings either a positive resolution or a neutral resolution.

Reenter the dream using the suggestions in the section above. Instead of asking the dream figures who they are and why they're in your dream, though, follow the dream events as you originally dreamt them. When you get to the end of your original dream, add your own imagined ending, or resolution. Try to experience the ending deeply, imagining it by using two or more of your senses. For instance, do not only envision the resolution, but also imagine what you might hear from the dream figures, or what you might smell. Might you feel the wind across your arms, or the heat of a fire? The more senses you involve, the more your imagined ending will feel satisfying, and "real". When your story is complete, come back up from the reentered dream, and write the dream again, including your new ending.

Very occasionally, your dream characters might seem to "have a mind of their own", and decide not to cooperate with your imagined ending. If this were to happen, don't be alarmed by their "independence". What has most probably happened is that you dropped a little deeper into your dream and actually fell asleep. You are then not re-imagining the dream, but actually dreaming a new dream. If this happens, you may not awaken until your timer goes off. In any case, when you come into awake life, write down in words or in images this "new" old dream, and work with it as you would with any new dream. If it is disturbing or a nightmare, analyze how it compares with your previous reentry where you collected new information. What more information has come to you? If it is a neutral or pleasant dream, thank your Dreammaker for its creativity. You can now decide whether or not to work with the dream any more. Sometimes this new dream brings a delightful and humorous resolution to the original nightmare we'd never have consciously thought of, and I can only wonder at this display of originality within us!

Many, many volumes have been written about dreams, recurring dreams, nightmares, and working with them all. I hope that this introduction to dream analysis has given you some practical ideas as to how to understand what's going on in the second half of our lives, our sleeping lives. Always, stay grounded, go slowly in a respectful manner towards yourself and Dreammaker, stay open and curious, but if you find yourself confused, frightened, or disturbed, ask for help from a wise counselor or therapist.

Oh, and remember my recurring dreams of moving into a new house? Though I still sometimes have one, their frequency has greatly diminished. In the past few years I have "moved into" a new season of life and have now become comfortable in my new work and how I direct my energies. After several years of primarily facilitating small groups and seeing people in person, I have shifted into writing regularly, hoping to share what I've learned through the years of working with others and exploring my own passion for the inner life, and its connection with our small "p" political selves and what we choose to do in our awake lives.

It's been challenging for me to shift from seeing many people in person and getting feedback on some of the effects of my work, to the more solitary task of writing, not knowing if I will ever finish my book or be able to get it published, or knowing if it will ever be helpful to anyone. This has all been done with the Covid-19 pandemic, climate change, and a societal reckoning with racism as background, adding to the uncertainty of knowing what life may be like in the future. I think my dreams of moving into a new home were my psyche's way of coming up with all sorts of possibilities of how I might find a new sense of "home" in all that was, and is, changing, including health challenges and my son moving into his own adulthood. I think the dreams were telling me I would find my new home, a sense of where and how I might live, with the promise that though unknown, it would be a positive change.

Daydreams and the Stories We Tell Ourselves Spontaneously

Noticing What We Think About All Day

Just as working with our night dreams can reveal much about our inner selves, our spontaneous daydreams can do the same. The trick here is "catching" them, and believing enough in their importance to us to make the time to record and to work with them. If you become aware during the day that you've been off on a fantasy of living on a tropical island, you can send yourself a quick email to remind yourself later to record it in your Dream Journal.

One of the best ways I've found to keep track of my daydreams and the stories I tell myself is to have developed the habit of reviewing my day each evening, either at a particular time, say, after supper, or as I'm preparing for bed. For this to work well, though, I must do this before I'm too sleepy to be able to write down my observations.

Making a little time to review your day can become a really useful habit. It works best to do it somewhere where you have at hand your daily planner and calendar, your to-do list, your journal, your dream journal, and some post-it notes. As you review your day, you'll no doubtedly remember all sorts of small details that are important enough to note so that your next days run a little more smoothly.

Picture in your mind all the activities of the day in chronological order starting from when you awoke. You might remember that you wanted to turn down the volume of your radio alarm, and change the station from a news station to a classical music one. Right then as you remember that, make a note of it on your to-do list or do it right now. There will be other chores that you remember to note down, promises of appointments that you need to record, or other details that are easy to forget. Write them down as you remember them. If there were emotional altercations with others, you can process them a little in your journal, and this allows you to determine if you need to follow up with an apology or a word of encouragement to someone. You can "clean up" messes before they threaten valued relationships.

As you review the day, pay attention not only to the events that happened but to your emotions and whatever you were thinking about as the day wore on. If you notice that you were really worried about something in the morning, or that you were fantasizing what you'd really like to say to your boss at the lunch meeting, or imagining how wonderful your next job is going to be, make a note of those daydreams in your Dream Journal. Write the date, label it "Daydreams", or "DD", and quickly note the topic. Most of the topics you remember don't need any more analysis than this, because you'll immediately know how those thoughts were a response to immediate actions, upcoming concerns, or expressions of frustrations or preferred futures.

You'll know which daydreams to record in more detail because they will either have a lot of energy in them, or they will be the same daydream that you've recorded many times previously. Pay particular attention to any daydream that causes you to have a lot of curiosity about it, or that has you asking yourself "I wonder why I was thinking of that!?!" Some days, on a little reflection, it will be obvious why you particularly noticed the daydream. Perhaps you always start to think about food when you pass the Lebanese restaurant on your way out for lunch, or you perseverate on living as an artist on a tropical island for so long because you were reminded that your colleague had told you about their recent vacation in Hawaii. These daydreams also no longer need analysis as you've been able to identify their origin.

Pay attention to the topics that recur, even if you can identify what prompted your daydream. For instance, if you have several daydreams over a period of time about escaping to a tropical island, perhaps that is a clue that, at the least, you need a vacation, or that you might consider a different work situation. Or if you have several daydreams over a period of time about escaping to a tropical island and being an artist, you might consider taking a class in painting. Or pull out your paints and canvases long abandoned in the basement closet.

The Daydreams and Stories that Bring Us Down

Occasionally, though, there will still be curious fantasies or recurring stories that don't seem to make a lot of sense to you. Those are the ones to write down in more detail, the same way that you would write down a dream report. Try to write it in the present tense, to help you immerse yourself in the daydream and remember details you might otherwise overlook.

Once you've got either a story or a series of impressions, go ahead and work with it just as you would work with a night dream. Either then or at a later time, use all the analysis skills you've already learned. Does the whole situation of the daydream remind you of anything? How does it make you feel? What does it make you think of? Circle and then associate to the nouns in your daydream. Issues will often come up in our day thoughts especially if we do not remember dreaming of them at night, due to over-tiredness, medications, or a habit of not remembering any dreams. Paying attention to these thoughts and stories that arise during the day can yield many of the same benefits as working with your nightdreams.

Then there is the phenomenon of intrusive thoughts. These are ideas or scenarios that seem to have no connection with the consensual reality of your day-to-day life, but are thoughts and stories, often negative or frightening, that intrude into your attention when you least expect them. These are usually a symptom of current or post-traumatic stresses, and, though upsetting and inconvenient, they serve a valuable purpose in reminding you that there is something that you badly need to attend to in order to live in peace. Please remember that you don't have to suffer these intrusive thoughts by yourself in silence, and please reach out for support from a wise counselor or therapist.

If, however, you have intrusive thoughts but cannot identify any current or past stress or trauma that could be causing them, look carefully at what you are feeding your psyche. Have you watched a horror movie lately that has been simmering in the back of your brain, creating its own sequels? What's been the overriding theme of your social media lately? What about recent advertising that's captured your attention?

Regarding our consumption of media, it's wise to periodically review our sources and ensure that they are truly what we want to bring into ourselves. While I consider it important to know what's going on in the world, I've determined that watching most forms of a daily newscast isn't an effective way of actually finding out. Different sources have different biases, and mainstream media just doesn't cover events that disagree with the narrative that their owners want to put out to the world. Even infotainment is more geared toward delivering audiences to advertisers than it is in informing the public about anything important to know about. Especially if the media coming to you is "free", be sure to ask yourself the age-old question "Cui bono?" Who benefits? Who benefits from you consuming this particular information or entertainment?

Besides this phenomenon of being manipulated for someone else's benefit, most news still adheres to the principle that if it bleeds, it leads. So not only is our attention skewed to get the impression that everything is so dangerous all the time, the images are not ones that I particularly want rolling around in my head as I try to fall asleep at night, nor intrude upon my daytime events. If I, practically and usefully, could do something to help the victims of tragedies, that would be a reason to know all the details. But when I am powerless to help, it does no good for me to be secondarily traumatized by too much exposure. We become numb, and are even less empowered to figure out what we can actively do to prevent any next tragedies.

In order to have a mind as peaceful and effective as possible, I think we need to be conscious of what comes at us, and to exercise what control we may have in order to not be drained of any ability to help, but to discern where our abilities and passions can meet the world's needs. Who benefits from keeping our thoughts and decent good will in perpetual agitation? Not us, and not the people and situations where we can devote our assistance.

So it's worth doing some serious investigation if you suffer from low-level anxieties, intrusive thoughts, and ongoing agitation. There is so much that happens that is out of our control, but we owe it to ourselves, and to all we come in contact with, to not suffer unnecessarily. Paying attention to daydreams as well as our night dreams is one way to figure out what we, in the midst of our own busy lives, can do something about.

Connected to this issue of ongoing agitation are the stories we hear from our colleagues and friends in casual conversations. Even if we work hard to ensure that most of the information we consume is helpful to us, most of the people around us are not that diligent. Many of the people around us live their lives in constant agitation, and seek to feel better by talking about it to anyone who will listen. It's very easy to get into what I call the "Ain't it awful?!" conversations, with others around us corroborating and extending the awfulness with "And you know what else?!"

I don't ever want to blame people for this, because most of the time we're all doing just the best we can, and so many people are suffering in quiet desperation. Yet being mired in these feelings points out how important it is to do whatever we can to be happier, to encourage ourselves and others in making good choices about what we take in, whether it's media, conversation, images, or our food and drink. There are so many forces that deplete and weaken us, such as overwork, exhaustion, constant exposure to addictive short-term pleasures, and living in discouragement, that it's very difficult to be conscious, to see clearly, and to choose things that keep us strong and able to be a positive force in the world. This whole book is about ways to become conscious and to see more clearly, so that we are capable of making the choices that are within our power to do.

Something that will sometimes happen if you attend to your daydreams is that you may become aware of the content of your daydream at the time that you're actually "dreaming" it. You can be having daydreams not only in your idle moments during the day, but also while you're in the middle of a conversation, or in the middle of a meeting. As you're doing whatever it is that you're doing, sometimes a series of thoughts or snatches of story will come to you about the person you're speaking with or about the topic that you're addressing. You may suddenly "see" the person in an 1800's period dress, or imagine the person, who does not have children, surrounded by four children of various ages. You may "see" all the participants of your meeting as performers in a circus. If we can catch those daydreams in the moment, then we can quickly notice whether they are giving us insights into the situation at hand. This type of intuition can sometimes be extremely useful. Though usually not literally true, there may be insights into either what's objectively going on in the situation, or about your own subjective responses to these people and situations. Sometimes you may be amused at your own psyche's sense of humor in entertaining you with associations that in hindsight are often perceptively accurate. In those moments, it's as though you are observing how it is that your mind works in picking up present stimuli and mixing it with memories, other impressions, and both your own and others' emotions.

The Stories Other People Tell About Us

So many of us are less than free to fully pay attention to what's going on as it's going on. Our minds are busy, not only with the daydreams that are stimulated by our everyday interactions, but also with figuring out who we are and what we think about life, and one of the ways we figure that out is by listening to what the important people in our lives say about us. We're always interested in what our colleagues and friends have said about us, and most of us still think we're the people that our parents and teachers have said that we are. But is that still true? Was their assessment of us ever really accurate?

How do you think your best friends would complete this sentence: "[Insert your name]? Oh, she's the person who … "? Would your spouse complete the sentence in the same way? What about your work mates? Your boss? Your parents and relatives? Can they all possibly be describing the same person? We all have many aspects of our personalities, and we show different aspects of ourselves in different contexts. In our lives as adults with people whom we meet as adults, we ourselves are mostly responsible for how our friends and co-workers complete that sentence. They see us now, as we are and how we reveal ourselves to them.

But it's also true that other people don't always see us as we are, but as how we fit into whatever it is that they need at the moment. This is especially the case if we were raised by parents who had strong needs of their own and were not able to parent us in ways that allowed a full flowering of who we are. Or, if we had parents who wanted and needed us to fulfill certain roles, we may have done our best to live up to their expectations. Subsequently, we may not have ever let ourselves do certain things or develop different talents other than the expected ones. How true, then, are the stories that they tell about us?

If we've been told all our lives that we are a person who does such and such, but we think we may want to do something or be someone else, then that inner conflict can first reveal itself by our finding ourselves focused on the stories our family tells about us. Often, things in our environment will bring up memories of how you were told to be in the world, of what your talents are, or how "people like us" are treated by the world.

Whether or not we are bothered by these kinds of stories, it's helpful to consciously think through how accurate these stories are, and if we want to live by them or not. Make room in your regular journal to record the stories you remember from your childhood. What did your parents say about you? Was it true, or partially true, or not true at all? Were the stories, the family vignettes, told with love or with so-called humor but at your expense? Were you the "responsible one", or the "wild child"? Were you the "straight-A student" held up as an example to your siblings and cousins? Did your siblings and cousins appreciate your example as "the smart one"? Each of us will have our own experiences to record. Whatever they are, get a clear sense of them, and their truth, now.

Beyond your nuclear family, what were the stories told about your extended family? Do you have stories of how your grandparents immigrated? Are they stories of hardship or of success upon success? Were there implications for you as to how you were supposed to be, or your vocation as you grew older? Did you fulfill those expectations, or not? How does your extended family view you now, whether you fulfilled the family tradition or rebelled?

What about the stories of your group, your society, your ethnic ancestry? Where was your family, "your people", vis a vis the dominant culture in the area you grew up? Look at who carried the archetypes of the "hero", the "fool", the "rebel", the "savior", the "warrior" among your people. How do all these stories make you feel, now? Has your family kept up your people's traditions, or did your family join the melting pot of contemporary culture? Are you happy with how it has turned out, or do you want to live differently now that you've thought about it?

In my own family, every generation in memory became more affluent with professional occupations and an emphasis on an academic education. Things like art, even music, were seen as of little value, or of no value unless you made a "good" living at it. It's not surprising, then, that it took until I was over 55 years old before I allowed myself to explore my artistic longings.

Note, too, the stories that should have been told, but weren't. Was your mother a closet artist, painting only in secret and destroying her work because she didn't think it was good enough? Did your father come home from the war a different person from the dad you remembered before he left? Whatever happened to your maiden aunt's best friend, who lived with your aunt until her death? Did anyone from the family ever stay in touch? What about your cousin who disappeared for a year when she was 16? Why didn't your grandmother's brother move to the United States when the rest of the family did?

Were there stories that everyone knew, but no one talked about? Why did your grandmother divorce her first husband back in 1924, when women didn't do that sort of thing? Whatever happened to your mom's older brother, the one you've never met? What questions were met with silence? Which topics brought the cold response, "We do not speak of those things"?

Are there any stories about you, or stories that you tell about yourself, that you're tired of? Do you feel that whether you're tired of them or not, that you just have to accept them? Or do you yearn to be seen differently? When you meet a new person, what do you tell them about yourself? Do you feel good about what you say about yourself, or are you embarrassed? Do you feel good about how your life has turned out so far, or do you feel you have so much potential that has never been lived out?

All these kinds of stories are the subject matter for countless novels and movies, and you could spend the rest of your life remembering, unearthing, and recording the endless stories of yourself within your community, and your community's history and its influence on you. What I'm focusing on now is encouraging you to become aware of how you've thought of yourself within your own history and within the histories of your family and your people, however you would define "your people". Has your self image enabled you to build the kind of life and community that you've wanted? Has it limited you? How much of that must you simply accept, and how much can you change it now to create the life and community you want?

I also hope that you've noticed that there are various ways to tell a story. Depending on who's telling it and what is important to them, the same incident can be described in a variety of ways. Who's telling the "Truth"? Are they all true? How would one find out which story is true-est, or closest to what really happened? How does someone else's telling of a story matter to you? Do you have any choices about how the stories are told? Is it important for you to tell your own stories?

Yet another way to reflect on our stories and become aware of how stories have affected us is to look at our favorite stories at different times in our lives. Or, if you don't remember many stories from your childhood, did you find new stories when you were reading books to your own children? Who were your heroes or heroines? What book or movie did you take in over and over again, until you knew almost all of the dialogue? And are those the same types of heroes and stories that you enjoy now? If not, when did it change for you? Can you identify why it changed, if it did?

As a girl, I loved the Nancy Drew mystery stories. With her friends Bess and George (both young women), driving through town in her blue roadster, Nancy would calmly solve whatever problems came her way. I would never own as many of those books as I wanted to read, but then I found out that our public library carried some. I was so excited! Yet I was reduced to tears and stifled sobs when, by the time my mother finally took me to the library, there were none available to be checked out. It was a very sad day in my 11-year-old life. I loved Nancy's intelligence, her confidence, and her independence, and those stories provided a model for me to grow into.

What about you? Why did you love the stories you did? Did you grow up to become any of your early heroines or heroes? What about their characteristics or interests? Have they influenced your own qualities and interests?

Some people say we're the sum of all the stories told to us and about us. I tend to think we're more than that, but it helps to become aware of and reflect upon all those stories. We come to feel more a part of the people and of the world around us, and we can come to choose which stories we will keep as identity markers, and which ones we will abandon in the freedom of becoming who we want to be and in living how we want to live.

Daydreams and the Stories We Tell Ourselves Intentionally

Now that we've looked at the stories in our lives that we haven't had much control over, that is, dreams, daydreams, the stories that other people have told about us, and some stories that we have naturally gravitated toward, we've had a glimpse at how powerful stories are for our general self-esteem as well as our moods during the day. We can also use that power of stories intentionally, though, to affect our self-esteem, our moods, and our energy to bring into our lives the people and situations that we want, all in the service of creating the life each of us wants to live within ourselves and within our extended communities of beings in this world.

These kinds of stories are related to our identifying how we want to live in the world, which is part of the reason to choose to live a reflective life nourishing our own inner lives. As we understand more and more deeply who we are, the kind of world we want to live in, and how we've been influenced without our conscious awareness, we are then free to discover how we can contribute to the kind of world we want, imagine our place in the world, and move closer and closer aligning our outer lives with the inner lives we've been exploring and developing. This is living in integrity, and knowing our power to create change for the benefit of all. There's no better way to live, in my opinion. But it sometimes takes a long time and a lot of exploration before we believe it is possible, along with becoming wise enough to accept that there is only so much under our control as individuals. Even though we don't have complete control, it's wonderful to consciously take responsibility for what we do have control over, and know that we are serving not only our own good, but the good of many beings on this fragile planet.

Creating these kinds of daydreams and stories is very much related to creating affirmations, which I talked about in Chapter 5. Instead of coming up with a succinct phrase, though, I'm suggesting that you create full stories by playing the game of "What if ...?" or "What would my life be like if ...?" or "What would the world be like if ...?" You use the power of your imagination to come up with pictures of a desirable future for yourself and/or for the world. And then you further imagine what it is that you could do to help bring about those desirable futures. You think about what you would need to know, the kind of people you would need to have with you, the resources it would take to bring these stories into reality. It's fantasizing in a very practical way.

As you daydream about these things, the inner critic part of you will no doubt be telling you how silly it all is, how you couldn't possibly do x, y, or z. But this is where all the reflection you've done by looking at the stories that people have told about you, all the family stories, all the figuring out of who you are in relation to "your people" can pay off. When the inner critic fills you with its criticism, you can truthfully remember that you've had difficult times before, but have come through them, that you've been able to learn new things in the past, that you've been able to find people to help you, and that you've already proven some naysayers wrong in your life. You have the evidence from your own life to know that when hard things arise, you are resourceful, and that when excrement is thrown your way, you are a gardener taking that excrement, composting it, alchemizing it, and transforming it into something that you can plant your seeds in. You know that with attention and work, you can bring in a harvest.

One practical way to do this is to look at your Dream Journal and see if there are hints or indications that there is something you need to address in your day-to-day life. Let's use that daydream of becoming an artist and living on a tropical island as an example. Say you have no savings, that you've never even sketched a picture, much less painted one, and that you've never been to a tropical island.

The daydream is certainly unrealistic and impractical. Yet if you've been having that daydream recurrently, and it has a charge for you, meaning that you really like it and can't just forget about it, then that daydream is telling you something important, something practical. It's time to imagine how you might make it real, and in the imagining, take a few baby-steps in awake life to see how you might like that reality. If you're an artist in the daydream, try becoming an artist in your awake life in consensual reality. Take a course from the community college in beginning acrylic painting and see what happens. You might find that you love it. You might find that you'd rather wash the kitchen floor than make a mud fest of mixed-up colors on a canvas. But you got to talking to a guy in the class who takes photos in the river valley and you decide to spend a Saturday morning accompanying him in his small adventure. You drop the painting course and instead take a course on the art of black and white photography. Start telling yourself a new daydream about the photographer on that tropical island.

You can plan to go on a packaged tour of Hawaii to check out what a tropical island feels like. You could save up the money by bringing your lunch from home rather than eating out, or deciding to drink peppermint tea rather than getting pop from the machine two or three times a day. You enjoy telling yourself the story of how you sacrificed to make your dreams come true. When you do finally get to Hawaii, you might find that the humidity of tropical islands is not something you want to live in. So tell yourself a new story of the photographer who lives in the desert of the American southwest. But after a while you realize that you don't really want to move away from your friends and family who all live within a convenient three hours of the apartment you really love here in the city. How to shift your daydream now?

Dream about the nature photographer who became an internet sensation in his spare time until he built up his side business enough to go part-time in his day job, then actually quit it. Now that is a daydream that energizes you, and has practical guidance on what to try next, and then after that, next again.

Besides trying out the baby-steps that can bring your daydream into consensual reality, you can focus on a challenge you have either at work or in your personal life, and daydream as to how one of your childhood heroes might solve it. While you might not get any practical ideas from the daydream where Superman picks up your supervisor and flies him to a new job in Australia, making your work challenge disappear with him, the humor from imagining your supervisor flying over the Pacific Ocean flapping his arms and legs while Superman holds him by the back of his shirt just might loosen up some new ideas that shift how you approach your challenge. Asking yourself "What would so and so do?" helps you imagine what you can do, because our heroes do reflect some of the qualities that we have or at the least have in potential. If you had access to those qualities, what might be possible now?

Yet another way to come up with a new daydream is to list some of what you deeply dislike about the world as it is now. Once you've got a list, pick the top two or three that bother you the most, and then daydream about some solutions to those things that are not working. Tell yourself the stories of how those situations were turned around, and include yourself as one of the characters who act to change those situations. Come up with many dreams as to what could happen if …

Another option would be to take any of these ideas and look through the images that you've been collecting. Imagine the people in those images uniting to solve your challenges, or imagine how the world could be if the images that inspired you were common realities in the world. Would you have the same challenges? What would be different? Are there ways that you could be now that would make that world more likely to become our future? Do you have an image of someone who looks like they are already living whatever it is that you're hoping to live? Post it in your journal and write about it. If you don't have a collection of images to sort through, draw a scene, or lay down different colors that reflect that chosen desired future. Go back to your journal and use the image to inspire your chosen daydreams.

Dream big, and then take one tiny step after another. Seeing change, any change, happen in our lives brings hope and new energy. Most of the changes will either be of the "developing of a new habit" type, or the "exploring of what options might be available for us" type. In either case, imagining ourselves already having the habit established, or imagining ourselves stepping forth into exploring options, helps us create a new story that we can live into. One of the mental games that I like to play is the "If my life were a novel, what would be the next scene?" In order to imagine that, I need to know what kind of a novel I'm metaphorically writing with my life. If it's an adventure novel, certain possibilities open; if it's a mystery thriller, other options show up; if it's a redemption narrative, yet other possibilities are on offer. While I know that I can't just make reality conform to my dreams, by consciously creating these dreams or stories I am then on the lookout for any openings, any new opportunities, that would move me forward toward the fulfillment of my dream.

I'm not describing the "law of attraction" where people act to create their own reality. There is far too much that is simply out of our control to offer false promises that we can surely manifest whatever we want by imagining it and believing in it. If this process is followed too simplistically, then when circumstances intervene to get in the way of fulfilling our daydream, it's easy to blame ourselves for not doing the manifesting in the right way, or not wishing hard enough, or of sabotaging ourselves. There is far too much in the world that is not under our individual control that can get in the way of our desires. Yet, by identifying how we want to be living and the kind of world we want to have, then dreaming a story of how we can participate in creating the conditions for these ways of being to exist, we not only show ourselves what to look for in our daily lives that can move us in that direction, but we are gathering up all of our powers to actually follow those openings and possibilities, and gathering up all of our energies to keep taking the next step, and then the step after that.

I'm also talking more about how you want to live, or what kind of world you want to live in, than manifesting "things". Yes, "things" may be needed in order to create conditions of being, but imaging how the world might be a more just place, or how our city might create a thriving community where drug use is minimized, is usually a longer-term dream than telling a story to yourself about the late-model sports car that you want.

Creating a story to live into works not just for individuals, but for groups of people as well, whether families or organizations. We can share our individual hopes and dreams for the group with the other people in the organization, and solicit others' hopes and ideas as to what we all might do next, or what we would like the future to be. If you can together create a story of what could be, the story will bring hope and energy to all who invest in it, and then can become a map as to how to bring it into reality. Without a vision, a dream, life often gets stuck into a stagnant, then hopeless story that extends whatever we don't like, don't want, into a neverending future of dissatisfaction. We begin to believe that nothing will ever change, and that we, ourselves, can't do anything to change things. We notice all the stories around us that are stagnant, all the examples of discouragement. This often happens without our being aware of it, and causes us to feel discouraged, helpless, and tired. Enlisting the power of conscious daydreaming is one tool to help us out of that sense of "ain't it all awful?"

When daydreaming like this, it's helpful to hold all the details lightly. Remind yourself that you're "just" daydreaming, and let the dream change as reality around you opens up or closes off different possibilities. Dead ends aren't failures, but are just an indication that your direction needs to shift a little. It's like a dance; it's definitely an exercise in creativity, or like playing a strategy game, only real-life strategy: "Okay, this way is blocked. What other roads are open? If I do this, what happens? Let me give it a try!"

Guided Meditations and Visualizations

Guided Meditations and Visualizations are terms that I use interchangeably. While they are done silently, you are actively using your imagination to visualize yourself participating in the story that the author of the guided meditation has prepared. You start off by allowing your body and your busy mind to become as relaxed as possible in the moment, and then follow the suggestions to imagine yourself in a very pleasant place, strong and empowered. It is a short vacation in the middle of your day, and you come back to the rest of your day refreshed, relaxed, and ready to do whatever is next.

Guided meditations can easily be found on the internet for a variety of topics such as healing, prosperity, creativity, and many others, including many by well-known spiritual teachers. But you can also write your own, and use them in intentional ways to nurture relaxation, support your goals, and to develop your inner spirituality. Start by leading yourself into deep relaxation, then picturing yourself in a scene where you are successful in living the life that you want, with ease and with grace. Keep the vision filled with sensory experiences: what will you be seeing and hearing, what might you be smelling or tasting, and what are you tangibly feeling? Have your story keep you in the pleasant state of living your desired life for several minutes, letting all the sensory cues really sink in. With practice, try to increase the amount of time that you are imagining this desired life. Feel and notice the details.

So how is this anything more than just a fantasy and an escape from your daily circumstances? Many of us live in circumstances that feel chaotic and out of our control. Every step forward seems to be met with resistance. It seems that it is impossible to live the kind of life we desire, it's impossible to create a life that is really good. What happens is that in your guided meditation you've now deeply imagined your desired state, you've experienced what that feels like, and you can decide whether you really want that in your daily life, if it's what you thought it might be like. You're free to modify the circumstances that you're imagining until you really feel, even if just in those 15 - 20 minutes of meditation, how it is that you desire to feel and be.

Then, in your everyday awake consciousness, you can anticipate where you might feel that way or do the types of things you are desiring to do. You can recognize when you're moving toward that, and you can strategize how you can achieve that more and more in the chaos and challenges of your own daily life. Your recognition then gives you the clues and the directions as to where and how you can experience that feeling and do those activities, and you can then give yourself permission to believe that your desired future state really is possible for you as you feel into it more and more.

All of this helps you to overcome, little by little, the discouragement that comes when we experience the inevitable setbacks. Little by little you access more energy to work within the limitations of your life to achieve as closely as possible the life that, until you experience yourself moving into it, you've only imagined.

A Guided Meditation for You

Here's an example of the type of Guided Meditation that you could write for yourself. It might work best if you were to record it, then listen to your own voice guiding yourself through it. If you're listening rather than reading, you're usually less distractible than if you have your eyes open, and it might be easier to deeply relax if you're not also doing the work of reading it. Most of the time, people listen to guided meditations while sitting, yet you could also listen to this while you are walking at a rhythmic pace. Just modify the wording of this to reflect walking instead of sitting. But even if you simply slowly read this rather than recording and then listening to it, if you are able to imagine into it, you will be receiving most of the benefits.

As you begin to allow your body to relax in a way that suits you right now, just notice your breath. Allow yourself to discover what is most comfortable for you as you slow down. Notice as you inhale that it takes a bit of effort to bring the air into your lungs and belly, but that when you exhale, all you have to do is let go. Your shoulders may drop a bit as you exhale; just notice. Some people prefer to breathe with their mouths closed while others prefer to exhale through their mouths. There is no one correct way to breathe in and then out. Just notice and discover what feels most relaxing for you. And here, now, start your visualization:

I am taking some slow deep breaths. One breath after another. As I feel myself slowing down, I sink into my body more and more, letting go of the concerns of the day. — Breathe — As I start this meditation, I think of my allies, the people both alive and passed who are guides to me, and the animals and plants whom I resonate with, and I imagine them here with me, I ask them to be here with me in spirit. — Breathe — I relax my muscles, and in rhythm with my breath, I scan my body to allow each area to deeply relax. — Breathe — I bring my attention to my toes, and relax them. — Breathe — I let the muscles in my ankles and lower legs let go and relax. — Breathe — I let my knees relax, both the left knee — and the right knee. — Breathe — I let my thighs relax — and my hips. — Breathe — I let all the organs in my pelvis relax. —I let my stomach relax. — Breathe — I feel my lower back relaxing — and as I move my inner sight up my back, I feel relaxation moving up my spine. — Breathe — I let my chest and heart relax — and let my neck and throat relax. — Breathe — I let my shoulders relax, and then my upper arms, left side — and then right side. — I let my elbows relax — and my forearms. — Breathe — I let my wrists relax, and my fingers relax — left hand — and then right hand. — Breathe — I slowly let my attention move back up my arms to my chin — and let my chin and my jaws relax. — Breathe — I move my jaw back and forth to help it to relax — and then let it rest. — Breathe — I let my eyes relax — letting my eyes close or stay open slightly, whatever feels better. — Breathe — I let all the muscles around my eyes and in my forehead relax. — Breathe — I let my scalp relax — and I let the base of my brain and the back of my head relax. — Breathe — I notice that my breath now feels slow and effortless. — Breathe —

I gently bring my attention to my desire to live in a good way, to live consciously, mindfully. — Breathe — I bring my attention to my desire to live a meaningful life, to be happy and to somehow make the world a better place. — Breathe — I know that I live in a deeply interconnected world, that I am able to eat because the plants and the grain I eat grew in sunlight and rain. — Breathe — I can smell the rain that nourishes the plants. — Breathe — And now I feel the sunshine after the rain, drying the raindrops and warming the soil. — Breathe — I am thankful that someone, many someones, picked the fruits and vegetables that nourish me. — Breathe — I know that someone brought the foods to the store for me to buy and bring them home for my family. — Breathe — I'm tasting my favorite meal right now, enjoying it with a loved one. — Breathe — I acknowledge that countless individuals did their work to make possible my feeding my family and myself. — Breathe — I am grateful that

I am able to nourish myself and my family with the help of all those individuals and the earth and the sun and the rain. — Breathe — I know that I need the earth and the rain to be free of toxins so that the food I eat is nourishing. — Breathe — I know that all the people involved in bringing my food to me and to my family must also be nourished and have well-being. — Breathe — I acknowledge that I am connected to dozens of people in my everyday life, the workers who built my car or run the transit system, my co-workers at my place of work, and all who receive the benefits of my work. — Breathe — I can hear us laughing and telling stories as we work together. — Breathe — I am conscious that I am connected with all of the people I know, and that I am also connected with everyone who has been involved with building and bringing to me all the things that fill my life with joy. — Breathe —I am connected with people from around the world who built my computers and phone. — Breathe — I am connected with all the elements of the earth that make up all that I am surrounded by, the furniture made from the trees and steel made from metals, the plastic case of my computer and plastic food containers made from the oil from the earth, the clothing made from plants and wool and oil and the labor of countless workers. — Breathe — I can picture so many people who have made the things that I use every day.

I am embedded in a vast interconnection of people — and animals — and plants — and all that comes from the earth. — Breathe — I want to be aware of my connection with all of life, all the earth, with all that is. — Breathe — I want to take my part in this interconnected family of things. — I want to contribute and live in such a way that benefits all of us. — Breathe — I want all to thrive, — myself, my family, — all the people and all the world. — Breathe — I want to know the cycle of life, death, life, — I want to understand the transformation that is always happening, all the time, all around me. — Breathe —

I want to participate in this mystery. — I want to take my place, consciously, in this interconnected mystery. — Breathe — I make the time to think about these things. — Breathe — Almost every day I make the time to reflect on my life, on how I use my energy and resources. — Breathe — Almost every day I make a little time to get to know my inner life, what makes me happy, what gives me joy, what inspires my mind and my spirit. — Breathe — Almost every day I learn a little more about my own skills, my own gifts and interests that I contribute to the common good. — Breathe — I am aware that as I more deeply know who I really am and how interconnected I am with all that is, I make choices as I can that are good for all of us. — Breathe — I deeply want a world that is good for all of us. — Breathe — We are all here together on this beautiful blue planet. — Breathe — I do what I can to care for our home. — Breathe — I feel my love for this earth. — Breathe — I learn more and more how my choices have effects on other people, on other animals, on the earth. — Breathe — As I learn better, I do better, and I learn by making the time to reflect and think and ponder on all these things. — Breathe — I am becoming more and more conscious of my real power. — Breathe — I am one person, only one person, but I steward all that I am to bring awareness, understanding, life, and love into this world, into my world. — Breathe — I see us working together, I hear us laughing. — Breathe — I see the children running to me, I feel their hugs. — Breathe — I taste the clean, cool water as it quenches my thirst. — Breathe — I want to live in this world. — Breathe —

It's time to come back into this room, into this day, right here, right now. — Breathe — I slowly open my eyes and look around this room. I stretch my arms and legs, feeling refreshed and energized. I am thankful to have this vision of the world, and I feel my desire to live this every day.

To finish, tap your thighs with your hands, tap your feet on the floor, and recite your phone number backwards. Doing this shifts your brain rhythms from deep relaxation back into gentle alertness. It will bring you back into your day, refreshed and ready to attend to your next tasks.

Conclusion

There's no question that all of this analysis, all of this writing and dreaming takes time and effort, and that many people simply don't have the luxury of enough time to do more than record their strongest and most impressive dreams or nightmares, if even that. For me, different seasons in my life have offered more or fewer opportunities to explore all of these stories. There is no right or wrong judgment about this, not even a "It would be better if you could work with your dreams more." Some people do not remember their dreams or stories, others make the choice to focus on their awake lives and the concerns directly in front of them. There are no "shoulds" in this, only "mights", "coulds", and "what ifs?"

Look upon these ideas as possibilities you can explore in order to become more aware of your inner life, to become conscious and intentional about transforming your stories or creating new ones. Especially if there are certain issues in your life that keep bothering you, or problems that never seem to be resolved, then it may be quite helpful to examine your inner stories to see whether there's something influencing you that just isn't true, or isn't true anymore. I like to use the analogy of learning about nutrition and becoming physically fit. Almost every one of us could be doing more to take care of our physical bodies, but the priority to do so differs in different people. Yet, when we struggle with an illness, we suddenly have a lot of motivation to do more. Just so with dreams and stories. Almost every one of us could be doing more to understand the stories that come to us and that we tell ourselves, but the priority to do that competes with the many other things that we could do with our time and attention. Yet, there are times when this exploration might be particularly helpful. Especially for those of us who want to live reflectively and intentionally, it helps to know how we might go about learning how to do so.

But just as there are thousands of new towns or cities we can move to, and thousands of new people we can meet, there are thousands of ways to know ourselves better. The best way to discern how to respond to all of our inner stories is to follow our own curiosity and inner urgency. Sometimes, for any of many different reasons, a particular dream will pull at our attention. Then is the time to use some of these techniques to explore more. Just being aware of how night dreams and daydreams work in our lives is enough to notice when a closer look at them might be useful in our lives. I am constantly amazed at how creative our own psyches are. We never need to be bored with life!

6 Silence

Rather than following the admonishment "Don't just sit there, do something!" sometimes it is truly better to just sit there and do nothing — at least for a while.

This chapter is called "Silence" and not "Meditation" because while the two categories overlap quite a bit, this chapter focuses on more ways into silence than just meditation. The term meditation itself can refer to everything from thoughtful pondering on a particular topic, to mantra meditation, breath meditation, meditating on a phrase from a song or a poem, mindfulness meditation, guided meditation, focusing on an image, using prayer beads, centering, or resting. Many of those forms of meditation keep an active mind going, even if directed to specific topics such as carefully noticing all that is going on within and around us as in mindfulness meditation, or following the story and direction of a guided meditation.

Another reason that I want to focus on the silence part rather than the meditation part is because the practice of meditation has been increasingly used and sometimes hijacked by the workplace and by capitalism. Wellness programs, in general a very good movement in the workplace, often encourage the practice of meditation for stress reduction and focus. Increasingly though, it has been touted as a tool for success in the pursuit of corporate profits and individual profits, and has been strong-armed into a way to play the game of capitalism, economic success, and winning against the competition rather than as a method of stopping to question that world of individualism. I believe that meditation, at its best, is a great tool for wrenching ourselves free of the shaping of our values and the details of our lives from the influence of our overculture's focus on profits before people. Meditation, or rather, silence, gives us the space to be who we truly are and strengthens us to live life by our own values.

Sometimes, people who advocate silence and meditation are accused of spiritual bypassing, which is when people use their spiritual practices to bypass the challenges and suffering in front of them. Spiritual bypassing is focusing on the comfort, calm, and growth one gets from spiritual practice, a falling into thinking that a concern about material reality or social systems is somehow not worthy of being thought of as spiritual. In this way of thinking, spirituality should not concern itself with daily life — unless God sees fit to reward me for being such a "spiritual" person. It trusts that "karma" or "God" will take care of suffering and injustice, and that our own enlightenment or salvation is what we should be working on, to the exclusion of any political issues.

In some forms of more traditional religious thought, spiritual bypassing is seen as desirable, as there is the admonition "Judge not, lest ye be judged" (Matthew 7:1 of the Christian bible). There is the belief that God will deal with people in God's own ways, and that justice, punishment, or rewards will come in the next life.

Spiritual bypassing can be subtle, as calm and rest in our lives are truly needed and are only problematic when they are our only focus and goal. Spiritual practices become the kind of depth dimension practices that I'm describing, though, when there is a true balance sought between the more contemplative, quiet practices, and those that more actively help us identify and discern what is truly ours to do, and then doing it.

By silence, I'm going to be talking about different ways that we can get our busy minds to quiet down and to rest without skipping off from one fantasy to another. Our busy mind is often referred to as "monkey mind," reminding us of the primate swinging from one tree to another, curious about everything, picking up one thing after another, tiring with things quickly and always looking for novelty. For many people, meditation feels just like imprisoning that monkey in the cage of our brains. But monkeys can still make quite the racket as they rattle the bars trying to get out. Silence is when the monkeys calm down and quit rattling those bars, pausing, resting, and perhaps even listening.

Not that we can ever have a completely blank mind. When people tell me they can't meditate, they're often referring to an expectation that their minds will stop thinking completely. That's just not possible, because minds are made to think thoughts. We notice, remember, and compare constantly, and even in some of the deepest contemplation thoughts will arise. One is successful in silence, though, if you're able to notice the thought and let it go, sinking back into a quiet, centered, listening consciousness. And so, by silence, I'm referring to a holy pause for rest, refreshment, and for possibly gaining access to the mysterious worlds of alternate consciousness that mystics and masters have described.

There is much more to life than what we see and interact with daily, and there are ways to touch, to "know," these "other worlds." I have an image of a little boy standing in a forest, sticking out his finger and touching an almost invisible web of light and interconnection. That image reminds me that even though I don't see that web all around me, I can somehow "know" it, and that the way that I know it, the way I can apprehend this mystery in some way, is through the quieting of all that constant nattering self-talk; that is, in silence. There is more to life than only what is measurable, and the most common way we know this is in our experience of love. Though we can measure blood pressure changes and the release of different hormones that happen when we are with someone we love deeply, the actual human experience is not known through those numbers. While we can describe love in thousands of words, there is also a mystery about it that measurement, and even description, does not touch. It is this kind of mystery of worlds other than our conscious daily consensual reality that I'm speaking of here. I think it's important to realize that the word "mystery" does not refer to something that is totally un-understandable, but rather to something that is infinitely understandable, and that we can always sink further into mystery to experience and know more and more deeply. Silence is one of the surest ways to get there.

Almost all of us have a resistance to silence, even while we crave it on those busy days when we're overwhelmed with errands, tasks, and people wanting things from us. If we haven't yet developed some type of meditation practice, we can approach a craved hour of silence with "Oh! I didn't mean SILENT silence! So what do I do NOW?" And if I respond that you don't have to do anything, just sit in silence, very few people in our developed world can sit much more than 30 seconds without wanting to jump up and do something, anything! Even I, who have a practice of silence, have days where I feel like a horse yearning to run free, galloping at top speed, and I'm straining against the bit tearing at my gums and the reins holding me back. Other people who suffer from anxiety often find that it's very difficult to meditate or enter into silence. The silence seems to give full range to the anxiety that they are otherwise trying to keep at bay with constant activity.

It takes some time to slow down and move into a different state of consciousness. So many of my days feel like I'm a steam engine, slow to fire up and get the steam building. Then as the day proceeds, I'm moving full steam ahead, getting lots accomplished. Just as a steam engine at full speed cannot stop on a dime, neither can I, nor you. We have to slow down, let off the steam, and eventually come to a place where we can move into the wordless zone, the unknown. We live in a holographic universe where in some mysterious but very real way the whole is present in each of its parts, and we slow down to notice that we hold within us the entire universe. Powerful gifts are there in that experience, but we're no longer in direct control.

So why would we want to make the effort when it can be hard to do this slowing down, where we can't control what happens, and where the first thing we meet is ourselves and our own shadows which are sometimes scary and painful?

Well, we make the effort because we get to know our full selves, heal our negative shadow and incorporate our golden shadow. We become a calm seer of the dramas within us and around us. We watch ourselves as a compassionate witness, almost as if we're watching someone else. We're not so pulled by emotional noise. We can drop to a level deeper than the passing theater of the everyday. We get to go beyond ourselves to touch the entire universe in some mysterious way. We get to intuit the web of connections in which we are embedded. We begin to feel this broader sense of "me," what we can call our "soul" or our True Self, as the bedrock of who we truly are. Silent emptiness and fullness begin to feel like the same thing, and we sense that we participate in something much larger than our individual selves. We come to know this vastness as our true home.

So how? In the last 50 years we in the west have been taught by many Buddhist and Hindu meditation teachers how to reach these states of consciousness. Yet the same contemplative awareness is the legacy of the Christian mystics as well as of Islamic Sufi mystics. There are many resources, and I will here offer some simple openings to this vast well of teachings. As I said at the beginning of this chapter, the most basic practice is, in a reversal of our culture's call to action: "Don't just do something, sit there!"

Basic Sitting Practice

Sit comfortably with your back straight but not rigid. If you're comfortable sitting cross-legged on the floor on a cushion, that is another possibility, but not at all necessary. The picture of yogis sitting cross legged is based as much in the cultural practice in many Eastern countries of everyone sitting on the floor for all sorts of activities as it is in its assistance in helping you keep your back straight. If sitting in a chair, do not cross your legs or ankles. Position yourself so that you can be relaxed without any constrictions. Aim to sit still for the entire time you've devoted to your "sit." Loosen or remove tight belts or constricting clothing. Let your tummy relax so that you can breathe deeply, letting your diaphragm expand completely with each breath. Let your eyes close, or let them be unfocused and lowered toward the ground. Allow your hands to sit comfortably, or you can place them in some meaningful position, such as open with palms upward in a receptive pose, or palms together near your heart in a traditional prayer position. The main thing is to allow your body enough comfort and ease so that you are not distracted by it during your sit, yet also allowing you to breathe fully and easily. Have your notebook or journal within reach so that you can write yourself a note with a minimum of movement.

Start by taking a few slow, deep breaths, letting your exhales be long and slow. Fill your diaphragm fully with each in-breath, letting your stomach expand as your diaphragm expands, then let go into the exhale. After three or four conscious slow breaths, just allow yourself to breathe naturally, but remember to breathe deeply.

Remember your intention in your sitting practice. You might say a short prayer to open yourself to the spirit of the Divine, or simply affirm to yourself that you are giving yourself over to relaxation and inner mystery. Know that you are safe in that moment and that you are fully able to relax for the next 5 to 10 minutes.

I find it very helpful to mentally scan my body from my toes up to the top of my head to notice and to let go of any tension I may be holding. We often don't even notice all the tightness in our muscles, and spending the time of a breath on each area of the body helps us to notice and relax. Breathe in and focus on your toes and let them relax as you exhale. In your mind's eye, move your attention to your feet, then ankles, lower legs, knees, upper legs, buttocks, stomach muscles, inner organs, and on up through your body, including your jaws, cheeks, eyebrows, and scalp. You can focus first on the toes of one foot, then the other, alternating sides of the body all the way up, or you can focus first on your left side of the body all the way up, then allow your attention to go back down to focus on the right side of your body on up.

By about this time in my sitting practice my brain suddenly remembers something "really important" that I don't want to forget. After many times of being distracted during my whole "sit" by the worry that I will forget, I've learned to have paper and pencil next to me in order to quickly jot a short note as a reminder. I then feel free to let go of those thoughts and worries knowing that I can attend to them later.

After the short body scan, just rest into the silence. When thoughts come up, as soon as you're aware of the thought, let it go. A beautiful metaphor to imagine is that you're sitting at the side of the river where boats occasionally go by. Imagine your thoughts as the boats, and let them go on their way. Don't stop the boats, have a conversation with the people inside, or get on the boat and continue on down the river in the boat. Just notice the boat/thought, and watch it pass by you. Another boat/thought will undoubtedly pass by, but again, don't get on that boat/thought, and just let it pass by you. Just so you don't have unrealistic expectations, know that this is easier said than done. Before we even "come to," and become aware that we're even having a thought, we're often all caught up in the thoughts and having imaginary conversations with all sorts of people about all sorts of things! Don't berate yourself. This is normal. It's what brains do: think thoughts. Whenever you become aware of the thought, let it go and relax again. Affirm your intention, and let it go. It really does become easier with practice and patience.

When your timer goes off at the end of your five minutes or ten minutes, take a couple of deep breaths again, and offer a thought of thanks that you've had this time to relax and to refresh, to be open to more than the everyday bustle of activity. Do try to have a timer with a gentle alarm or vibration when it goes off, otherwise it's easy to be startled and adrenalize yourself completely, negating the relaxation you've just allowed yourself to have.

If you want to and have time, this is a good opportunity to now write in your journal. I've found that if I write after a sit, then I seem to be able to access deeper thoughts and am clearer about whatever it is I am writing about. If I journal before my sit, however, I often bring whatever I've been writing about into my meditation, and have an even harder time letting go of the thoughts that come up. This differs with different people and different seasons in life. Notice in yourself what works well for you.

As you become more proficient, expand the time to about 20 minutes. Twenty minutes once or twice a day proves to be a fine practice to receive the benefits of a meditation practice while still being short enough to live a regular life with job, family, and ordinary concerns.

Addressing Difficulties

Physical aches and pains — If you're uncomfortable during your sit, gently move yourself into a more comfortable position. Our bodies are not used to being still for extended periods of time, or if you have an idealized idea of meditation, you may be trying to sit in a lotus position. No extra points for suffering through preventable pain! Ensure that you're not putting pressure on particular points in the body where you may be cutting off your circulation and have limbs "fall asleep." Sometimes, sitting in meditation helps us become aware of the pain we have chronically been carrying in our body. In self-compassion, try to address that with stretching beforehand or checking with a health-care practitioner. Persons with chronic back pain may find lying down flat or even standing to be positions that they can best meditate in. Adapt. Do whatever works for you to be as comfortable as possible.

Outer distractions — Ensure as best you can that you will not be disrupted for the 5, 10, or 20 minutes you will be meditating. Turn your cellphone notifications off; don't answer the phone. For distractions such as traffic noise or other people talking, deal with them as with thoughts: notice them, then let them go. Tell your family that this is important to you and ask to not be disturbed. Ensure that small children and companion animals are tended to and will not need you for those few minutes. If that simply does not work, find another place or time in which to have your sit.

Falling asleep — This is surprisingly common! I think it's an indication of how sleep deprived we are as a culture. If this happens more than once or twice, do not meditate while lying down, or try sitting in a straight-backed chair rather than a cushioned one, and don't slump. Don't be giving your body the idea that it's time to nap. Don't meditate right after a meal. Try meditating earlier in the day. Prioritize getting adequate sleep for your own personal needs (8 hours might not be enough for you).

Boredom — This, too, is common, especially for beginners. Meditating seldom brings ecstatic experiences or mind-expanding visions, though that would be nice, and does happen on occasion. Our psyches are so stimulated most of the time that the lack of stimulation feels, well, boring. That's okay. As you persevere in your sitting practice, you will come to appreciate the quiet and inner spaciousness of your psyche. As you develop the silent witness of yourself within yourself, you begin to touch, in a quite subtle way, the interconnections that exist within the web of being. It's not usually firework-worthy excitement, but it has its own gifts. Be patient with yourself. Try not to give up too soon. Remember, some sort of meditation has been a reflective/spiritual practice for thousands of years. Don't give up before you've had a chance to see what the benefits might be for you.

Inner distractions — Most of the time, inner distractions are the thoughts that keep coming back even after you try to let them go. If they are about things that you need to attend to, make a quick note to address them later, and then, address them later. If you are living a life that is just filled with urgencies, address these urgencies so that you can legitimately take a break. No one of us is so important that we cannot be "offline" for a few minutes each day. A life filled with urgencies is simply not sustainable over the long term. Something's gotta give. But once your psyche gets the message that you're not forgetting to do something important by taking the time to meditate, and that you can trust yourself to deal later with whatever concerns arise during your sit, these persistent distracting thoughts tend to settle.

Take note of what these inner distractions are. Ask yourself if there's something within you that seems to be running away from this time of quiet. One of the opportunities in meditation is that all sorts of limiting beliefs and outgrown stories we've told ourselves tend to come up in the silence. If that's true for you, especially if you can identify that you often have the same sort of self-talk when trying to meditate, it might be helpful to bring it to your journal. Do the same for any anxieties that come up. Ask yourself the same sorts of questions that I suggested in the previous chapter on dreams and stories. Ask if what you're saying to yourself in these stories is true. If it was true at one time, is it true now? If it's partially true, what is the part that isn't applicable to you? Can you let that part go? Might you design a simple ritual or ceremony to let it go? I'll be talking more about rituals in the next chapter. Meditation is a way to gently let all sorts of early conditioning and stories that are no longer meaningful for you to work themselves through. I often think of meditation as a type of metabolizing of our thoughts and of the stories by which we've organized our lives and made meaning out of all the bits of our experiences.

Let me give a simple example of this. Let's say that when you try to meditate, you find yourself thinking that it's boring and that you're just wasting your time. You're not doing anything to get your goals accomplished; you're not even doing anything good for anybody else. If you were to take this time and instead of wasting it here in this quiet room you were to volunteer to rock babies who are sick in the hospital, at least you'd be helping someone else. And that would be quiet, too, wouldn't it? Maybe it would be just as good as meditation, and there'd be an extra benefit for the babies in it, too. And so on. On one level these are simply the kinds of thoughts that come up when we're not engaged in our usual activities and their stimulation. Yet if you were to have these same sorts of thoughts whenever you tried to meditate, perhaps you might ask yourself why you think that you have to be getting something accomplished in every moment of your life. Is that belief at the root of these thoughts? Many of us have been thoroughly indoctrinated in a capitalistic, Protestant work ethic which looks upon something like "just sitting there" as not only a waste of time, but as the sin of laziness, or sloth. But is it true that taking twenty minutes to sit quietly is evidence of your slothfulness? What about the contemplative tradition in all of the major religious traditions of the world, including Christianity? Don't you have any right to determine how you will spend your time in your life? Must you be defined by what you do or what you accomplish? Are you a human doing? Can you let yourself be a human being? Let yourself investigate these questions in your journal, and see how that changes the kinds of inner distractions that you may experience.

Sometimes, though, issues come up that are urgently calling for attention. They can be flashbacks of unhappy or abusive experiences, or they can be persistent images of horror or an obsession with really dark and scary thoughts. These are basically waking life analogies to the nightmares that come in dreaming life. The methods that I've included here in this book on how to deal with nightmares can be helpful in resolving these thoughts.

If, however, these strategies don't help you to resolve whatever is disturbing you while you try to meditate, please reach out to a wise person whom you can talk with in person, and explore all of this with up close support and skill in dealing with these experiences. You deserve to live a calm inner life and not be hounded by anxiety to the point where you cannot sit in silence with yourself. There is help available, and there are ways to resolve these painful issues. In a world that seems to multiply trauma, where many of us have experienced or witnessed horrendous things, we are certainly not alone in our need to address and heal the traumas. Don't just hang on each day, surviving — barely — from one day to another. Please find the helps that will assist you to heal.

Some Suggestions for Other Practices of Silence

While sitting in meditation may be the simplest practice of silence, and is the basis for the different kinds of meditations that are found in various traditions, it's not for everybody. Or, at least it's not for everybody at all times in their lives. Yet silence is deeply beneficial for everyone. Even little children do better in the rest of their day when they have had a chance for downtime — a nap or a quiet rest. As adults we rarely let ourselves do that, though, saddled as we are with the expectation of more and faster accomplishment. Even vacations have become marathons of activity and competition with the carefully curated Instagram images uploaded several times a day. If traditional sitting meditation is not for you, try some of these alternatives.

Shaking the Snow Globe, or, "No Mud, No Lotus"

Do you have a Snow Globe? If not, you can fill a small jar with water and add a tablespoon or so of dirt. Make sure the jar is closed tightly. Sit comfortably, and then shake the snow globe or jar. Quietly watch the "snow" or the dirt swirl around and then slowly settle to the bottom. Watch until there is no more movement in the globe or jar.

Simple. Effective. I find this to be a perfect analogy of my mind and spirit on days when I'm going, going, going, and finally decide to become centered and quiet. It takes a little while to settle, but I can be confident that I will settle as long as I don't keep jostling, and going, going, going.

I read many years ago that in meditation, we are to become so still that, sitting by a pond of water, the animals become so relaxed in our presence that they return to the water to drink. I find that to be a lovely image to imagine as I'm waiting for the "snow" or dirt to settle. One time I was sitting on the ground in a clearing in a small wooded area attached to a retreat center. I was meditating with my eyes closed. When I opened them at the end of my meditation, I was looking face to face into the eyes of a mother deer, with her fawn also looking at me, curious as to what strange creature I might be! It was one of the most wondrous moments I remember! They were less than ten feet away from me. After a few moments of mutual staring, I spoke softly to them in greeting, and after a few more moments, they moved off and continued munching the plants there in the clearing.

Another idea I've found in many places is the reminder that the beautiful lotus plant lives in clouded, plant-filled, sometimes dirty water, with its roots many feet down in the mud at the bottom of the pond. The analogy is that even out of a cluttered, chaotic, or even a "dirty" life, great beauty can arise, and that beauty often relies upon things that we disregard as noble or valuable, such as the mud in our lives. Hence: no mud, no lotus. This is another good thought to consider as we watch the mud settle to the bottom of the jar. What beauty might grow out of the mud of your life?

Coloring and Simple Artwork

Several of the practices in the chapter on images can be used to let your mind and body relax and open to a different kind of consciousness. Here we're not focusing on images that tell a story, that express an emotion, or that reverberate with symbolism. Here we're looking for activities that invite you to NOT think about anything in particular. I have included scrap paper and pen in the supply list because it's very common, anytime we come into quiet, to have many thoughts rush up to fill the void. I've found that while it's one thing to bat away most of the random thoughts, some of the thoughts are important to remember. Things I've forgotten that I promised to do, a sudden insight into how to solve a problem I've been stewing about, or an appointment I'd forgotten to put into my calendar are examples of things that I don't want to just trust that I'll remember again after my quiet time. That's what the paper and pen are for, to quickly jot down the items in order to then be free to forget about them during the time I've allocated for this quiet.

Adult coloring books are filling a need that many are beginning to recognize: that we as humans need regular moments of quiet, undemanding, unproductive time — or at least "unproductive" in terms of how the modern world defines productivity.

Playing with watercolor or colored pencils, allowing the colors to simply cover the white paper, to mix and blend, is another way to slip underneath the incessant conversations we have with ourselves. Colored pencils often blend into fascinating new colors, and watching how two or three colors transform leads us into calmness. I find watercolor especially satisfying because as the pigments move across the page depending on how wet your brush or paper is, the colors seem almost alive with a mind of their own. Enjoy their unpredictability, and watch their wordless magic lead you into a meditative space, a light trance. Playing with watercolors is the closest I've gotten to the feeling I had as a young girl while I watched a lava lamp move in its mesmerizing way. My father, who was always gaining weight then trying to lose it, would often need to have his clothes altered. He used to take his clothes to a tailor, and while he and the tailor discussed their business I'd sit and watch the lava lamp the tailor had there in his shop. I still remember how the lava lamp would calm me, allowing my mind to stop the inner conversations and just flow as the colors in the lamp moved and transformed.

There aren't many lava lamps around anymore, but fortunately, there are watercolors.

Mandalas

In Chapter Four I gave directions as to how to make both free-form and more formal mandalas. Mindfully creating the circles and the repeated motifs can bring us into peace and a wordless quiet. But there are ways to make more three-dimensional mandalas, too.

In various places around the world, monks and holy people used colored sands to construct mandalas as prayers or as healing places. After a period of time, the mandalas were deconstructed and the sands returned to the earth or released into the flowing water of a river. There is also the ancient custom of the mother in a home making a mandala at the entrance. She would make the design out of sand, flour, or ground corn, sifting them onto the ground with her hand. Each morning a new one was made as people walking into and out of the home would eventually obliterate the day's design. These temporary mandalas reminded people not to hold onto things, situations, or conditions in their lives, teaching that all things pass away and the way to happiness and contentment lies in accepting change. All is impermanent.

One way to reflect those practices in our own life is to create nature mandalas in our yard or as we walk in nature. A friend of mine made a new small nature mandala each day for a whole season, posting a photo of each one on social media to allow all of us viewing the photos to share in her moment of meditation and quiet. She used what was already there in her yard, incorporating small stones, leaves, berries, flowers, and small twigs.

Prayer Beads

Throughout the world, in many traditional religions people have used strings of beads to count prayers or to settle the mind into a quiet, receptive state. Hindus have their malas of 108 beads which mark the repetition of a mantra. Muslims have their beads on which they recite the 99 Names of God that are enumerated in the Quran. Christians, especially Catholic Christians, have their rosary which is a mixture of the traditional prayers of the Our Father and the Hail Mary. And how many visitors to Greece come home with "worry beads" for a souvenir? I'm sure that worry beads started out as prayer beads.

Beads feel good to hold and handle. They can be slipped into a pocket or under a pillow. They can facilitate a calming rhythm in your breath, in your thoughts in the form of memorized prayers, and in the moving of the beads between your fingers. This is especially noticeable when you use the beads while you're walking. There is the tactile memory of gathering berries from bushes, eating some of the sweet fruit and collecting some, a motion repeated over and over by people through millennia. There might also be a strong sense of a mother's love, if you were fortunate enough to have been nursed by a loving mother when you were an infant. You may have a nonverbal tactile memory of grabbing at your mother's nipple as you suckled on the other one.

The beads can be symbolic in either their source or their color, and many prayer beads have added items such as medals, crosses, crucifixes, or tassels. Each of those is associated with symbols in different spiritual traditions, and, of course, we can choose our own symbolism to associate to them.

It can be a meditative or depth dimension practice to construct your own set of beads, beads chosen by you, in colors or shapes symbolic to you, in numbers that are significant to you, and with added objects that are meaningful to you. Beads can be found in craft stores or in old jewelry that you or your mother or grandmother are no longer using. You can make beads from clay, homemade playdough, or the polymer clay such as FIMO gotten from craft stores. Rosaries are called such because roses were used in hand-crafted crowns on statues of the Holy Mother, and their petals were then dried and ground to make beads with an exquisite scent. And many rosaries were made simply from knotted string instead of beads.

It is meaningful to dedicate your set of prayer beads to a certain intention. The traditional sets of beads have their historical intentions, and you can either affirm those, add your own intention along with the historical, or completely substitute your own intention. Prayer beads are tools, and we make them prayerful, holy, or meaningful objects by our intentions and the history of how human beings have used these tools for millennia. For instance, the rosary comes from the Catholic Christian tradition, and is a devotion to the Holy Mother. It consists of two main prayers that most Christians would have known by heart: the Our Father, the prayer of Jesus recorded in the Gospels of the bible; and the Hail Mary, consisting of lines from the Gospel that refer to Mary along with a petition that the Holy Mother pray for us "now and at the hour of our death". Other prayers, the "Glory Be" and the "Apostles' Creed," were added as time went by.

Priests and monks of the Catholic Church were obligated to pray the Divine Office every day, which is a set of different readings from the bible recited several times a day. Most common people in the Middle Ages, though, did not know how to read, nor were they encouraged to read the bible even if they were rich enough to have (a hand-copied) one. They were encouraged to pray the rosary instead. The rosary was very popular for centuries precisely because of its simplicity (only two prayers needed), but I think also because in an agrarian society, people were close to the land and the knowledge that we depend upon the earth for our survival. The earth is our mother, and Jesus's mother, according to scripture, was given to us as our mother. I believe that there was a visceral truth that was satisfying for people to affirm and to meditate upon in uniting the two ideas into a Holy Mother. Later in the Middle Ages, the church encouraged people to meditate on the different events of Mary's life in relation to Jesus's life, each defined event to be thought about while praying each decade of the Hail Mary prayers. These were then codified into the Joyful, Sorrowful, and Glorious Mysteries of the Rosary, with each set of five Mysteries assigned to certain days of the week. If people said the rosary each day, as was encouraged, they would go through all fifteen mysteries a couple of times during the course of the week. Things got more complicated through the years with added prayers, indulgences assigned to praying the rosary, public recitations of the rosary, etc.

But the simple act of reciting two well memorized prayers, one Our Father followed by ten Hail Mary's, remains the core of these prayer beads. A person doesn't pay attention anymore to the words of a very familiar prayer, and they become sounds or directed pathways of thought that lead into a quiet, receptive, reflective state of mind and spirit. It usually takes about 15-20 minutes to go through the 55 to 60 prayers (depending on which version of a rosary you might use), which is a traditional amount of time that is recommended once or twice a day in other traditions worldwide for meditation. This amount of time allows us to let our nervous systems calm down, entrain our brain rhythms to a calmer pace, and sink into a blessed silence that allows the rising of other kinds of wisdom beyond our daily thoughts.

I made a set of prayer beads from agate and other semi-precious stone beads I bought at a craft store. I divided them into four groups of seven, with a slightly larger purple amethyst stone between the groups of seven. I chose seven and four because they are numbers with a significant amount of symbolism to each one. Seven was the traditional number of planets that were known before the more powerful telescopes were available, and four is the number associated, among other things, to the four elements of our world. The four sets of seven beads are colored brown and beige for earth, blue for the sky symbolizing air, red for fire, and blue-green for the water of the oceans. I included two pendants: a tree of life sculpted into an oval medallion, and a traditional medal of Our Lady of Guadalupe. Our Lady of Guadalupe, also known as La Conquista, is said to have appeared to a poor indigenous man in "The New World" of Mexico in 1531. She is a symbol reminding me to resist the oppression of colonialism and other injustices. My intention in creating this set of beads was to remember how I am held by the earth and by the heavens, and by this remembering, to continue to commit to the healing of the environment in any way available to me. Using the symbolism that the earth is our Mother, this is also a reminder to me that I am in relationship with all that is around me as chosen, beloved family, and that I am cared for, and care for others, through a kind of a Holy Mother.

The two prayers or intentions that I usually use with this set of prayer beads are short quotations from two holy women whose lives I admire: Hildegard of Bingen and Julian of Norwich, both strong and influential independent women (independent for the Middle Ages, that is). I consider them to be the very human spiritual ancestors who can be models and helpers for us here in this world. The quote from Hildegard I use for the larger beads is "God hugs us. I am encircled in the arms of the Mystery of God." It is Julian's quote that I use for the groups of seven: "All shall be well, and all shall be well, and all manner of thing shall be well." Julian's quote, especially, brings me into a calmer frame of mind. The repetition does its work. I do not consider this light trance to be a kind of false consolation, or even brainwashing, at all, though, because I consider it a reminder that my efforts in life should not be judged on outcome, and that if I continue to do what I can do to the extent of my ability, in authenticity and integrity to the best discernment I am able to make, that, indeed, all shall be well. The outcome may not be to my liking, but it will be the best outcome that I will have had any power to make happen. All we can do truly is all we can do, and I can be at peace with that. (Well, at least most of the time!)

The rosary, on the other hand, is a type of prayer that I use in the middle of the night when I can't sleep. Though I am not a church-goer nor conventional believer, I was raised Catholic. I am very familiar with the prayers of the rosary, and I support its intention as a connection with the symbolic Holy Mother of all. I don't have to think about the wording of the prayers at all — it's almost like reciting a "spell" in another language that brings about my awareness of that which we call the Divine or the Mystery in life. In the middle of the night the rosary calms worries I might be carrying and soothes whatever pain my dear body is experiencing. Holding the beads reminds me that I am not alone, no matter how alone I may feel at the moment. Tens of thousands of people with good intention, thousands of my direct familial and cultural ancestors, and tens of thousands, perhaps millions of well-intentioned people all over the world, throughout time, have all used beads to utter their prayers to the Great Mystery. I stand in a long line of humans who have reached out for whatever help and comfort may be available in this mysterious world. Might you want to as well?

You can purchase traditional prayer beads at religious supply stores in bigger cities, as well as online. I often find old rosaries at thrift stores in the jewelry section. If you are using prayer beads from a tradition that is not your own, invest some time in finding out how they are used in those traditions, what prayers are traditional, and what the intention of the practice has been. You can certainly substitute your own prayers and intentions if you do so with respect, but it is a sign of respect, courtesy and justice to not just take a tradition from another culture to use as our own. There is a history to these items, and it is not appropriate to use them frivolously or unthinkingly.

Once you have your beads, decide what words or prayers you will use on each bead as you finger them. You can use an affirmation or prayer that you have composed, or you can use a traditional prayer if its words ring true for you. "Help me, please, Great Mystery of Life" works too. You can also use a short quotation that you find inspiring, or words from a person whom you admire. Just ensure that it is easy to memorize so that you are not distracted by trying to remember the wording. The point is not to have to think about what the words mean, but to have a phrase or prayer that comes so easily that you don't have to think about it at all.

If you have just a circular set of beads with no beginning or ending spot, attach a small medal or symbol at a certain place so that you will feel with your fingers when you have completed a round. Even a small piece of string tied in the right spot will serve the purpose. Red thread is a very symbolic choice.

Either sit yourself comfortably or walk at an easy, steady pace. The more boring the walk, the better, as the intent is to drop into a quiet state of mind rather than enjoying the scenery. Start your prayer or intention and recite it as you hold the first bead. Then move your fingers to the next bead and repeat the prayer or intention. Continue until you come to the end. If you have different prayers for different beads, you should be able to feel the difference in the bead either through its size or by means of a larger space between that bead and the surrounding beads. You shouldn't have to look down at the beads to know where you are or what prayer to say. As you continue you will probably find that your breath synchronizes to the rhythm of your words. If not, feel free to modify some words so that it fits better for you.

If you make mistakes or get lost, don't give up. Though prayer beads may not be for everybody, if you're not used to using them it takes a while before it comes easily. Give them a good chance before giving up on them. And as I have suggested before, having some paper and pen close at hand is helpful to record those important reminders that come up as soon as we calm our busy minds.

Afterwards, you may want to record your impressions or insights into your journal.

Pulling In Your Extended Attention

There are times that I feel just too busy and overwhelmed with life to take the time to sit in silence or to meditate. Yet I've certainly found that it is always worth my while to make the attempt. In order not to be constantly distracted by a busy life, though, I've had to learn how to bring my sphere of attention into a much smaller and quieter sphere, and to do so responsibly. By responsibly, I mean staying true to my commitments or to renegotiate them, and to not use spirituality as a way to escape from the complexities and pain of the world — also known as spiritual bypassing. As a "for instance," the words of Julian of Norwich, "All shall be well, and all shall be well, and all manner of thing shall be well" can be used as a type of mantra, brainwashing ourselves into a Pollyanna state of mind where I don't have to worry about or do anything because "God" will just take care of it all. I can go on to think that the world is not my responsibility, it's "God's," and I can go my merry way without committing to help clean up the messes all around us.

That is certainly true in one sense: we are not in charge of the world and that whatever happens, life is far bigger and more mysterious than we know, and "all will be well" for each of us even if, or when, it ends in death. We are limited in our desires to heal the pain of the world and we have to let go of thinking that our actions will certainly change the world in ways that we define as "better." As long as we are as responsibly informed as possible, all we can do is the best that we can do, and we focus on discerning and doing that, rather than solely focussing on the outcomes of our actions. We need to let go into trusting that life, love, and goodness will go on without our constant interventions.

On the other hand, though, our work, our intentions, and our relationships do matter, and do change the world, at least as much as the proverbial butterfly's wingbeat contributes to the hurricane on the other side of the world! What we do and how we do it, even what we think matters, and it's our responsibility as a human being to become more and more conscious of how this is so, and to choose how we will be, how we will think, what we will stand for in life, and what we will do. I spoke above as to how I use Julian's words to remind myself that if I live in radical authenticity, then I can be confident that I am doing all that is possible for me to do in order that "all manner of thing shall be well." Here is one way to pull in our extended attention while responsibly attending to all that is in our circle of influence.

Do a Brain Dump: Either in your personal journal or on a separate piece of paper, list in point form everything that's on your mind that you're trying to remember to do. Then list things you would like to do, list chores and errands that you don't want to forget, list everything that's nagging at you. Write them all down. Then think of all the major areas of your life, such as family and children, your communities, work, personal interests, health, etc. What are the special projects that you would love to do, such as genealogy, or painting the kitchen, or writing a book? Those are the dreams that pull at you, but often you never do anything about them because they are not urgent, nor will anything fall apart if you neglect them. They are still important in your life, though, and deserve to be on your lists even if you choose not to do anything with them for now. Does anything else come up that you want to remember? List them. Get them out of the back of your mind, where they nag at you in quiet moments, and onto paper where they are now something that you can deal with in a purposeful and intentional way.

Look at your list. Designate with a symbol, such as an asterisk, all the items that you must do something about soon (within the next few weeks). Designate with another symbol, perhaps a plus sign, any item that you have to do or any project that is coming up that you are involved in that is not urgent, but that needs your involvement in the next six months or so. Put a question mark in front of items that would be nice to do, but are not strictly necessary. In my journal I have a list in the back where I keep these ideas. I call it my "Possibilities" list.

As much as you can, shift items from this brain dump onto your calendars or lists where they won't get lost. As soon as you do this for an item, cross the item off your brain dump. Ideally, you will process every item from the brain dump. If you can't, your brain dump can simply be added to your "To Do" list, to be checked whenever you next organize your affairs. The whole point of doing this brain dump is to allow yourself to trust that there aren't little things that you're forgetting, nor that there are quieter desires or callings that you're ignoring just because they're not screaming at you.

With your newfound peace of mind, imagine each area of your life one by one, and imagine pulling inward your "tentacle of attention" or your outstretched arm of concern, and letting that area of concern just be. Knowing that you are not ignoring any commitments or urgencies in those areas, let yourself put all your concerns down for a few minutes. Imagine yourself spiraling inward, pulling in all your expanded attention until you are settled in a cozy circle, centered within yourself, like a cat curled up napping. Settle into a cozy chair or other comfortable position. Notice how it feels to know that, for at least this moment, all is taken care of and you have nothing pulling at you right now. Take three slow, deep breaths, and just rest. Depending on how much time you have, you can now enter into meditation with a calm mind and a calm body.

Between Earth and the Heavens, Between an Atom and a Star

This is a simple calming practice to remember who you are and where you are right now. Sit comfortably and attend to your breathing. Take a couple of deep breaths, then bring your attention to your feet and imagine that you are growing roots down from your feet deep into the earth. Imagine yourself well planted in fertile soil.

Move your attention to your root chakra. Chakras, the Sanskrit word for "wheels" or "circles", are different energy centers within our bodies that also correspond with all the ways that we grow and develop as human beings. The reality and the symbolism of the traditional seven chakras can be a life's study in themselves, but for right now we'll use them as reminders to ourselves of the different areas in our bodies up along our spine. The root chakra is at the base of our spines, and symbolizes our basic security as a person rooted in life, having a place in the world with the right of being here. Notice that area of your body and picture yourself healthy there with the color of deep red. Rest there for a moment or two.

Move your attention upward to where your genitals are. Imagine health within all your relationships and in your sexual and reproductive self with the color orange. Linger at each chakra with a few deep breaths, imagining the healing energy of the earth moving into each area of your body and knowing our deep connectedness with all that is around us and supporting us. When you are ready, move your attention upward to your solar plexus area, just around your navel. This chakra is associated with your self-esteem and self-confidence, and how you present yourself in the world. Imagine full health in this area of your body and life with the color of bright yellow, like the sun shining fully and warmly.

When you are ready, move your attention up to your heart area, the symbol of love and your connections with all the people, animals, and growing things in your life. Imagine the earth's healing energy bathing your heart chakra with green life, the color of growth and fertility. Take a few deep breaths, and when ready, move your attention upward to your throat center. This is your voice center, your ability to speak out, to communicate who you are with authenticity and with being heard. Bathe this chakra with translucent blue light, imagining clarity and health in all the ways that you speak out and communicate your self into the world.

After a moment or two, bring your attention to your third eye, the space between your eyebrows. This chakra is the center out of which you see into, behind, beneath, and around all that is within your center of concern. Imagine this chakra glowing with a gentle but very strong indigo light, bringing the earth's energy of healing and fertility into your ability to see all that you need to see, with clarity and accuracy.

When you are ready, bring your attention to your crown chakra which is situated just above the crown of your head. Imagine it pulsing with violet light as a many petalled lotus, or as a rose, fully blossomed and fully opened to the energy of the heavens. Imagine bringing the earth's energy upward to mix with the light of the heavens and with your connection with all that surrounds you. Imagine then the light of the heavens streaming down and mixing with all that earth energy that you brought up through your body and your chakras. Now imagine that the light of the heavens is coming down into all your chakras one by one, and slowly changing colors as it reaches each chakra, down through the indigo of your third eye, down to the clear blue of your throat chakra. Then it trickles down into the pure green light of your heart, and then down to the pulsing yellow sunlight of your solar plexus. After swirling there for a few moments, imagine the light moving down into the bright orange of your reproductive chakra corresponding to the generation of new life, whether that of human babies or of art or work, whatever is the result of your love and passion. Then bring your attention to the deep red of your root chakra, and feel the energy move down your legs and into the earth, mixing the light of the heavens with the energy of the earth.

Spend a few moments, and a few deep breaths, feeling the energies swirl and move downward, and then upward, and know that you are a nexus of communication between the heavens and the earth. Allow the energy to mix, and feel yourself as the important creature that you are, a conduit between all that is, within and without, underneath and above, between heaven and earth.

Then imagine that you are at the center of the universe. It has been said that we humans are halfway between the size of an atom and the size of a star. I don't know whether that is literally true or not, but it is symbolically true that we as humans are right in the middle of things, from the tiniest particle that we know of, to the largest that we know of. We are literally made of stardust, the atoms in our bodies coming from the same elements making up the rest of the universe. We belong here; the universe is our home. We know and receive out of our own center, and we act and influence out of the center of who we are. Each of us, within our own selves, are the centers of our own universe. Feel the reality of that as much as possible. When it is time, take another deep breath and return to your everyday life.

Mantra Meditation

It is probable that only a few of the readers of this book will have the chance to be initiated into a traditional Mantra Meditation. A traditional practice would entail learning meditation from a Hindu guru ("guru" simply means "teacher") and then being given by the guru a personal Sanskrit word to use as a concentration device in your meditations. The guru himself would be able to trace his lineage through a long line of teachers reaching back several hundred or more years. And you, too, would now be part of that lineage.

Yet even though few of us will have that experience, the word "mantra" has become part of our everyday lexicon, and the general intent of the traditional practice can be very useful in our perhaps naive adaptations of it. A mantra is a word or short phrase that you repeat in rhythm with your breath as you sit in meditation. Most of the time the mantra is not said aloud or vocalized in your body, though there are methods of mantra meditation that have a whole group of monks chanting together a particular mantra, very often the sacred word "aum" or "om." We usually see it spelled as "om", but "aum" reflects the proper pronunciation which is actually made up of the three sounds of "ah", "oh" and "mmm." Very simply, or very complexly, it refers to the essence of ultimate reality, the Atman, our soul or inner self, and Brahman, ultimate reality or the entirety of all. The concept to which it refers is huge, as big as the word "God" or "Great Mystery," holding the meanings ascribed to it by many cultures and thousands of years of development.

We can, in a very simple way, easily adapt this rich and ancient practice into a help in our own practices of silence. We can choose a word or very short phrase and repeat it with each breath as we sit in silence for 10 to 20 minutes. It helps to keep the mind from running off into our usual fantasies or worrying. It doesn't really matter if the word or short phrase is meaningful to us or not. We can even use a nonsense syllable or word. There are pros and cons each way. Both work, as the mantra is symbolic of a general intention and movement of your spirit. If it is a meaningful word or phrase, we can be distracted (as well as enriched) by pondering its meanings and extending its examples and analogies. If it's a nonsense word, we won't be distracted by philosophical thoughts, but we might very well be distracted by wondering if we chose a "good" mantra, or by undervaluing its use by thinking it's all rather silly and childish, sitting in the silence repeating nonsense words when there's important work to be done.

One school of thought is that once you are given or you pick your mantra, you keep it forever. Others say you can change your mantra as you want or need to. The only caveat is to not get into the futility of never settling on one, always looking for the "perfect" mantra. There's no such thing as a perfect mantra, just as there is no perfect spouse; some are much better than others, though. You can use "It's okay" on the inbreath, and "It's all okay" on the outbreath. "All shall be well," a quote from the holy woman Julian of Norwich, works well, too. Another that can be used is "I accept this" on the inbreath, and "I can manage this" on the outbreath. Single words that can be used are "Love" or "Peace." I use the words "Here I am," which has a resonance from biblical scripture of responding to a call from the Divine, as well as indicating my intentional turn towards silence rather than toward the hundred other things that are pulling at my attention. The primary use of the mantra is to simply calm the inner rattling of the cage of our consciousness by the monkeys running around in our dear monkey-mind.

The use of mantras and short prayers has a long history in Christianity, as well, though not referred to as "mantras." They're called "Aspirations", reflecting by the syllable "spir-" that they are said with our breath or spirit, not our voices. I remember ones like "Jesus, Mary, and Joseph," "Sacred Heart of Jesus, have mercy on me," or "Jesus, meek and mild of heart, make my heart like unto thine." When I was a young girl in Catholic grade school these short prayers were referred to by another term that was just fine for the very young grades as well as for adults, but these prayers then known as "Ejaculations" were often not emphasized as much in our pubescent years!

There is a long tradition in the Eastern Orthodox branches of Christianity of hesychastic prayer. This is a mystical tradition of contemplative prayer where one of the primary practices is to repeat the prayer "Lord Jesus Christ, son of the Living God, have mercy on me a poor sinner" in concert with your breath, all during the day whether working, walking, or sitting in prayer. The idea is that it would become your heart/mind's accompaniment, or response to the gift of life, and that it would fulfill the biblical injunction of 1 Thessalonians 5: 16-18 to pray unceasingly: "Rejoice always, pray without ceasing, give thanks in all circumstances; for this is the will of God in Christ Jesus for you." This prayer takes as its inspiration the words of Jesus in the gospel of Matthew where he says "whenever you pray, go into your room and shut the door and pray to your Father who is in secret, and your Father who sees in secret will reward you" (Matt 6:6).

Though these prayers are not exactly the form of meditation as we find in Hinduism and Buddhism, Christianity does have these ancient traditions of silence and contemplative prayer so similar to those of other traditions. Unfortunately, much of this knowledge was not talked about much in daily expressions of Catholicism, and almost not at all in Protestant Christianity. The only way to learn about this was in some of the most hermetic and contemplative religious orders of monks and nuns. When meditation began to be known in the west, brought here by Eastern gurus often as a consequence of the political unrest in their own countries of origin, many people thought of meditation as new and different. Some Christians abandoned their own tradition and embraced this "new" form of spirituality; other Christians labeled it as "from the devil," all without realizing that these practices of silence have always been a part of those people who were intent on developing the inner life and our relationship with the great mysteries of life, including Christians.

Choose your mantra. Sit comfortably, yet keep your back upright. Sit (or stand or lie down) where you won't be distracted, with your pen and paper close by so you can write yourself a reminder with the minimum of distraction. Set your timer for as long as you intend to meditate. Start with five minutes; twenty minutes gives your nervous system a chance to completely relax, allowing you to move into a different type of consciousness.

Breathe naturally, slowing your breath as you become calm. Recite your mantra in synchrony with your breathing. Repeat until you are done or your timer rings. Meditation is a practice, not a guarantee of any fantastic mystical experience. Yet you should feel refreshed and calmed by this practice, and see these effects in your life beyond your time seated in meditation. On the other hand, you may experience sudden insights or enthralling or compelling visions. If that happens, be calmly thankful. This is a normal phenomenon, and does not indicate that you are suddenly a saint or an enlightened being. It is what it is. Of course, it doesn't mean that you are NOT a saint or enlightened being, either!

Variation:

Counting Meditation
Another type of mantra I haven't yet spoken about is to count your breaths from one to ten, and then go back to one. Repeat this for the entire time you sit in meditation. You may be surprised to find how often your mind goes off on its own and you "remember" your count only when it's up into the 20's or 30's. If this happens, simply begin at one again, attempting to stay conscious of your count.

Meditating on a Koan
A koan is a question or short parable used in some forms of Zen Buddhism to help the student attain a sudden enlightenment. The question or parable is often paradoxical, does not make rational sense, and so the meditator has to completely let go of logical solutions. By letting go of our habitual ways of thought, we may be suddenly open to seeing something new, something perhaps not even possible to have been known in the previous mindset. Koans were used in the training of Zen monks also as a means of evaluating the student's progress. Was a student still trying to find the "right answer?" Was the student's response one of frustration, or delight?

You may have come across a couple of the more traditional koans: "What is the sound of one hand clapping?" or "What was your original face before you were born?" These seemingly nonsensical, yet strangely wise stories are found not only in Zen Buddhism, but across cultures. Among First Nations people in the Americas there are the Trickster Stories, and in Islam there are the Mulla Nasruddin stories. These stories or questions are not equivalent by any means, but are examples of ways that teachers across humanity can challenge common wisdoms, ordinary ways of thought, even challenge our ideas of morality and sanity. While often used as entertainment even for small children, who delight in the nonsensical paradoxes, these stories and questions can disrupt your train of thought in the most delightful as well as in the most infuriating of ways.

While we may not be able to study with traditional Zen masters and be challenged by the koans of that tradition, we can make a point of noticing the everyday types of koans that arise in our lives. We can then bring them into a sitting meditation, holding the question or the story lightly, and invite a new insight or a different take on whatever the subject of your home-made koan might be. These modern day koans can also be really interesting in incubating dreams, where dream logic is most people's way of experiencing these nonsensical ways of knowing. You can discover koans in the midst of daily conversations, as you are reading deep philosophy, or in the midst of watching the news. They can be both simple and profound. When you hear them, write them down and assemble a collection of them. It is often very insightful to ask them of young children. Here are a few examples of ones that I've found recently:

- What else could I be thinking other than what I ordinarily am thinking?
- When there's nothing that can be done, what can I do?
- "So, are we both crazy, or are we intensely sane?" "Yes!"
- Is world peace possible?
- When there's no place to go, how do I get there?
- "Good God!" screamed the woman as she saw the bomb drop from the plane.
- Whose crisis is the world's climate crisis?
- All shall be well, and all shall be well, and all manner of thing shall be well.

Decide on your koan or question that does not have a logical answer. Sit comfortably with pen and paper available. Let the question sit lightly in your mind. When you find yourself trying to logically answer the question or find yourself trying to analyze the question, let go of your thinking and just repeat the original question to yourself. Continue to keep the question in front of you while letting go of distracting thoughts. If you suddenly have a strong insight, write down a word or two so that you can remember it after your time of silence. Then go back to keeping the original question in front of you until you are done or the timer goes off. Sit for a few moments pondering any insights or discoveries you may have had. If you have time, write about your experience.

Centering Prayer

Centering Prayer is a contemporary practice of sitting in silence for about 20 minutes, usually twice a day, where you intentionally allow the presence of God to work within you. Though Centering may look from the outside as if it is another form of sitting meditation, the difference is that it is self-consciously a prayer, where allowing the Divine Presence to work within you is the central understanding and intent of the prayer. I mention it here because it is currently the most well-known example of contemporary Christianity that is seeking to revivify its vast contemplative tradition of mystical prayer.

In the mid 1970's three monks, Thomas Keating, William Meninger, and Basil Pennington began teaching first priests and then lay people the contemplative prayer practice found in the medieval classic *The Cloud of Unknowing*. They were U.S. Catholic Trappist monks, members of a strict enclosed contemplative religious order. They had observed the hunger in people for silence and for meditation as manifest in the large interest in Eastern meditation, and decided to teach anyone who wanted to learn the tradition of this silent prayer that continued on, though not well known, in Christianity. There are now many resources available to learn more about Centering, as not only each of the three, but many others, have written books on this ancient tradition made contemporary.

This method is simple, though not easy. You choose a Sacred Word of one or two syllables which symbolizes your consent to God's action in your life. You begin the prayer by focusing on your Sacred Word, but unlike a mantra, you do not keep repeating it during the duration of your meditation. When you notice that your mind has wandered, you return to the Sacred Word as a recommitment to the presence of God. The prayer is often described as resting in God, with God, in silence. You let go of all thoughts and stories, even pious or religious ones. Centering Prayer groups are found at some Catholic churches and retreat centers, though they are not exclusively Catholic. All are welcome. Most people learn about Centering in small group introductions, and groups often meet once a week. Members of the groups are encouraged to continue their Centering practice twice daily in their own homes between the group sessions.

There is no "goal" or sense of success that you look for in this prayer. It is simply a time of resting in the Holy Mystery of life and love. A famous story is told that a woman was complaining to Thomas Keating that she just could not do Centering, that she must have been distracted at least a hundred times during the prayer. Father Keating responded with a big smile, assuring her that indeed she had been doing Centering in exactly the right way. How fortunate she was to return to God a hundred times, over and over again!

And there is definitely not a goal to have mystical experiences during the prayer. Thomas Keating has said that even if you should have a vision of the Mother of God herself, you are not to engage in thoughts and conversation, but to say, "Not now, dear, I'm Centering," and return to your silent abiding with the Holy One.

Another reason that I particularly mention Centering Prayer here is that while there are many apps and guided meditations available to support you in whatever practice of silence you may choose, I have found the Centering Prayer app from Contemplative Outreach to be very helpful. I have not included outside resources in this book, because almost anything you may be interested in is within a few clicks on the internet or a simple search on amazon.com. But you may not otherwise come across this app, which is why I include it here. The Centering Prayer app is free, you can choose how long you want the timer on, and there are chimes that begin and end the sessions. It includes basic instruction in Centering, and of course the app can be used in many other types of silent practice. There are other options available, but I find this to be the gentlest timer appropriate for silent meditations.

Other Ways of Finding the Benefits of Silence

There are many ways to enter into silence, and I've included only a few basic ones to get you started and over the most common of difficulties you may face. Two other useful ways to move into the quiet, though, bear mentioning here. I will speak more about them in the next chapter on embodiment. Both music and walking the labyrinth are common ways that people are finding the silence we need in practical ways. Both of these methods, though, require a little bit more than just yourself and a few simple supplies that once gotten, will serve you for a long time with nothing else needed. In this book I've focussed primarily on ways to live a reflective life that are under your own control and that need few resources, need nothing exotic, and that don't need other people or a community in order for you to access them.

The kind of music that brings you into a quiet space for letting go of thinking, thinking, thinking may be different for each of us, and it may take awhile to find what's most helpful to you. Steer away from songs and words; steer away even from wordless music that evokes lots of images and emotions, or that bring up memories from the past. All of those types of music engage the thinking mind or stir up emotions, which are not helpful for entering into the rest and spaciousness of silence.

Nature sounds or other kinds of ambient music might be quite suitable, unless the music prompts you to alertness and action: for instance, whale songs are beautiful, but they may inspire you to rush out to start a campaign to "Save endangered whales!" Now that might be just the thing to do, but ideally that impulse would come from your deepest self, not from a sudden urge inspired by the music. Listening to your deepest self is what you're looking for in silence, coming to know yourself, and with space for discerning what is authentically yours to do out of all the good things that you could possibly be doing. There is no end of good things that sorely need to be done, but it's in the silence where you will find the match of your deepest passion with the urgent needs of your family, your neighborhood, or the world.

A labyrinth is a walking path that looks a little bit like a maze, but unlike a maze, a labyrinth has only one path forward. There are no dead ends, no choices to follow different paths in a labyrinth. There's no way to get lost. Labyrinths were originally designed as patterns embedded in the patterns of the floor tiles of a great church, as an alternative to a pilgrimage to Jerusalem for those who could not actually leave their daily lives to travel. They are a great way to move into silence — your feet literally take you to the center, where you can ponder and listen, then literally move back out into your everyday life with the wisdom or refreshment received in the silence.

Yet, not everyone has access to a labyrinth. They are increasingly available at churches, in church parking lots or retreat center lawns, and even in some community places. Yes, you can access one and "walk" it online, but as soon as you get online you are vulnerable to all the other distractions pulling at your attention. Let me just close by saying that if you have access to a labyrinth in your community, definitely check it out and experiment with how it can work with your own needs and schedule.

Closing

In the ways that some people talk about meditation, it's easy to think that it's the best and fastest way to "enlightenment" and psychedelic experience, especially if ayahuasca or peyote is included! Well, that's not been my experience, and I've had a mostly daily meditation practice for more than forty years. (Full disclosure: I've not tried the ayahuasca or peyote options!)

What I have found, though, is that it is the practice of silence that always helps me to get in touch with my deepest self and to somehow be in communion with whatever is the "all that is" of the great mystery of life. It's the surest reset to the scramblings of ideas, motivations, pressures and pulls that we all experience in our day to day lives. It's the place that has the answer to the question of what is standing between you and the peace that you seek. And it's accessible to all of us and to any of us. It's a wonderful way to explore all of who we are, especially outside of the tyranny of tasks and the weariness of words.

Most of us are completely inundated with a neverending backdrop of sounds and words. It's common to say "I can't hear myself think!" All of the practices in this book are about creating the space and the conditions to indeed hear ourselves think, but more than that, there are some things we cannot know until we let go even of the tether of words and logic. Silence is the way to do that. Most of us will never live as hermits or in encompassing silence except for a few minutes or a few days at a time. So let us choose what freedoms we do have in our lives in order to sit in silence and to discover what we cannot know in any other way. We often feel as if we have no freedom to do what we want with our lives, and it is true that our lives are constricted by obligations, injustices, poverty, lack of health, and various types of captivity, but almost all of us have more choices than we think we do. It is in silence that we can be free of some of the overculture's brainwashing, in order for us to truly discern our own response to the well-known Serenity Prayer of Reinhold Niebuhr: "Grant me the serenity to accept the things I cannot change, the courage to change the things I can, and the wisdom to know the difference."

7 Embodiment

In this chapter I invite you to consider how, in order to survive as a productive member of our less-than-healthy civilization, we are encouraged to constantly act as the oppressor towards our own oppressed physical selves. I often have felt as though I've been a slave driver with a whip, forcing my crouched body to do one more thing, finish one more task before I collapse. I've told myself "I'm strong, I can do it, I can do this one last thing." How is it that we learn to do this to ourselves, somehow thinking that we're winning the battle against time and successfully finishing all the things on our to-do lists? I want us to examine how we are encouraged by the culture to ignore the real needs of and the real signals from our bodies, how we are encouraged to overindulge in foods and products that appeal to superficial desires as well as distract us from the pain that ignoring our real needs leaves us with. And I want us to strategize ways we can awaken from this numbing out to use what choices we do have to access that which is truly nourishing, and to work to ensure that all of us have access to that as well.

I offer reflective questions to consider what our bodies are, how we extend beyond our skin boundary, and how to come to know our embodiment more deeply. Then I offer a series of things you can choose to do *with* your body that can help you become more aware of your physicality, and finally offer several ways that by doing or making things, we can embody ourselves into the world around us.

Who Are We?

When we do reflect on our physical bodies, what is it, exactly, that we are thinking about? We almost always focus exclusively on the aspects of ourselves that are enclosed within our skin, the boundary that separates you from me. Yet none of us can survive more than a few days if we're not taking into ourselves parts of our earth in the form of water and food. What we take in becomes the cells and organs enclosed within our skin. So, how are we separate from the waters in the rivers that we use as our drinking water? How are we separate from the plants and animals that will become a part of our physical bodies, even though at this moment they might still be growing in the fields around our cities? What we excrete from our bodies breaks down into nourishment and moisture for the soil or for microorganisms. Gases within our bodies are excreted by our breath and nourish the plants which rely on this carbon dioxide. The plants and trees then excrete through their pores the oxygen which we ourselves so need in order to survive.

Yet many of us have become so numb or so distracted from these processes that we don't even notice when the new coal companies bring new poisons into the watershed along with the few new jobs they promised. Clearcut forests are literally hidden behind strips of trees lining the highways so that the public doesn't get upset seeing all those bare stumps. When there are few trees to absorb carbon, where will the carbon go? Where do our own bodies begin and end, when even our skin boundaries absorb sunlight — and the chemicals in the sunscreen lotions along with?

So as I talk about embodiment, keep the question of where your own body begins and ends in mind. How does your own awareness of what constitutes your body impact what choices you make? Do you even know what choices you may have? I am aware that each of us has huge limitations as to choice. But I also know that I haven't yet met anyone, including myself, who is aware of and makes use of all the choices that we do have in each day that can influence our own bodies/the world. How might we know more, become aware of so much more without becoming overwhelmed? How do I do what I can, when at the end of a stressful day just figuring out what to make for dinner reduces me to tears?

And always, we need to accept the limitations that all bodies have, if not in the present moment, then in the process of aging, and death. If I asked you in this moment, what picture comes to mind when I talk of the human body, what would you say? I immediately have two responses: Leonardo da Vinci's drawing of the Vitruvian man, and the body of any one of the many young and exquisitely toned female actresses fed to us as models of how we "should" look. Neither of those two images are like the bodies we see on the buses in any big city, nor in the Walmart's of any North American town. Though we may compare ourselves against some young ideal picture of a human body, the truth is that most of us are kind of lumpy or kind of achy or kind of struggling with this dear body of ours. As much as I might want to go bungee jumping or climb Crowsnest Mountain, I'd be wiser to accept my limitations, limitations that get in the way of sleeping through the night, much less climbing up or jumping off of high places.

Well, here we are, in bodies that often don't work quite right, in environments that are often less than pristine. Any of us can point to bodies that are in much better condition than our own, as well as pointing to bodies that make us look pretty darn fine. Yet, isn't it amazing that even here, even now, we can, through these imperfect sacks of bones, sense in at least five different ways so much that is outside our own selves? Isn't it amazing that we can sense and know so much within our bodies as well as around our own sacks of skin, enclosing this always moving and changing locus of biological processes? And isn't it amazing that these skin sacks themselves are semi-permeable organisms within a much larger organism, the earth? And our earth, of course, is but one small station in an unimaginably vast universe.

Though we are our bodies, we are not only our bodies. When we speak of the self, different cultures have described who we are in several ways. In the recent Western materialistic and scientific mindset, the body has been seen as a machine with the mind as the computer giving it instructions. But this idea of the body as a machine has been shifting with more respect for the mystery of human consciousness, which is now described as "body-mind" and includes our emotions. This term is an increasing acknowledgement that how we think and feel, and what we think and feel, affect the functioning of our physical bodies. It goes the other way, too, where a body, broken and limited in some way, affects our feelings and thoughts in myriad ways. Our sense of ourselves on a day we awaken with pain is certainly different than when we awaken fully rested and glowing with health.

Before the prominence of materialism, most religions taught that we are a mixture of body, mind, and spirit. My own teacher, Dr. Estés, teaches that we are body, mind, heart, soul, and spirit. The difference between spirit and soul in this model is that "the soul is like the receiving and broadcasting station of our connection with that which is greater than us, and spirit is like the spirit of a child, the life force that is determined to live and express itself, that perseveres and never gives up until the last surrender. The heart symbolizes our ability to have relationships of love and connection with others as a constituent fact of who we are as humans." I've found this model very helpful, and it gives a language to enquire of others, specifically my spouse and my son, as to how they're doing, and at the same time reminding them, and myself, that each of these aspects of self are important and worth attending to.

Each of us is incredibly complex, and everything that we are and know is mediated through this physical body. Not only our minds and hearts, but also our bodies hold sensations and memories as well. As we move, stretch, dance, and embrace, notice how each sensation relates to memory and to all other aspects of who we are. Yet so many of us can't allow ourselves to notice these sensations, because the memories they evoke are so painful. Touch any inch of skin, and a memory comes up to be acknowledged, accepted, loved, and healed. But life comes at us with a deafening roar, and we rarely have time to process these memories. We too often need to numb ourselves just to get through the day.

I believe that it is both a spiritual practice and a political act to create for ourselves the possibility of exploring these memories stored within, and to open ourselves fully to the pleasures that are mediated through our bodies. I think that if we can do so, and model to our friends and teach our children how to do this, eventually a critical mass of humans will arise who know ourselves, inside and out. We can become conscious of what was done to us and what we do to others, and we can heal from the traumas we have lived through. We can become increasingly aware that though we think of ourselves as bound by our sacks of skin, "we" do not end there.

We also extend backwards and forwards in time. We come from generations who never had the chance to heal from their traumas and unknowingly passed those on to us, here, now, in addition to our flesh and genetic codes. As we become more conscious and open to healing, we won't pass on all that unhealed trauma to future generations. Not only will we not pass on the ancestral trauma, but by transforming ourselves we will heal the past as well; we are part of the healing of the world. We will become not only aware and cognizant of each other, but in important ways we will know that we *are* each other, and *are* this earth which surrounds, sustains and supports us. When we know those things, we can more easily imagine how our choices and actions matter; we will know that we belong, that we are not apart from matter, that is, "mater" (Latin for "mother", the root of words such as matter and material), our mother earth. We can learn from the earth, from that part of our larger selves that creates in abundance and shares with deep generosity. We can surround, sustain, and support each other in abundance and more than enoughness. We can become like dandelions, whose roots are a powerful medicine, or a single apple tree feeding people, animals, and, finally, the earth. And each apple contains the seeds for many more apples.

We can then remind ourselves that our human-made story about scarcity, lack of resources, and money are made up. We can come to know and believe, on the deepest level, that things as they are don't have to be like this. We can change, we can act, and we can each do whatever we can to be in alignment with our earth's, our *mater's,* abundance and generosity. This won't happen by next month or by next year, but just as we've told ourselves false stories of never enoughness, we can tell ourselves, over time, other, truer stories. As they resonate within, those truer stories can take deeper root. As we take our embodiment seriously, we will heal, feel more pleasure in our bodies, make meaning with new stories, and know all of who we are.

What's Your Current Relationship with Your Body?

However we might consider our bodies, we can't get out of them. Even though many of us seem to do a good job of living only in the top 12 inches or so of our bodies, the rest of our body cries for attention. When it does, what is our response? Are you happy to give your upset stomach some gentler food and a rest? What do you do when you get a headache? Can you rest in some quiet with a cool drink? Or do you have to take two pills and just get on with it? There have been many days when I wish I could just unscrew my body from myself, so that I didn't have to feel its achiness, and get on with what I either wanted to do, or felt I had to do. Alas, I dragged my dear body around on those days and tried to ignore it the best I could. It took me years to learn to care for my body, my self, with as much kindness and tenderness as I would care for a child whom I dearly loved. In fact, it was the experience of caring for my own child that prompted so many of these reflections, as I sought to encourage in him a healthy experience of embodiment.

What about you? What is your relationship with your body? Settle yourself comfortably, relax, and be silent for a few minutes. Scan your body in your mind's eye, starting with your feet and moving upwards until you've paid attention to every part of it. How are you feeling? Begin to write the answers to these questions in your journal. There are many questions here, and many more that I didn't include but that may come up for you in this practice. Be gentle with yourself, and keep to your time limit. You may find yourself feeling badly about how you used to treat yourself, but please remember that these questions are for exploring and bringing to consciousness ideas and attitudes that you may not have ever thought of. Do not use these questions to accuse yourself of not being your best. Remember, no shame, no blame; it's information. This information is valuable because it can help you become freer to choose how you *want* to respond.

You can come back to these questions over and over again. Writing about these questions will bring up memories, and some of those memories probably won't be happy ones. Please take good care of yourself and if you start to feel overwhelmed, stop to take a breather. Go slowly, or do these questions with a dear friend whom you feel comfortable with. Ask for support from a friend or spouse, or from a wise person or counselor when needed. Our bodies hold memories, and if you touch any part of them, either directly or with your thought, care, and attention, you may wring surprises out of yourself. This is not to be feared, but it does help to be prepared and to reach out for support if the surprises are difficult ones. Remember that our bodies know how to heal. When we cut ourselves, the skin heals on its own, as long as we notice it enough to clean the wound and not keep re-injuring ourselves in the same spot. So, too, not only the body, but the mind, heart, spirit and soul know how to heal ourselves, as we notice and not keep re-injuring ourselves in the same ways. And just to remind ourselves, not only people but whole ecosystems can heal by themselves, as long as we don't keep damaging them in the same ways.

Basic daily needs

Is today an average day for you, or is it particularly difficult or particularly relaxed and easy? How have you cared for your body, your self, in the last while? Do you feed yourself well? If not, why not? Are you able to take a lunch break away from your workplace, or do you just munch on a protein bar between tasks? Do you move and stretch in the ways that make your body, your self, feel good? If not, why not? Do you provide pleasant sensations for your (at least) five senses? Do you find beautiful things to look at? Do you listen to good music or enjoy your silence? How about what you smell and taste? Do you have lovely textures touching your skin, at least some of the day? If not, why not? After a full day of work, do you get to relax when you get home, or do you face a second work shift of laundry, cooking, homework help, and finalizing that report due tomorrow morning?

Speaking about your body

How do you talk to your self, your body? I have come to speak of my own body as "dear body", especially when I'm feeling pain or am uncomfortably stressed or tired. I know that I, and my dear body, are doing just the best we can with what the days bring. And I can speak kindly to the achy parts and the parts that won't do what I want them to. Yet it took me a long time to not drive myself as the slave driver with a whip. I was afraid that if I let myself rest, I might not ever get up. I was needed at work, and I didn't want to let anyone down.

Caring for yourself when ill

Can you easily take a sick day when you need one? What about taking a week off if you're ill? If you can't, or would hesitate, why? Do you push yourself to go to work anyway because you really love your work that much, or do you push yourself because you don't have paid sick days and can't afford the loss of a day's pay? Or do you push yourself because if you took a day or two off, you'd return to a chaotic workplace with all your undone work waiting for you? Do you push yourself to produce because you're self-employed, and nothing produced means nothing earned? Or do you go to work even when sick because of peer pressure, knowing you'll be subtly punished by the others who would have to cover for you? Your body will work hard for you for a very long time. It takes a long time for dear body to protest how it's mistreated. We may feel, though, that we had no choice in pushing ourselves so hard, that that is just what we had to do to survive. And sometimes, that's the honest-to-God truth. Rarely do any of us work in conditions that are sustainable and nourishing for the long haul. But at least knowing that gives us the motivation to change for the better whatever it is that is in our control.

Embodied pleasure

Ask yourself when you last experienced bodily pleasure. Write that down, and figure out exactly what it was about that situation that made it so pleasurable. Write down all the things that make your body, your self, feel good. Include the pleasures that cancel themselves out because while good in the moment, the long-term consequences aren't good, like splurging on Oreos in the evening, or staying up till 3 a.m. talking with a friend. Figure out what it was that you liked so much that you were willing to treat yourself poorly in order to experience that pleasure. Make a list of all the pleasures that make you feel good. Which of those things are under your control to give to yourself? For the others, what is it that you need? More money, another person, a particular person, a healthier or stronger body? Can you simply ask for what you need? If you get a *no* from the first person you ask, can you ask someone else? Can you just buy a chair that you are completely comfortable in, or shoes that are both pretty and comfortable? Can you better control the stress in your life, or would you have to change situations drastically? Could you get a different job if you needed to? What really might be under your control? What would need a revolution, or a change in the law?

Accessing the body's knowing

When you make decisions, what feels like a yes in your body? Do you pay heed to that? What feels like a no? When have you most recently overridden that and did what you didn't want to do? Why did you override your no? What happened next? What feels like a *maybe*? What do you do then? How do you decide?

Bodily shame

Do you feel shame in your body or shame about your body? What is it like? Where do you feel it? What were you told about your body? What were you taught about being a good girl or a good boy? What were some of the things that you wanted but people said you shouldn't want those things? Were they trying to protect you? Did they actually protect you? How was your body treated by others? By your parents? By teachers or by doctors? By others your own age? By the opposite gender? By the same gender?

How do you feel about sexual arousal? Do you think that being aroused is dangerous, that it is the source of evil, or the "near occasion of sin" as I was taught in Catholic school? Do you think that this idea of sexual arousal being dangerous is somehow connected with the stories of Adam and Eve, of Original Sin? How has your religion of origin, if you have one, looked at the functions of the body? What has it taught you about sex and sexuality? How does that resonate with your own values, your own experience? If you believe in a personal God, do you think that God disapproves of your responses to your body's sexual arousal? Might you see arousal as a gift from God, and that God delights in humans who express their sexuality in ways that are both respectful and pleasurable?

If your body does not match your culture's current model of who is beautiful or acceptable, how do you feel about yourself? Do you think of yourself as wrong, or just different? Is different good, or is different unacceptable? Have you had any responses from other people about your difference from your culture's model? Has anyone rejected you because of your difference? Have you kept yourself hidden because you are different? Have you not been able to do some desired activities because of this difference? Have you been able to get your clothing needs met with beautiful options?

Who taught you about the needs of changing bodies?

Where did you learn to care for your body? Who taught you about grooming, puberty, sexuality, contraception, pregnancy and child bearing, menopause (both male as well as female), and aging? Was it a person, or a teacher at school, or a magazine article or a book? Who taught you about the sometimes embarrassing issues of unwanted attention, of menstrual accidents, of incontinence, of bad breath or other bodily smells? These are value-free realities of a human body, yet are the source of embarrassment and pain because of the unhelpful and often harmful attitudes of the culture. (Just this question alone could be the topic of a whole library of books!)

Illness and disability

When you have been ill, how have you felt about your body? That it has let you down? Or are you accepting and responsive to your own needs? Are you tremendously frustrated, thinking, "I don't have time to get sick!"? Do you take the time you need for rest and for medical consultation, or do you wait until you collapse, metaphorically or literally? Are you around people who encourage you to recuperate when you are ill, or do the people around you treat you as a snowflake or as weak if you rest? I've been in communities where one is expected to just keep working hard, no matter what. And when someone ended up in hospital because of exhaustion, the community treated her as a hero because she was so devoted to her duty.

What about chronic conditions you live with? Do you feel you have to hide any special needs you might have? How do you feel about asking for accommodations at work? How easy is it to ask for help with your chores at home? Do you feel less than others if you have a visible disability? Do you feel respected and believed if you have an invisible disability? All of us are only temporarily in full health or fully physically able, yet all of our institutions and workplaces assume full health and youthful passion and energy. All the time. Did you have that full health and abundant energy when young? If so, how did you then perceive older workers and community members? If you didn't have full health and energy, how did it feel to not fulfill unstated expectations?

If you have an ongoing disability that prevents you from working or contributing full time in paid work, how do you feel about that? How do other peoples' attitudes toward you and your disability affect you? Do you feel disabled? What does *disabled* mean to you? If you are disabled, how do you experience that? Is it more of an ongoing condition that is just the way you experience life, such as paralyzation or blindness? Or is it something that came on into a relatively healthy body, such as chronic pain or multiple sclerosis? Is your disabled condition stable, or is it ever changing? Is it a matter of ongoing deterioration or of different levels of pain and disability?

If disabled, do you still feel that you are contributing to life? How do the people around you think about your contribution? If you can't contribute in meaningful ways, or in ways that you consider meaningful, how do you feel about that?

As a young person, I was taught that even the profoundly disabled contribute to this world by offering an opportunity for others to be of service in meaningful ways. I used to visit the religious sisters in their nursing home, and I noticed a life-giving attitude among most of them. As their health declined, they embraced contributing in different ways. The college professor now crocheted caps to keep newborn babies warm, and another made greeting cards that were given to all the other sisters to use. When increasingly disabled, the sisters visited and cheered the other residents, and when not able to do even that, they prayed for others. For the most part, every sister was honored and loved in every way they contributed. Experiencing that has helped me deal with increasing disability in my own life, knowing that there are many, many ways to contribute, as well as knowing that my worth as a human being does not depend on what I can offer to others.

Are you able to get the care and the support you need from your health providers? From your workplace? From your family and friends? Are services accessible to you financially, and physically? Do you feel other than or less than others? Do you ever use your disability to more easily get other legitimate needs met? For instance, do you ever use your disability to get out of visiting with family members who do not treat you respectfully? Do you ever use your disability to escape from doing chores that other people have prioritized or that you don't think need to be done? Whatever the case, do you feel that other people judge you poorly if they assume that you are using your disability as an excuse?

Illness and death

It would be nice if all of us could live fully with bodies that do anything we desire until sometime, when we're really, really old, we go to sleep and just never wake up. Unfortunately, we can't count on that scenario. Oftentimes our bodies break down long before our minds do (and vice versa). Have you been around family members or friends who have had life threatening illnesses or significant ongoing illness and disability? Have you thought about what that might be like if that were to happen to you? Have you thought about what's important for you to be able to do as long as you can? What actions can you take now that would make that more likely as you age? How would you feel about yourself if you couldn't do whatever it is that you do now? What kinds of things make your life worth living? Which of these are dependent on a fully functioning body? How do you view the elderly, the ones who live in long-term care facilities? If that were you, how would you like to be treated?

Have you thought about and made provisions for what would happen if you were to become seriously ill and not be able to make your own decisions? This is not only a concern for the elderly, as serious illness and accidents happen to the young and healthy as well as to the old. Have you thought about who might speak for you? Do they know what your preferences are and what your values are? Do you know the legal requirements and limitations for caregivers if or when you cannot speak for yourself? Have you had these kinds of conversations with your family members? One of the greatest gifts you can give your family members is clear information for how you want to be cared for should they have to make decisions for you. If you love them, then put this information in writing! At a time of crisis, it is a tragedy when family members disagree about Grandma or Grandpa's treatment options. When is too much, too much? When is enough, enough?

Use your current relative health to consider all these aspects of embodiment, and get whatever assistance you may need in order to do so.

Why do all this?

Examining your current relationship with your body has almost unending questions to consider. Please pace yourself, and don't think of this exploration as something with a finish line. All answers, including ones about your wishes for your final days of life, are provisional — the best you have for now. Revisit these questions, because your answers will change as you change. These are all in the service of helping you to better know your own self, your body, your soul, your spirit, your mind, and your heart, and to treat yourself with utmost acceptance and compassion.

But these reflections go far beyond your personal self, of course. What you care about might depend on a community's effort to make it happen. If you suffered from inadequate knowledge about puberty and sexuality, how can you assure, now, that young people won't have to suffer the same way? If you care about the conditions in long-term care facilities, how can you be part of advocating for excellent care? How can you join with others who have similar concerns to make possible that which is most important to you? You may not be able to address all your concerns through working for change, or advocating for adequate funding, or ensuring accurate information at the right time, but by reflecting on these aspects of our human life, we can clarify how we will choose to use our own life energy, now. To a very great extent, we can choose what we leave as our life's legacy. This truly is a depth dimension practice.

As I offer more reflective exercises regarding our embodiment, I have divided them into two general, yet sometimes overlapping categories. The first set of activities is about our experiences within our bodies, and how we can create meaning and access soul knowledge through this embodiment. The second set of activities are things we can do, make, or build by means of our bodies. Most of the previous exercises in this book can be thought of within that category as well, but here I will focus more on creating in a three-dimensional way.

With Our Bodies

Mindfulness of the Body

You can do this exercise wherever you are, at home, outside, in a quiet pause at work, or on a bus, train, or plane. Don't turn inward while you are driving, as you might become so relaxed that you drift off. If you think you may fall asleep, set your alarm for as long as you have time for this exercise. If you do fall asleep as soon as you relax your muscles, take note that you are most probably not getting enough rest and nurturing sleep, and make a resolution to correct that as soon as possible.

Take three slow, long breaths. Loosen your stomach muscles and let the air in all the way down to fill your diaphragm. Loosen your shoulder and neck muscles. Breathe out slowly. After those three long breaths, allow yourself to breathe naturally. Just observe your breath. Is it smooth or a bit ragged? Does it speed up or does it stay loose and relaxed?

Focus on your body. Thank your body for the wisdom that it holds, for all it does for you, letting you experience reality in a myriad of ways, allowing you to move from one place to another. When you're ready, focus on your toes and feet, thanking them for allowing you to stand, to walk, and to run, or for whatever mobility you have. When you're ready, bring your attention upward, focusing on your shins and calves. If you notice tension anywhere, release the tightening as though you're letting a damned river flow freely. In actual fact, when your muscles are relaxed your blood can now flow more freely to bring nutrients to your muscles and inner organs and take toxins away to be flushed out of the body.

Continue to slowly move your attention upward to the different parts of your body. Make note of any impressions or nudges to care for any particular part of your body. Where there is tension, allow release. If there is pain, take a little more time to ask your body what you need to do to help alleviate the pain. Release any fear, and trust that your body is always doing what it can to move toward healing. Make yourself a promise to act on whatever intuition arises in response to the question, if you can. Then imagine that the pain is dissolving as your blood vessels branch out to every part of your body and remove the chemicals that signal pain to your spine and brain.

As you move your attention to the different parts of your body, accept each part with as much love as you can muster. Thank each part for what it does and how it works in cooperation with all the other areas of your body. Bless each part of your dear body, sending an intention of care and compassion to each area as it comes into your consciousness.

When you have brought your attention to all parts of your body, imagine that the top of your head is opening up to receive all the goodness and beauty that is around you. Rest in that goodness until it is time to move on to the rest of your day.

Variations:

Grounding

Start with your three long, slow breaths. Let your awareness move down through your body and imagine an invisible golden cord of light that moves down your legs, through the chair and floor, through the structures of whatever building you might be in, and deep into the ground. Imagine your cord moving down through the dirt, through any underground rivers or aquifers, down into the rock and then bedrock, all the way down into the molten metal of the earth's core. Imagine then that your cord is bringing back up to your body all the energy of the earth, filling you and grounding you as you go into your next activity.

Cosmic Grounding

Proceed with the Grounding exercise, but as you bring the earth's energy into your body, imagine that the invisible golden cord of light extends up through your spine and head as well, and opens through the top of your head. It extends up into the clouds and up until it reaches the sun. Extend the cord further into the Milky Way galaxy and out and beyond throughout the whole extent of the cosmos. Bring that awareness of sublime spaciousness into your body and feel it mix with the earth energy that you've drawn into yourself. Know that you are held within this home of your physical body on and of the earth while at the same time, a part of yourself, your awareness, can extend to the edges of the universe and to all that is. As I mentioned previously, how big you are is situated somewhere between the size of an atom and the size of a star, yet your awareness can extend even further. What a mind-blowing thought!

Sense Mindfulness

Sit comfortably somewhere where you can close your eyes safely. Start with simply noticing that you are breathing. Look around wherever you are, gently noticing all that is in your field of vision. Close your eyes and slowly identify all that you are hearing. Is that a car radio? Birdsong? Traffic noises or computers humming? When you feel confident that you've noticed all that is making any noise around you, bring your awareness to what you are touching. Is it the arms of your chair? Is the fabric smooth or nubbly? Or are you holding on to something? Feel all of its contours and edges. Is it cool or warm to the touch? What are your feet resting on? Can you feel your socks and shoes? Are the backs of your legs touching anything? If so, is it soft or is it hard? What is supporting your seat? Is it the boards of a bench, or a soft, plumped chair?

Is it a plastic seat or are you on the floor? If you are on the floor, are you on a rug or on wood? Or linoleum? Is your back being supported by anything? Now, what are you feeling from the inside of your skin? Do you have pain anywhere? Do you feel your muscles flexing, or your organs pushing against each other? Are you aware of your stomach and intestines digesting your last meal? Are there any other sensations that you are aware of within your body?

Once you've explored your sense of touch, bring your attention to your sense of smell. Are you noticing cooking smells, or are you smelling traffic fumes? Are you smelling lilacs or balsam? Are you smelling any of the products that you've smeared on your dear body this morning, like facial cream, deodorant, or hand cream? Move your attention now to your sense of taste. Do any of the smells that you're aware of have a component of taste for you? If the cooking smells that you are aware of include garlic, are you imagining the taste of the garlic this instant? Do you taste the lingering flavors of lunch? What about the taste of the chewing gum, or of your acid reflux? Is there a hint of the coffee you had on your break?

Now just rest in the awareness that you have many ways of knowing, of taking in the world around you as well as the world within you. Most of the time we are aware of only a fraction of these sensations, often because we are doing so many things that we can't consider everything that is available to us. Otherwise we'd be completely overwhelmed. Try doing this exercise in a variety of situations: at work in a quiet moment, outside in a forest, outside at a beach or river, at a concert, at a meal, or while sitting quietly with a loved one. Reflect for a moment on how a sudden sensation can remind us of a special moment in the past, or a favorite smell can conjure up our grandparent's home.

Stretching

Start out with a few long, slow, deep breaths, and then when it comes time to notice the different parts of the body, do some gentle and slow stretches in whatever part of the body that you are focusing on. Flex your toes and feet when you begin, then move and stretch the different muscles in your legs. If you don't know any stretches for a particular part of the body, simply consciously tighten and then release the muscles in that part of your body. As you move up into your head area, open your mouth wide to stretch your jaw muscles, grin widely and then purse your lips, wrinkle your nose, open your eyes wide and stretch your eyebrows upward as if suddenly surprised. You can amuse yourself by imagining what you must look like if someone were watching you at that moment!

You can stretch anywhere: while waiting for a bus, while cooking, while brushing your teeth, while watching videos. You can stretch in bed before falling asleep, and stretch in the morning before you rise. This kind of mindful stretching is not only pleasant, but is an excellent warm up for your next activity, whether exercising or giving an important presentation. It can keep us supple and ensure our range of motion. It is also an excellent way to notice any subtle changes in the body before they can tighten into disease, helping us to be aware of how emotions may be lodged into our body until we deal with them as best we may. This awareness reminds us to both do what we can to keep ourselves healthy, and to be aware that the nature of physicality is always transforming from life to decline to death to life again. This awareness of our bodily changes reminds us that since we do not live forever, we can and perhaps should live with intention.

Soothing Yourself

We each need friendly touch, but sometimes it's just not available. My son was recently telling me about his martial arts classes, where almost all the touch is wrestling, kicking, or an attack of some kind. He says that if that were all the touch someone was getting, it would really do a bad number on their mind. It made me think of all those who either live alone or with an abusive partner, especially during the recent pandemic.

As much as possible, remind yourself that you are not simply a brain on a stick, but are a fully enfleshed human being. When doing your mindfulness or grounding throughout the day, touch yourself kindly. Pat your body, comfort yourself with love. When you come out of the shower or bath, dry yourself mindfully. Feel the pleasure of being cared for, notice the areas that are needing more attention. Use your body lotion mindfully, and take in the scent. Notice the beauty you sense around you.

Hold your chin in the palms of both hands, remember that you are a valuable person, and that you belong here on this earth with the rest of us. Imagine at times that you're platonically hugging a friend, a relative, or a mentor or guide. Imagine holding hands with a dear friend as you're talking on the phone or zooming together. And then do so in person, if you can and if it is appropriate.

If you are a survivor of physical or sexual violence, recover your sense of your sacred self by focussing on each part of your body, touching it with love and gentleness, even giving that part of your body a special gift. Dedicate a week at a time to care for the different parts of your physical self. For instance, if you're focusing on your arms, you may want to gently hug yourself whenever you remember during the day, or you might leave little Post it notes to remind you to do so. You may pat your arms and marvel at how the muscles work together, how your arms serve you by getting and holding so much. Gently squeeze your upper arms to remind yourself what respectful touch feels like. At the end of the week you might buy a new long-sleeved shirt that is beautiful and that makes you feel good. Or if you are focusing on your neck, you might stroke your neck gently while putting on moisturizer cream. You may meditate on how an unrestricted throat can talk with others, can sing and soar, and can yell for help when needed. Your gift to your throat might be to wear a beautiful scarf or select a piece of jewelry to adorn your neck. Continue this honoring of all the parts of yourself until you have a genuinely appreciative sense of all of who you are.

Humility of the Body: Stuff, Resources, Clutter, Airtime

How much space do we take up in this life? How many resources? How much airtime? By our mere presence, do we take these things from others? By meditating on how we express our physicality beyond the boundaries of our skin, we can understand a bit more how some of us thoughtlessly take more than our fair share. By analogy, we can meditate on how some groups of people encroach on others' space, land, resources, and ways of being; how colonialism starts and spreads. We can meditate and repudiate our current culture's obsession with accumulating, of always wanting bigger and wanting more. Pondering these things allows us to choose to live according to the abundance of the earth, and make our identity as a citizen of the world, sharing the resources sustainably rather than as mindless consumers who eat up resources then spit out garbage.

This exercise started for me with a family discussion on the stuff that other people left for Mom (me) to clean up, that there was no place to sit as every horizontal surface was covered with … stuff. One family member quipped, "See, I've been telling you we need a bigger house!" Another lamented, "But I don't have anywhere to put this in my room!" And, insulted, added, "Stuff, whaddya mean 'stuff'? These are very important papers!"

This discussion got me thinking about the discrepancies in house sizes among the various people in the world. I thought about the culture of accumulation I live in, about what we really need in life, and my mother's old admonition to finish my vegetables because there are poor children in Africa, or China, or India, who don't have enough to eat. I thought about how holy people in some places in the world own nothing except the clothes on their backs, who wander from place to place as they pray, and who depend on the charity of others in order to eat. I thought about the idea of need, and how advertisements try to convince me that I need whatever product they are selling. It's easy to point to the homes of wealthy people and judge that they are taking far more than their share of the world's resources, but what about you and me? What is my role in the sharing of resources? Is there enough for everyone, really? Well, certainly not if every person demands one thousand square feet, the toys to fill them, plus the gas guzzler in the garage! What about those of us who need more than an average person? What about artists who need room for their big sculptures, or hobbyists who build things in their backyard studios? Should they relinquish their space? Should I quit painting since the canvases take up lots of room, not to mention the paints, and the papers, and all the rest of the supplies I (try not to) hoard in the storage room? Should any of us even need a storage room?

We won't come to answers to all these questions just by doing this exercise. But if we can develop this reflective habit, we may be better able to identify what kind of stuff contributes to our flourishing, to the expression of all of who we are and what we bring to the world, and what kind of stuff really is excess (I'm talking to you, chocolate fondue pot!). As we consume only the resources that contribute to our own flourishing, we can become more committed to ensuring that all of us have not only what we need to survive, but to thrive, and become more committed to the international justice that this would demand. We won't individually solve the problems of the world, but we will become better able to see the problems and contribute to a greater justice than we have now.

Humility comes from the word 'humus', which means earth. We are of the earth among many other people, animals, and plants that share the earth. How are we to be humble? How are we to survive, and thrive, yet not encroach on what others need? Is there room for all in our individual houses? Can three adults survive and thrive in my own modest home? Can all of us survive and thrive in our larger home of this earth?

- ◆ Become grounded and relaxed. Bring to mind some of the activities that you love, and the materials that are needed to be able to do those activities. Feel your appreciation for these things that bring value into your life, these things that you love to do. As you are relaxed and ready, consider the following questions, and respond to them in your journal.

- ◆ What are some of the things, beyond yourself, that you love? Which ones do you enjoy by yourself? Which are enjoyed with a community? What are their costs, to you yourself, to the city or community, to the earth? How much are these things that you enjoy accessible to people who are different from you, or who have fewer resources? Can everyone who has the desire access these things in some way? If not, what are some of the barriers?

- ◆ Where you live, how do you share physical space? How many people live in your home? Are all of your rooms used regularly? How much storage space do you have? Do you use it all? How many square feet, approximately, do you claim for your own use? If you feel ambitious, take the square footage of your home, figure out how many square feet are common areas, and then divide that by the number of people in the home. Add to that how much square footage you have for your own use, such as a bedroom, an office, or workshop or studio. Then do some research to get an idea of house size and occupancy rates in other countries, especially those that you've considered to be less developed or poorer than your own country. Do some comparisons, but don't give in to any blame or shame. This is just information for you to consider. Think about the mitigating factors that might make a straight comparison inaccurate, such as whether the people in that country spend much of their days outside, or whether they do their work inside of their homes. Do this same comparison (necessarily provisional and inaccurate) with other families in your own country. Just strive for some estimate of where you are in the usage of resources, but try to go beyond categories such as middle-class, lower middle-class, poor, and upper-class. Have you uncovered any surprises?

◆ Most people imagine their stuff as extensions of themselves. With this in mind, do you spread your stuff all over the place? Do you leave your stuff on the kitchen table, or do you put stuff on the empty chairs? How much of this is just a bad habit, and how much of this seems genuinely necessary? How much of what is in storage is your own stuff? Or do you squeeze yourself or bow out to make room for others? What might be a fair and just division of space in your home? Is your room bigger than what you need? How did that happen? Do you want to do anything about it?

◆ Extend this informal analysis to any other areas you use, such as garages or sheds, or storage space in relatives' homes, etc. Remember to consider the sports supplies, your workshop areas, and your craft areas. Again, please, no shame, no blame. Just awareness. Regarding supplies for hobbies, which seem to multiply by themselves when we're not looking, it's reasonable to keep a stash of supplies for future sessions. However, many of us have what I call SABLE supplies: Stash Acquired Beyond Life Expectancy! (On the other side of that, though, I've occasionally found in thrift stores a huge stash of wonderful supplies that are both delightful and affordable, donated, I assume, by the family of some crafter who didn't live long enough to use up her stash!) For the purpose of this exploration, you may want to go through your supplies and storage places, just to remind yourself of all that you have.

◆ Now consider how much airtime you take up. How much or how often are you the center of attention? Do you need that much attention? Do you demand it, or do you simply want that much attention? You may have heard the expression, "So and so just sucks all the air out of the room!" Might that be you, some or all of the time? Think about how you are in your home and among your friends. Or are you the wallflower? Remember, no shame, no blame. It will be appropriate that the amount of attention you get, or need, will vary in relation to whatever your role is in any given situation. How much airtime you take up among friends will probably be different than at where you work; after all, a college instructor's job is to be the center of attention when giving instruction to the students. Just reflect on how you share time and attention with others. Notice if there is someone or some group that is never heard from. Why might that be? How much space do you take up, and is that how you want to be?

If you do this exercise as part of a group discussion, do your utmost to keep people from judging or blaming either themselves or others. This exercise is about awareness, not about right or wrong, good or bad. Keep the focus, as much as possible, on the virtue of sharing more or less equitably whatever are the available resources, along with familiarizing people with the idea that we use our stuff as part of our own identities.

Situating Your Body in Time and Space, and Recognizing the Cost of That

In many ways, most of us have lots of choices about how we understand ourselves, how big we are, how we extend beyond our own sack of skin. But in other ways, we don't. We are the recipients of whatever the world around us thought about people who looked like us or were our ancestors. If you are a person of color, people who share the color of your skin have been judged by some others as lesser than, as exotic, or not quite human. Even if you are a white person, unless you descended purely from the old aristocracies, you hold within ancestral memory the humiliations, the starvations, and the arbitrary violence of feudal life in the Middle Ages in Europe. In many places it was the right of the local baron or landowner to have sex with each bride in the domain on her wedding night, before she could be with her husband. This practice asserted the landowner's ownership of the people, and engendered doubt in every new family as to who really was the biological father of the first born. And so, if you're a woman, you hold memories of sexual violence and witch hunts; if a man, memories of humiliations, injustices, and lynchings; if LGBTQIA2S+, memories of the physical consequences that you, and others like you, barely survived. Many of the people like us never survived what happened, and their stories are lost to us except in our dreams at night, or in the eccentricities and sufferings in our bodies.

We are learning more and more each day about the science of what many of us have intuitively known, that we carry the unresolved trauma of our ancestors and that we live in a world so formed by trauma and violence that we don't acknowledge it any more than we acknowledge the increasingly toxic air we breathe. Most of us won't live long enough to resolve and heal our own personal violations, much less heal and resolve the trauma in our family lineage. But, we can do our part. Every bit helps, and helps to create a little piece of a non-traumatized world. If I can raise my son so that I have not passed on my own sufferings and trauma, that's a blessing that may allow him to do greater work in the healing of our ancestors and in the healing of the world made by these ancestors.

I don't have specific exercises for this sort of healing, as that would require another book. Or a library! But I acknowledge it here, though, as the ignored elephant in the rooms of our lives. Whatever is good for our personal healing is good for ancestral healing; whatever is loving to ourselves and to others, is good and right. Whatever brings reconciliation within and among ourselves is needed. Please remember this shadow that most of us carry along with us everywhere we go, with every person we love. Heal yourself enough that you can be a force of healing, love and justice among all of us. Thank you for your work. Thank you to our ancestors for surviving long enough for us to be here now.

Feeling 'Colonized' by Other People's Ideas, Needs, or Expectations

I've spoken a lot about reflecting on our interconnectedness, even our extension of self with those who are around us, and with all that is around us. While many of us will benefit by reflecting more on our interconnectedness with other people and with the earth, it is also true that not all that is around us is thoroughly good for us. I can meditate on my connection with the grizzly bears — fellow mammals, eating many of the same foods, needing most of the things that humans need — but I'm not going out into the bush to find a grizzly bear to sit with. Of course, we need to exercise common sense and discretion.

This goes for the fellow humans in our lives, too. We are so often deeply damaged by those around us, even more deeply at times by those who are supposed to love us.

If we are carrying many introjects from parents, teachers, and other voices of, "you *must* be this, or that", then some of the imaginary cords that connect us with each other need to be respectfully, yet thoroughly, severed. Introjects are best described as imaginary poisoned barbed arrows that others have shot into us at various times of our lives, most commonly in early childhood. They are the voiced or unvoiced expectations and demands for us to be a certain something, or to act in a certain way, without regard for who we truly are or who we want to be.

For instance, I now understand that my parents were not mature enough to be skilled parents when I came along, and they desperately wanted and needed me to entertain them, to make them feel loved and needed, and to hold their marriage together. As a young child, I got approval when I cared for them, or made them laugh or feel proud of the family by my accomplishments. When I acted in an independent manner, or in any way they could not immediately understand, I was treated with indifference or reprimand. Or worse. So the poisoned arrow, or introject, for me is feeling that it's my job to respond to the needs of everyone around me, or else I will not get the resources I need to survive.

There are many, many ways that we are shot-through with the ideas and expectations of others, and most of us carry many such poisoned arrows. Some people are raised by abusers and shot with the self-definition that they are only good for others to sexually use them. Others get the arrow of certain educational achievements, or carrying on the family tradition of working in a particular vocation, a vocation that may not be your own calling.

One way of dealing with this poison is to become aware of the introject, and redefine who you are in relation to it and who you are in your true self. And then finally, in sacred imagination, cut the cords that have bound you to the other person, pull that barbed arrow out and soothe the pain of its removal with the healing tinctures of self-care and blessing. And then do this with each introject that you become aware of. Many introjects are too painful or too deep to handle alone, though, in which case you need to explore these introjects with a counselor, therapist, or wise person who can help you.

Though we may think that these introjects are mere ideas, they work within us over the years, circumscribing our possibilities and our radiance in being who we truly are. The effects can be physical in the stress responses of inner conflict and pain of dealing with disappointed others who actually caused the pain when they shot those arrows in the first place. Cutting those cords that they captured us with, and pulling out those poisoned arrows can certainly *feel* as though they were physical objects within us, even to the point of our feeling that something is missing when they've finally been dealt with. That's why it's so important to prepare to fill their space with the healthy medicine of new ideas, intentions, and behavior.

It's also the case that sometimes we have people in our current lives who are not healthy for us. With these people, we must enforce boundaries, and sometimes, must end contact so as not to continue to be abused. These people must be kept at arm's length. We can treat them kindly while also protecting ourselves. But often these people seem to have a hold over us that must be severed. By using our imagination in a deep and sacred context, we can find the will and the strength to accomplish this severance in our everyday mundane lives. Using symbols and acting symbolically are not simply imagining something. There is power and strength in the psychic imagination that can translate into daily life. The following exercise can be helpful in cutting those binding cords and extracting those poisoned arrows.

Sit quietly for a few minutes and become as relaxed as you can. In your journal on a new page, write the date and the title, "Cutting the Cords that Bind." Next, write freely about whoever it is who has bound you to them, who has shot the poisoned arrows into you. You can use initials or a pseudonym so as not to blatantly identify the person in your journal. There is no need here to rehash all the injuries inflicted, nor is there need to focus on your emotions. As simply as possible, write down how they have molded you and how they have wronged you. Point form or short phrases are fine. Keep this exercise only to three or four minutes.

When you're done, think about what kind of medicines you will put in place to help yourself heal from the wound that comes from wrenching out those barbed poison arrows. I'm speaking metaphorically here to describe what some of your real psychological needs will be. Pulling out these introjects will leave an emptiness that is too easily filled by going back to fix or strengthen the unhealthy bond between you and that person who has harmed you, or by creating unhealthy bonds with other people. In a way, it's as though we miss the old normal and think that it will be easier just to go back to the unhealthy relationship than to go through the work of healing and finding new ways to be in a relationship.

Think of what kinds of prayers, affirmations, or behaviors you will use to heal the wound and fill up the emptiness. You can compose a prayer to whomever or whatever you call Greater; you can create affirmations that carry your intentions for your life without the cords that bind you; you can design a simple ritual that you will perform regularly or whenever you notice the suffering in walking away from the old normal; you can make a list of the friends and allies you will call on, in person or in thought/prayer, to mirror back to you your strengthened self, your free self. Think through this carefully to discern what will be truly helpful for you. At the same time, your work needn't be perfect, and you can switch out this medicine whenever it's needed. Write this information down in your journal where you can remember to look back at it if or when things get hard.

Think a little bit about what the consequences might be if you remove the person who has harmed you from your life. Can you move forward and just not pay any attention to their words or actions? Do you think they will sense how you have moved out of their control or influence? Might there be anger on their part? Might you be in physical or psychological danger? Think about how to keep yourself safe and as strong as possible. Do you share assets with that person? If so, how will you ensure that you are able to keep your fair share if you end your relationship with them? Do you need to get a new job if the harmful person was your boss or co-worker? Might you need to move to a new home? If the harmful person is a parent or relative, how might this change how you relate to them? Will you need to cut off all contact? If so, how will you do that? Can you just bow out of their life, or will you need to actively let them know of your decision? If you do that, how will you handle the repercussions? You don't have to figure out all the details right now, as more will become clear as you move forward. However, don't go into this naively, and do be sure to put into place whatever measures you need to be safe and to keep your assets. This may mean losing access to some relatives whom you love, especially children such as nieces or nephews. You may need to consult a lawyer or prepare to look for a new job. You may not be able to finish this exercise in one sitting. That's okay. Nothing needs to be rushed.

Now, with at least a tentative plan in place, turn to a new page in your journal, signifying that you are turning the page on that relationship, and write down your intention or affirmation for cutting the ties. You can compose your own words, or use something like this:

"[Insert the name of the person who wronged you], I am cutting the cords which bind me to you. I am pulling out the poisoned arrow that you have shot me with. You have no right to have harmed me, and I now reject your negative influence. I walk on to a life without your interference, and claim my own sovereignty over my life. I walk away from you and I walk into goodness and freedom. I pour into my wounds sacred medicines that will help heal me as I recover my strength and my own self-determination."

As you say these words, imagine that the cords which bind you to that person are thick and tight. Imagine that you have some kind of cutting tool with which you will sever the cord. It can be a pair of scissors, a butcher knife, a utility knife, a sword, or a machete. The instrument doesn't matter here, it's your intent and your visualization of the cord being cut that is important. You may repeat your words 2 or 3 times, until the words feel authentic to you, and your strong-self believes them. You are letting go and moving on.

Now imagine that you are pulling out whatever poisoned arrows that they have shot into you. Yes, the arrows may cause pain as their barbed edges metaphorically tear into your skin. Those arrows, those ideas, were shot into you with the intention that they stay and become a part of you. It may take a while, a few days to a few months, to heal from this wrenching of yourself away from the person who harmed you. Be as kind as possible to yourself and all that you have gone through.

Now use the medicines that you have prepared. Say the prayer that you have composed, or the affirmations that you've written. Imagine them as the salve which cleanses the wound, that protects it from infection, and that helps you to heal. Check in with a friend or ally if you have planned that route. Once you have completed this simple ritual, rest awhile and do something particularly caring and special for yourself. Take a cleansing shower, meet friends for dinner, or indulge in that decadent ice cream.

Whenever the pain of severing the cords that have bound you to another person comes up, use your medicines again. If there are more actions you need to take, such as following up with a lawyer or looking for new work, continue them steadily. Every move forward helps you to heal and strengthen. As I mentioned before, if this necessary severance is overwhelming for you, please access whatever support you may need, whether from a mentor, counselor/therapist, or wise person in your life.

Healthy embodiment is always a dance of balancing our individual selves and needs with the selves and needs of others around us. We are each a unique person, and we ourselves are the ones who know best what is vital for us. We not only have to figure out how to balance our inner selves, but also to balance with whatever community we have around us, whether that's family, other people in our lives, or the ecosystems of animals and plants in which we live. Ideally, our creativity and mutual care, as humans, allow us to do this and address these needs. Not everyone, though, is healthy enough or clear enough to do so. We do need to work with others towards this balance, but we should not tolerate others encroaching on ourselves. This simple ritual is one means to strengthen ourselves as individuals without adding further harm. It can also help support us to have the inner strength to discern what we can do to bring into embodiment a world that supports the healthy life cycles of all that is around us.

These practices and rituals are depth dimension practices that can restore us to our True Selves. A single 20 minute session won't heal everything, but remember that we do have the rest of our lives for our daily depth dimension practices.

By Means of Our Bodies

These next ideas are activities and exercises that we can do only because we have a physical body that we can use to influence the world around us. When we build something new we are, in a sense, extending our bodies into the world, embedding our embodiment into the world outside of our physical bodies. Our presence remains in some way, because we have paid attention or brought something new into the world.

These depth dimension activities bring us out of our actively thinking head-space, and we can often achieve with them the flow state where we lose track of time (timers are helpful here if we need to stop by a certain time!), we lose ourselves in the activity, we're free of the never-ending chatter in our brains, and we're simply present with whatever it is that is in front of us, or that we are doing. Most of us have experienced this with activities such as dancing freely, gardening, gazing at a river, lake or ocean, or with needlework.

Most of us live much of our lives in our thinking brains. That of course brings great ideas and solves complex problems, but when we are in the flow state we end up refreshed and often, inspired. When do you experience those flow states? What might your life be like if you let yourself follow the natural flow of your own longings? Who would you be?

Where would you place your attention more often?

Being in Nature

Is there a safe enough natural place near where you live in which you can walk alone? Perhaps a populated city park during mid-day? Or do you have a friend who will walk with you in mutual contemplative silence? I would recommend not wearing ear buds in order that you can stay more aware of your surroundings and of any threat that may come your way.

Nature can inspire a wordless belonging, especially if you slow down to notice the smaller plants, the tiny animals, the birds. Imagine seeing the world from the perspective of the wren or robin, then from the perspective of a hawk or an eagle. Imagine yourself as one of the animals you see. What would it be like to live outside all the time? Where do they go when it rains or is freezing cold? Where are the nests and habitats in which they shelter? How do the creatures of a particular environment use the other creatures and plants that are around them to survive and shelter?

How do you feel in different natural environments? For instance, I love the outdoors – in theory! I fantasize about hiking the West Coast Trail, complete with campfires and whale sightings. Alas, the sun burns my skin no matter what sunscreen I use, the rain and humidity flare up my arthritis, I don't hike well at the best of times, the mosquitoes absolutely love the taste of my blood, and the perspiration makes me feel like I have bugs crawling all over me — and half the time I do! I do best sitting in the shade at a beach, occasionally dabbling in the waves that lap by. Or overlooking a river valley with a wide-brimmed hat. Or sitting under the shade of a tree. Where do you feel best? Do you feel that being outside is a natural habitat for you, or do you have to carefully pick where you place yourself so as not to be hopelessly distracted by your own bodily needs and quirks?

As you are in nature, you may want to receive photographic memories of that which you find beautiful. As opposed to the idea of taking pictures, receiving photographs means responding to what has caught your attention, and receiving, with gratitude, that beauty into your life. Urban sketching is another way to really see what is before you, and then choosing what to include in your sketchbook. You can get artistic and symbolic, as well as literal in your sketches or photos.

Variations:

Tree Meditation

Go to a tree, in person or in imagination, that is older and bigger than you.

With curiosity and respect, look deeply at the tree from its roots to its crown. Listen. Are there animals, birds, or insects that make that tree their home? Be still, and imagine what it would be like to be that tree. Imagine being flexible yet strong, deeply rooted with a rigid backbone trunk, yet sporting nimble branches that move in response to the wind. Imagine the sun shining on you, and you conveying the water and minerals from the earth up through your trunk, your branches, and to each papery leaf. Imagine receiving the sunlight and effortlessly converting it to the food that nourishes you. Know that so many creatures make their home in you, carving out spaces for themselves, building nests and dens in your trunk, branches and roots.

Know that you exist in harmony with humans and other mammals, with all life that needs your oxygen to live. As a tree, you purify the air by absorbing carbon dioxide and exuding the oxygen that humans and others need to breathe. Know that you, as tree, transform toxins to that which is needed by other beings. Know that you, as human, transform oxygen into the carbon dioxide needed by the tree.

Know that when the season turns to fall, the coolness signals you, the tree, to release all the fruit that you've produced, then all the greenery that you've produced. Know that you will go into a deep rest, yet awaken to the warmth of the next spring to produce leaves, fruit to share, and provide a stable place for many creatures to call home.

Walking Meditation

As taught by Thich Nhat Hanh, and also used in Centering Prayer circles, walking meditation usually punctuates sessions of sitting meditation. But it can be used anytime and anywhere, including in your home as you walk up and down your hallway. It is an especially unique experience if you can walk barefoot, directly onto the grass, earth, or sand. The exercise is to walk very, very slowly, mindfully aware of how your muscles cooperate as you place one foot on the ground after the other. You might synchronize your breathing as you walk, moving one foot on the slowed down in-breath, the other foot on the slowed-down out-breath. Notice how challenging it is to balance yourself as you fall forward so slowly. Imagine each footstep as massaging the earth or kissing the ground. Become mindfully aware of all that your senses are taking in, with no need to change anything, or to get anywhere. Continue for two to five minutes, or longer.

Walking in Rhythm

As you walk, chant a prayer or affirmation in time with the steps you take. You can compose a simple melody for your prayer, or sing, silently, a carefully curated song that is meaningful to you. Repeat for as long as your walk lasts.

Some people like to listen to playlists or podcasts while they are walking. That's a perfectly fine activity, but it's not necessarily a Depth Dimension embodiment practice because you are not listening to what is coming up from your inner depths. Rather, you are being entertained or distracted by stimulation that is coming from outside of you. As well, it's more difficult to be aware of the environment while listening to something through headphones. And this is not only an issue for Depth Dimension practice, but for your safety. You want to be able to sense, hear, and see if there is anything or anyone in the environment that might mean you harm.

Build a Relationship

As you walk through nature, it is common for a particular plant, tree, stone, or animal to become the object of your attention. If or when that happens, change your looking at that object into looking at it as a subject, that is, as a being in itself that may be capable of a relationship with you. Develop that relationship. Or, if nothing calls to your attention, pick one or two elements to get to know better. You can choose a particular element, such as this particular tree at the turn in the path, or the element as a category, such as roses as a group, or dandelions in general.

Talk to them in your imagination, paying attention to whether you feel them answering back. Don't get distracted as to whether the answers are really from the element or animal, or from your own imagination. You'll probably never know for sure, but humans have a long history of allyship with plants and animals. Tap into that history as best you can, and value the conversation for what it reveals, not whether you can prove scientifically the mutual communication. Pay attention to what other ideas arise as you speak to your element or animal, and take note. Pertinent information for our lives comes to us in all sorts of ways, and this will be a relationship that symbolically gives you new information and new ideas. This is a very good way to develop your intuition – another aspect of human experience that is not adequately understood by science. Reserve judgment, and just go with it. If the information that comes is useful and good, use it. If it's not understandable, ask for understanding. If it is negative or critical, disregard it and make a different friend.

Write down in your journal your observations, conversations, and new ideas. Watch the whole cycle of life of your element or animal. Go back many times to visit your plant or animal friend. You can take photographs of your friend throughout the year, getting to know them in the various seasons, watching how they survive and then grow again. You can do a little research on your friend, finding out what other people have observed and learned about your friend over the generations. As your relationship develops, ask for their help and guidance in understanding yourself. You will not need to always be with them in person, as you will have extended yourself by taking in their wisdom and messages to you. Just as you can ask a question of a good friend in your imagination, and know how they would respond, you can rely upon your nature friend's information and wisdom.

I have several of these natural friends. The greatest benefit I've received from them is the feeling that just as they belong in their own ecosystems, I, too, belong. It's not me alone vis-a-vis the whole of nature. I, too, am nature. I, too, belong. As you do, too. One of my friends is the ornamental crabapple tree in my front yard. I greet them every time that I go through the front door, and am grateful for their pink blossoms that last only for a short week in spring. I appreciate their beautiful limbs filled with leaves, and delight in the tiny fruit, the crabapples that feed the deer, and no doubt many other animals, all through the winter.

As a whole species, I love sunflowers. I've always loved their cheery faces in the last half of summer, and the golden way of how the young ones turn to follow the sun. How do they do that?! Then, mature, they usually face east, faithfully waiting for the sun to rise the next morning, confident that the light will always come. (Yes, I know I'm anthropomorphizing here!) One time when I was having a self-esteem mini-crisis, wondering whether I really had certain gifts or if I was just telling myself a story of my specialness in order to feel better, a vision of a field of sunflowers suddenly arose in my mind. At the time, I was wearing a bright green dress, just the color of sunflower leaves. My hair has a tinge of yellow gold, and I had a sudden insight that we, all of us humans, are like a huge field of sunflowers. Have you ever seen a sunflower that isn't gorgeous? Have you ever seen one that doesn't look special in its own way? Yes, I realized, we are all deeply gifted, with our own specialties. I thought more about sunflowers, listened as they spoke to me, and realized how they were not only beautiful, but deeply useful. Humans and other animals eat their highly nutritious seeds, and the crushed seeds make a wonderful oil that we use in cooking as well as sometimes even in industry. Their sturdy stalks make habitat for smaller animals, and humans have used the stalks for temporary fencing or as woven walls. The very placement of where and how the seeds grow reflects the pattern of the Fibonacci numbers, that pattern of numbers that fascinates humans as one of the principles of nature. The sunflower seeds spiral around the center in rays where each ray contains the number of seeds that are one of those Fibonacci numbers. To me, this pattern and organization feels wondrous, and a big reminder that there is so much that we cannot know at first glance, at a superficial glance. Where else are there patterns, wonders and mysteries close beside us? Every time I see a sunflower, whether cut for a bouquet or thousands in a field, I send out a greeting and a blessing of thanks.

And then there are the deer. When they come in small groups to find the crabapples under the snow, they peer into the window of my study. More than once I've had the feeling of being watched, only to look up and see a deer bending to look through my window! The deer remind me that it is possible to stay wild while roaming through the streets of the city. That they, and perhaps even myself, can survive quite well taking advantage of all that is around us. That one can be both familiar and other at the same time.

For thousands of years humans have befriended animals and plants, and claimed that those plants and animals have spoken to them, teaching us how they can heal us when ill, teaching us behaviors that enhance our survival and well-being. Much of this knowledge can still be found by either researching or talking with the people who are close to the animals and plants now, in our times. By opening ourselves to the possibility of deep friendship with beings around us, we can sense our embodiment as both the same as the plants and animals as well as different; that is, how we are each individual, but how we each also belong with each other.

Whoever is in what we might call our personal Soul Circle need not be exclusively humans. How would you describe your own Soul Circle?

Walking on Pilgrimage

Pilgrimages and their little sisters, processions, are deeply entrenched Depth Dimension practices in the human psyche. Just as the knights of old (and young people from almost all cultures) entered the woods for a journey and an adventure, people embark on pilgrimages as a sacred adventure. The idea is to leave what is well-known to go on a journey to a sacred place where it is known that people have received blessings, knowledge, or experiences that are a response to whatever is needed in the pilgrim. Another reason that people have gone on pilgrimages is to petition the Divine for a special favor, or in thanks that a special blessing has been received or a prayer answered.

There are still formal processions that different churches have throughout the year, such as to the Cathedral of Our Lady of Guadalupe in Mexico City every year on the feast day of December 12, or The Camino, a centuries old pilgrimage across Europe ending at the church of Santiago in Spain. The Camino has become particularly popular in the past few decades as all sorts of people choose to walk parts of it or all of it. Chaucer's Canterbury Tales are stories about what happened on a pilgrimage walk to the cathedral at Canterbury in England. For many pilgrims, what happens between themselves and the other pilgrims is often as eventful and meaningful as the actual inner transformation of the walk.

But it's not necessary to join a formal pilgrimage to receive many of its benefits. We may not have the experience of meeting other pilgrims, but we can experience a journey into the Sacred, and then the return to ordinary life, which is now made extraordinary by the walk. While walking, words aren't necessary, because it's your body which is doing the praying, or asking for wisdom or an answer to a deep question. It is a type of initiation experience.

There are many varieties of pilgrimage. Indigenous and aboriginal peoples have always made pilgrimages to sacred spots on the land, as well as going on Vision Quests. So one kind of pilgrimage is to go on a journey to a particular place; another is to go somewhere not so far away, but to stay in the spot to listen for a sacred message. One can go repeatedly to a regular space, getting to know it over the seasons and over the years. Muslims go on the Hajj to Mecca, where they circle the Kaaba, a central Holy Place for the faith. We can adapt that for ourselves by choosing a meaningful place that we might circle a certain number of times once a year, or on another regular basis. We might walk around our block, or around our neighborhood, as a way to sacralize it, to pray for all the life that is found within its bounds, and to claim this spot as where we will bring attention, love, and repair or renewal.

Labyrinths

In Christianity in the Middle Ages, it was considered the greatest of pilgrimages to go to Jerusalem, the center of the faith. Since this was an impossible undertaking for most people, different cathedrals created labyrinths for the faithful to walk as a substitution for the more elaborate pilgrimage. Walking a labyrinth has been revived in the past few decades not only for Christians but for anyone who wishes to have a bodily experience of centering or contemplation. A labyrinth is not like a maze; in a labyrinth it is impossible to be lost, since the only path to the center is the same path out again. No matter how many twists and turns there are, if you keep walking, you will get to the center. And once at the center, you cannot get lost again as you walk back into your ordinary life. The symbolism of this not-getting-lost or not-getting-distracted no matter how convoluted and complex the path, is a powerful metaphor as to how many of us wish to live our lives. Walking the labyrinth can also remind the walker that we go in with our questions and worries, then leave them at the center, where the Sacred can receive and bless us with new realizations or answers that we take back out into our everyday lives.

Many cities now have labyrinths that are open to the public, but if not, you can print out a copy of a labyrinth on paper, and "walk" it with your finger. There are many designs, from the ancient Hopi and Greek labyrinths, to the one from Chartres Cathedral, to new contemporary designs. Another finger labyrinth can be made by gluing the design of the labyrinth onto a large base of cardboard or wood using heavy twine or cord.

Even prayer beads can be a form of pilgrimage, as you meditatively walk your fingers around the circle of the beads. You can say a particular prayer or affirmation as you finger each bead, or you can drop the words as you proceed in silence.

Blessing Ourselves and Others

Here I am including so many ways that people have used their bodies in certain gestures and certain postures to bless themselves, and others, or to situate themselves in the presence of what is most meaningful, special, or sacred to them. Catholic Christians have used the Sign of the Cross to bless themselves, touching their head and heart, then each shoulder as they recite "In the name of the Father, and of the Son, and of the Holy Spirit, amen." Dr. Estés has reminded us that others have used the same gestures with different words, such as "May I see beyond ordinary Sight, may I love beyond ordinary Love, and may I listen beyond all ordinary Hearing. May it be so."

Christians have often knelt in prayer, signifying surrender of their own efforts to bring about something on their own, as well as their subservience to the will of God. Muslims prostrate themselves in prayer five times a day, reminding themselves that they surrender themselves to God's will. 'Muslim' means "one who submits or surrenders". Other common gestures are standing tall, with arms raised or spread over other people or objects while praying, such as when a holy person blesses a congregation, or a priest consecrates bread and wine at the altar. Hindus, Jains, and Buddhists have a tradition of mudras, symbolic ritual gestures and poses, most of them involving different hand positions.

Interestingly, even therapists and theatrical actors have tapped into the power of placing one's body in certain positions so that other bodily systems resonate to the meaning we give to the gestures. We can become aware of other memories or other feelings when we adopt those positions or gestures. We can tap into that power at any time, just by moving into those poses, and listening to the sensations, thoughts, and memories that arise. Sacred dance has also been used for thousands of years to express intention without words, and to shift our consciousness out of the mundane into something beyond our everyday awareness.

I'm focusing here on the blessing of self, others, and certain objects which carry a particular meaning for us, including our homes and places that we designate as sacred. To bless is to first bring to mind your gratitude for what is here and now, and then to imagine and invoke what goodness you intend toward whom or what you are blessing. In blessing your home, for example, you may invoke safety, comfort, rest and hospitality. As you go on to imagine these qualities in your home, you may come up with ideas of colors, objects, sound or music that express these qualities. When you then adorn your home with these colors and objects, you are manifesting your blessing on your home. You may also intend a welcoming atmosphere, acceptance, laughter, healing, and beauty for all the areas and all the inhabitants of that home.

Blessing is a way to participate in the joy of what others have received: gratitude for their abundance, well-being and joy, happiness, caring, and contentment.

Blessing is also a way to extend loving kindness to the people in front of you by noticing what they appear to need and sincerely praying that they are able to access that. And, whenever possible, ensure that they do have access to what they need by your charity, your knowledge and ability to refer to organizations that are of help to people, and by which leaders you support with your votes.

Variations:

Blessing Walks

I suggest that you regularly engage in Blessing Walks. Wherever you walk, become conscious that you can bless all that is in your environment. If you are walking through a beautiful nature space, bless the plants and animals that make up that space, and think about how that space can be accessible to more people as a beauty and mental health resource. If you are walking on the city streets, bless all who maintain the upkeep and the safety of those streets. Notice who else is there with you, and notice their needs. Intend that they have whatever is needed for them to be safe and have well-being. If there are persons who are homeless, think about how you might advocate for adequate housing, whether that's through your votes, volunteering, or other kinds of support. If you are in Walmart or the grocery store, notice and bless the other customers. Spread your own aura of calm and kindness as you do your own shopping. When watching the news, or scrolling through Facebook, do so with the intention of being grateful for whatever goodness you witness, and pray for whatever is needed in the people and situations you witness.

Become aware of your connection with others, and be aware of what boundaries you may need with others, too. Know what you can and cannot do, and do not feel as if you must solve all the problems in the world by yourself. For instance, if you regularly take medication for a condition, bless your meds with gratitude for what they do for you. And extend your blessing to all of those who live with the same illness or condition. Pray that all those who need that medication are able to access it, and extend gratitude to all of those who created the medicine. At the same time, know what you are able to offer to others, and what you can't. You may be able to advocate in a general way for those who have the same medical conditions, but you may not be able to be a support person who interacts personally with those who suffer. It is easy to feel resentful about having to take medications and live with side effects, but blessing these and other circumstances in our lives helps us to encourage gratitude where it is due, in order to live with more peace and contentment.

You can bless with words, spoken or silent. You can bless with feelings, or an inner movement towards an intention of well-being. You can bless with a gesture, whether obvious or subtle. Sometimes the greatest blessing is simply a smile and beholding the other person with genuine respect.

The practice of Tonglen, from Buddhism, is also a way of blessing that helps to develop compassion. With your breathing, you imagine that you are breathing in suffering, and then breathing out healing. You can start with your own suffering, or the suffering of someone whom you love. This practice helps us understand that suffering is universal but that an open heart of compassion contributes some relief. As you breathe in, imaginatively inhale what is dark, heavy, and hot. As you breathe out, imagine that the heavy energy has been transformed, and that you can now breathe out light, cool, and soothing energy.

Remember, each day as we go about our business, we run into all kinds of people. You've probably come across someone who has been through war, or who has lost children to war, addictions, or tragic illness. You may have passed someone who is still healing from having been tortured. You may have passed someone who just lost their job, or their best friend. We don't know the burdens that those all around us carry, but we can be kind and send out goodwill.

Simple Ritual and Ceremony

Some people find great meaning in the rituals of their faith traditions. Others are left cold, finding the rituals empty memorials of the past. Increasingly, people are creating new rituals and ceremonies, from creative original weddings to full moon dance ceremonies. The two words, ceremony and ritual, are often used interchangeably although some people use 'ritual' to refer to an action that is done repeatedly and regularly, whereas a 'ceremony' is a unique ritual to celebrate or commemorate a special, sometimes once-in-a-lifetime event. What's most important to remember, though, is that we neither need a crowd nor a designated leader in order to create our own ceremonies and rituals.

In a ritual, human beings are fastening two ideas together in a meaningful way using actions and objects; that is, using our bodies to move or manipulate physical things. At its most basic, a ritual takes an ordinary action or object, and attaches it to the meaning of something special, something set apart from regular life which reminds us of something deep within that we do not want to see lost from the world. Rituals remind us of something meaningful; they bring us into quietness and into the present. This practice is something that humans have done for thousands of years, perhaps before humans used language. Symbol making is what humans do. And the etymology of 'symbol' is "to throw [ideas] together."

We see this symbol-making in the making of altars. And even children make and decorate specific spaces as reminder places of specific meaning. Many adults have mantelpieces dedicated to family photos. And those grieving often have a special shelf that has photos and possessions of the person that has passed. Altars are places that hold our intentions, desires, and prayers. They can serve as meditation spots, invitation corners, or inspiration centers. We can infuse these spaces with the goal of reminding us of who we really are, and who we want to be.

Create your own altars around your home and in nature, on a tray for portability, or on a shelf in the corner. People usually add to their altars representations of one or more of the four elements, earth, air, water, and fire. You might add a special rock from the earth, a candle for both air and fire, and a small bowl of water, all chosen to remind you that we are of the earth and made from the elements. We belong with each other. You might add photos of special loved ones, or of a beloved teacher. You might add other meaningful objects such as jewelry, a drawing, or an item from nature such as a pine cone or flowers or herbs. You can let the actual making of your altar be your quiet time, your centering time. Perhaps you already have an altar or two in your home, and you can choose to enhance them, or clear them out to add a new energy and intention. If there is anything you don't particularly like at your altar, place it somewhere else. Everything on your altar should have meaning for you, so that you have a physical space that signifies a respite space, a calm place, a place that reinforces the qualities of your best self and your deepest desires. As you sit near your altar on a regular basis, it helps to focus your concentration and your energies toward what is most meaningful to you, creating a sacred space amongst the mundane.

If you create altars outside, ensure that all that you leave there is biodegradable, of natural origin. If you collect plants to include or to use as a kind of incense, be aware of whether they are an endangered or rare plant, and respond appropriately. You may gather only what has already fallen off the plant, or choose to take a photo rather than disturb the plant. You might collect blossoms, twigs, feathers, nuts or seed casings. As we collect these items, they remind us of the silent lives around us, and that the world is so much bigger than we're aware of. Several people I know have created small nature mandalas every day as their temporary altars, and then posted their photos of the mandalas online.

So creating an altar can be a ritual, but so can having a particular cup of tea at a particular place and time that you infuse with meaning and intention. Ringing a bell at a certain time, or to close a particular time of reading or prayer can be a ritual. Wearing a shawl can be a ritual if you envision its wearing as creating a little prayer hut around you. Even if worn around your shoulders, it may remind you that when a shawl is worn over one's head it encloses us away from distractions and creates a miniature tent of our own to dwell in. Others tie a scarf or bandana around their head as a physical reminder to hold the ego in place as they extend prayer and blessing to self and others. This bandana can 'lasso' the ego from judging or ridiculing our prayers and openness to Greater, and bar our ego from loudly commenting that, "this is ridiculous," "what I intend is not possible," and "I'm just making all this stuff up." Actually, "just making all this stuff up" is the first step of using our imaginations to envision a particular result and imagining the path from here to the desired result, as well as opening ourselves to receive that which we're requesting. And really, all of it is made up. We can make it up, too.

As we go about our day, we can infuse some of our regular activities with meaning, and therefore experience a deeper and richer life through these little rituals. As we walk through a doorway, we can offer the intention, "May all that is Sacred open its doors to me." When we put on our clothes for the day, we can be conscious of putting on the mantles of protection for our deepest selves, and when we take off our clothes at night, we can envision our taking off the layers of ego and false beliefs, so as to live with greater authenticity. When washing our hands we can set the intention, "May my hands be of use." And when we shower or bathe, we can imagine purifying our bodies, of letting go of everything that is not ours, of releasing all the detritus of the day.

We can incorporate fasting as part of our rituals, but include things other than the traditional food or drink to fast from. Having a regular day devoted to rest and the development of the inner life, a Sabbath, is itself a fast day from everyday life. You can fast from shopping, or gossiping, or from any particular activity if doing so is meaningful for you. Fasting from the news is something I recommend to each of us. A non-stop diet of Breaking News, hour after hour, day after day, week after week can paradoxically numb us to crises. Too much news encourages negativity, induces feelings of helplessness, and adds to depression. Taking respite from these jolts to our nervous systems can help us to develop greater real awareness of our Earth's and its people's needs – including what we might be able to do to respond in a helpful way. It's hard to breathe, though, when we're constantly inundated with sensationalized news stories. Take note of how you feel after a day, or a week, of respite from the news and/or social media.

We can create special personal rituals at any time. Put together an intention with symbols, ideas, and objects that resonate with that intention. Think of your senses, and collect objects that appeal to as many of your senses as you can. Will you use photos or drawings in your ritual? How about music, a special song, or a bell or whistle? I like to include a small square of chocolate with its bitter-sweet qualities, or sip a special beverage, in many of my rituals. Will you choose incense or essential oils to appeal to the sense of smell? When an intention is united with the experiences of our senses, the ritual is made stronger, meaning that our sense experience resonates with the meaning and intention of our ritual, settling into our heart and consciousness in a deeper way. This unity reminds us to hold our intention more deeply, and then whenever we have choice in our days, we choose whatever direction is most resonant with our intention. This makes our intention or desire more real, more embodied in our lives, day by day.

Let me give a bare bones example of how to go about creating a simple ritual. Feel free to recruit a friend or friends to participate in your ritual, or to simply witness you in your intention. In this book, however, I have concentrated on activities and practices that you can do alone.

Articulate your intention in words, if possible, or else in a symbol. Your intention might be "I want to be free from being pulled into the latest gossip at work." Or "I send healing and wholeness to my aunt who struggles with cancer." Or "I want to let go of my anger about the injustices of the world, yet still be a force of goodness." Or "I wish to be open to the nudges from Spirit throughout my days." I have often designed rituals to reinforce a new understanding or insight that I've come to, or to remind myself of something or some value that I know deep down is true, but is easy to forget in everyday life.

Let's choose "I want to let go of my anger about the injustices of the world, yet still be a force of goodness" as your intention for the ritual. So you want to symbolize both letting go of something, but also building or sustaining something. What actions or objects could symbolize letting go? Building and sustaining? You could collect some plain or ugly rocks to symbolize each of your angers, and you could choose a thriving plant to symbolize your intention to be a force of goodness. You might arrange the rocks around the thriving plant to symbolize the transformation of your anger into protection of that which you want to thrive (your ability to bring goodness). Or you can collect some old and dry leaves to write your angers on, then during the ritual, crumble and bury them around the plant as compost, transforming old stuff, the anger, into nourishment for your intention to bring goodness. This ritual is also then a representation of the life, death, life cycle that is all around us in nature, and reminds us that this cycle is within ourselves as well, in ideas and emotions that we wish to transform into something new.

Before you perform your ritual, plan what you might say, and plan your actions to include as many of your senses as possible. Think of how you will begin, what you will do or say in the middle, and how you will know that your ritual is at an end. You might start by saying your intention or prayer aloud, to have your intention go through your hearing. Your collection of rocks or writing your angers on old leaves use your sense of touch. The earth around the thriving plant will have a scent. So bring a small amount of the dirt to your nose to inhale the scent of soil, of what allows the plant to survive and grow. If you bury the leaves around the plant, sprinkle some water over them to start the composting process, or sprinkle some water over the rocks representing your angers, and have a sip of the water to remind yourself to let go of, purify yourself of, the anger. When you are done, be sure to take a little time to let the intention and action of your ritual sink in. You may want to record what you did and how you now feel about it all in your journal. You may also want to take a photo or a series of photos of the ritual.

When planning your ritual as well as in writing about it afterwards, record your intention, record the actions and objects you've used, as well as what they signify to you. You may include objects in your ritual that you can take away afterwards to place in a special spot in your home or to carry with you. These can be found objects or can be ornaments, jewelry, cloth, dolls, or sculptures that you create especially for this ritual. These talismans then carry the memory and the energy of the ritual into the future with you. Talismans are physical reminders of spiritual truths, doorways into the Depth Dimensions. As you look upon or finger the talisman in your pocket, you recommit to the ritual's intention. And slowly you increasingly embody your intention into the reality around you. You are embodying something new, something that you have chosen. Your ritual can be as simple or as complex as you want. Write about how you feel about the ritual. Ask what you are building or encouraging by performing the ritual. What does having done this say about you, if anything? Does this ritual express parts of yourself that you have not yet been able to express in other ways? What's next, after the ritual? What might you now need to do?

In Closing

With whatever intention we may have and by means of the movements, actions, and the creating we do to manifest that intention into the world, we are actively embodying ourselves into the world. All the works of our hands, whether cooking, gardening, crafting, building, woodworking, needlework, or sewing, embed ourselves more and more deeply into this world that we share with each other and all life. We are creating our world, building our environment with every action, with every intention. If we can bring consciousness and intention into these acts of creating and building, we can know and use the power of embodiment to build the type of world we want for ourselves and our children's children. Becoming conscious of and responsibly using our true power is what depth dimension practices are all about.

But there are many ways of understanding and practicing embodiment that I did not include here, such as dancing, various forms of bodywork such as yoga, chi gong, tai chi, and music, drumming, or chanting. There is also the mutual embodiment of sexuality, and all the nuances and power of relationships. We know anything, and everything, through our bodies. When we no longer are embodied, we are no longer alive. And of death we can say nothing certain. But who we are, what constitutes our bodies, and how we move into and make the world can be endlessly explored. I've included here just the beginnings of different ways to think of embodiment, and limited my examples to what an individual person can do without the need for like-minded colleagues or community.

What pondering embodiment can teach us is that there is ultimately no limit to how we might define what is "us." There are so many activities that humans have used to express a deeper meaning, a sacred intention, or prayer: lighting candles, building a fire, burning incense or plants, anointing with oil or holy water, bathing, immersion (as in baptism), rocking back and forth, making offerings, fingering prayer beads or knotted string, walking with deliberation, touching with intention, clapping, singing, chanting, rattling, drumming, dancing, building altars, and building just about anything. Through our body we understand creation, the relationship between the one and the many, and between separateness and unity. Within our bodies we know the individual hands therein, and our individual selves within one family. We explore our individual body within all of matter. All these ideas of self, all processes, and all activities are reminders of the multivalent symbolism of just about anything, and everything, and the relationships between everything within everything, and with each other.

We make meaning by becoming conscious of our intentions and attributions of meaning whenever we make altars, perform rituals, or join together two or more seemingly separate ideas. Furthermore, we make soul through both creating and discovering the depths of meanings, and embodying that within our Mater, our matter.

8 We're Breaking For Freedom

To be nobody-but-yourself – in a world which is
doing its best day and night to make you like everybody
else – is to fight the hardest battle that any human being
can fight and never stop fighting.

E.E. CUMMINGS, in *E.E. Cummings: A Miscellany Revised*

Having an Inner Life is a Political Act

We've looked at a plethora of ways that you can nurture your inner life through
the different modalities of word, image, dream, silence, and embodiment. I've
focused almost exclusively on activities and exercises that you can do yourself
at either no or low cost in order to remove the obstacles that stop most people
from moving forward either in their personal or collective lives, that is, of needing
particular types of people to talk with or do things with, or needing to access
a group, in-person, or online. Trying to find the perfect group to join is often
either exhausting or just impossible. Alternatively, when there are many resources
available, we can exhaust ourselves by trying to do it all, along with suffering from
'FOMO,' the Fear of Missing Out.

We often try to do it ourselves by reading, or writing, or learning to
meditate, with different levels of satisfaction or success. I wanted to give a variety
of activities and exercises so that the individual person can try new things to
enliven a personal practice, and so that different types of personalities might find
their own practices even if the most popular ones don't fit well in their own lives.

Remember, though, that what I have offered is only a beginning into exploring
the imagination, the analysis, the strength and wondrous depth of the inner life.
As we open into our inner resources, new questions and possibilities are always
coming into consciousness. Following these possibilities is a generative and
fulfilling way to live our precious few years in this material reality. There are many

varieties of wildflower seeds to plant, and the earth is full of places both internal and around us that need these beauties.

All of us need to know we have this inner well of resources that can buoy us up when the world is just too much, but we often need suggestions and guidance to explore those inner resources. Some of us have found this guidance in a larger context of group identity. There are wisdom streams contained within the great religious traditions, whether Christianity, Sufism, Kabbalah, or Vedanta. Others have found resources and guidance in political movements or specific streams of activism. These groups help us contextualize and interpret the inner experiences we may be having, and motivate us to keep on keeping on. But many of us aren't connected to larger contexts that can support and guide us. And we won't find that guidance in what relentlessly comes at us in our everyday lives. With work, family, children, email, internet, television, Netflix, Facebook, Instagram, Tik Tok and more, we can feel like that pinball launched every morning to be thrown here and there all day, feeling as though we have no control as to where we'll end up.

Add to that that the world is in a bad state: as I write this, we're in the fourth wave of the covid pandemic; cries for racial justice can no longer be ignored; we have a planet that is warming up, with unimaginable pressures of extreme weather events. Lowlands are being flooded by rising sea levels, and new waves of climate refugees just trying to find a place to live are becoming visible — not to mention wars and violence in myriad places of the world. The "haves" of this world consume unsustainably, while the "have nots" are ignored or silenced. It may well be that things get way worse before we see any significant change for the better. Compassion fatigue is real, and so is the creeping despair that none of us can really do anything about it all. Taking 20 minutes a day, a half an hour, an hour, feels impossible, but even if possible, can seem narcissistic or selfish, and even guilt-inducing for many of us.

In the midst of all this, *how* can we remember our humanity, explore our values, counter despair, and imagine what kind of world we want to live in? How can we not just survive all that comes at us, but actually take actions that can bring life, encouragement, and freedom? Some of us just happen to fall into groups or find friends who encourage that kind of thinking, but more of us seem to find ourselves in environments that just echo the fears and overwhelm of the overculture. "Overculture" is a term that Dr. Estés has coined to refer to the pervading influence in our lives of the mainstream, popular culture exemplified in the capitalistic and neoliberal culture of North America and Europe, but extending around the world as well. The overculture overwhelmingly sees people as means for wealth production (usually for the benefit of others), and ignores any aspects of human life that are not engaged in production, celebrity, or the distraction of the masses. It seeks also to entrain our nervous systems to its breakneck space, distracting us from inner soulful pursuits as well as from genuine community building for life.

Where can we find sustained motivation to both discover what we CAN do to be fully ensouled? Where can we find the strength to live out of that soul knowledge and do the things that are within our power and within our reach that would support the kind of world where all life can thrive, not just a few of the "haves"? While billionaires are building their space rockets on the quest to escape to a new home on Mars, abandoning earth when it is no longer livable is just not a wide scale solution to the problems that are in front of us.

Things are so urgent that we must move slowly, with deliberation and intention, otherwise our energy can so easily be dissipated. We need to be intentional, focussed, sustained, and most of all, soulful. Dr. Estés has often said "the most endangered being on earth today is the soul." Soul reminds us that while we might be the center of our own worlds, we are not THE center of the world, that there is "other", and "greater", and that we are connected with all that exists, with all that we know. And that there is more than what humans know right now. Soul reminds us that we are from and of the earth, from the humus, and that this knowledge can help us be appropriately humble. Whether we like it or not, we are here with each other, and we belong with each other.

Anything that one human might do is, yes, seemingly infinitely small, but the present world was made by many, many humans making seemingly infinitesimally small decisions, both personally and collectively, both purposefully and just by default. The way to a different world, a better world, is for each of us to become conscious of what we do have choice about, becoming aware of the implications of our choices, and then acting with intention and joining with others with similar intentions. We won't be perfect at it, and we may well not be able to do enough to prevent that which we fear from happening, but we will be making a difference in our own spheres of influence and living with authenticity and integrity. To me, that is a fully human way to live, ensouled, resourced, and intentional. The fullness of true self can be found by diving in, asking forbidden questions, and following through freely, with love and integrity.

But we can't do that if we live in a frantic state, barely getting enough sleep to go at it all again tomorrow, overwhelmed by the tyranny of tasks, and pushing away the awareness of the degree of suffering in the world lest we simply collapse under the weight of it all. When we are pushed beyond our coping abilities, we often react by yelling, screaming, or fighting back. Quick emotional responses are rarely the best responses, yet if we remain silent the powers that be take our silence as agreement. When humans are stressed and things get bad, we can fight, flee, or freeze. When humans are scared, we often get mean. Yet, when stressed, we can not only fight, flee, or freeze, but also form friendships, which is why and how many of us are here, now: because our ancestors cooperated. So how do you want to face our unknown future?

We too easily serve the predators in our overculture without knowing it, even sometimes in the name of peace. We stay silent on human rights issues; we ignore the politics where we can actually vote or otherwise influence outcomes. We misfocus. We obsess on our stomach issues when we work at a job that rapes the environment, because solving our digestive upsets seems easier than finding a different job. Or we try to make change using the same methods of hierarchy, power, overwork and anger that we're supposedly resisting. Noise, distraction, and advertising serve dominators and manipulators and those who want us to part with our money. The noise of the culture brainwashes and entrains our nervous systems if we don't have ongoing ways to defend against it.

Hierarchy, abuse, exploitation and domination cannot be trusted to act for our communal benefit. We know, or can discover, the things that don't work, that capture and entrain rather than nurture freedom and life, and we can avoid those things, at least in some ways some of the time. Breaking for freedom, that is, recollecting ourselves from the grasp of the overculture, is not a waste of time, nor is it selfish. It may well be the best possible thing we can do for ourselves and for all of life.

We can make soul grow in ourselves, 20 minutes or a sabbath at a time. Each of us is the only person whom we truly have control over, and then, often only to a certain extent, amidst the needs to care for children or satisfy our bosses. We need a practice, that is, something that we do repeatedly, that insists that we disengage ourselves from the machinery that drives us to work more, do more, and never think for ourselves. Just as we might love to sit among the wildflowers but won't smell their fragrance if we don't actually go out to find them, we won't enjoy the beauties of clear thinking or peace if we don't actually make the time for reflective depth dimension practices.

It is telling that George Orwell, in his novel *1984*, has his protagonist taking his first step toward freedom by buying and writing in an old-fashioned, outlawed journal. Part of any autocratic regime tries to get you to not trust your own perceptions. If people write their truths, ponder what they see, and think for themselves, the regime can't control them. They can begin to discern whether they are the crazy ones, or if it's the system that is crazy.

What many don't remember about the novel, though, is that Winston Smith didn't succeed in his break for freedom; the regime knew the danger of what Winston was trying to do, and succeeded in neutralizing him. But we can remember that *1984* is a novel, and not necessarily a map of the future. We can write and watch and dream and question, and though these won't necessarily guarantee a better future, they are an important way toward that future. It's the doing of these things, over and over and over again, asking yourself what you love, where you feel called to do something, letting your inner self reveal those things that feed your spirit, that breaks you out of the tranquilizing effect of groupthink. And in the practicing itself, aside from any visible outcomes, nurturing our inner lives and making our break for freedom can allow us to live well, make meaning, make soul, and find the true and renewable fuel that supports collective social activism in all its ways.

Three Helpful Questions

If individuals regularly invest time for their inner lives, and know that time will be free of being observed or judged, where what they write stays confidential, they begin to relax and let their minds wander out of the deep grooves that everyday thinking and just surviving tend to create. Asking questions that have never come up before becomes easier to do, and by exploring reflective questions freely, in detail and at length, you think thoughts and develop passions that you hadn't known were possible.

I have found that three questions are particularly valuable to return to over and over again. They are very helpful to many people in living lives of intention and integrity. The first question is "What if …?" The second question is "Does this (x, y, or z) bring about a bigger, more expansive, spacious and freer way of thinking and living?" And the third question is the old question beloved by sociologists and crime solvers, "Cui bono?" or "Who benefits?" It's often also phrased as "Follow the money!" By making an ongoing practice to ask yourself these questions, and by searching for the answers, you will find the values, people, and groups where you feel you truly belong to something worth believing in and living for, and belong with people who strive to live with consciousness and integrity in creating a world that works for all of us.

The first question, "What if …?" is a basic brainstorming question, meant to release creativity and help people to get out of the box of usual ways of thinking, usual ways of solving questions. If you get into the habit of asking this question, you switch yourself to possibility thinking rather than accepting everything just the way it is. Of course, it's easy to stop ourselves from allowing ourselves to ponder "what if's" that at first glance seem impossible or just too fanciful.

We can practice asking this question when we're with our friends, especially as an alternative to the "ain't it awful?" comments or doom and gloom complaining that seems to too often arise as our default way of conversing. We can ask it of our children and other family members over supper; we can remind ourselves to ask it every time we find ourselves frustrated and angered by a situation or policy. We can post it at the top of our daily to-do lists as a reminder. If we're too despondent to think creatively, or are feeling quite cynical, we can start with a little critiquing, such as "What if we never had to worry about that policy, or person, or situation?" "What would life be like if …?" As we further define our personal values and how it is we want to live in this world, the "What if …?" question gets us imagining what life would look like if the world operated, at least some of the time, according to our values. And that leads us to strategizing *how* things might get to be that way. Following that line of thought clarifies what we, ourselves, might do to help make that outcome more likely, opening up possibilities that might not have been possible without those leaps in imagination.

The second question, "Does this (x, y, or z) bring about a bigger, more expansive, spacious and freer way of thinking and living?" helps us discern the best choices we can make at any time, especially if we remember to consider how we might respond to the question in a week, month, year, or 5 years from now. For example, we may have a work situation that feels like a dead end and we decide to resign. But when our boss increases our pay, we try to convince ourselves that it's worth it to stay, because the extra money increases our ability to buy vacations and distractions that help us tolerate the dead-end job. Now, if we truly do not have any other options work-wise, this may well be the best choice *for the time being*. But if we don't also take steps to find another work situation, then we're choosing to stay in a situation that is making our life smaller.

It is not at all the case that bigger always equals better; if that were so, choosing more money would almost always be the better choice. This question refers rather to a more fulfilling life, a way of living that opens our lives to new ideas, new projects, new people, to personal growth and greater justice for ourselves and for others. If we are from settler families, then this is the question that our ancestors thought would be answered best by immigrating to the USA, Canada, or Australia. And for many settlers, it did result in much greater prosperity, and for some, greater security and justice. But the result wasn't at all the same for the peoples who were already living here.

In asking the question we must also remember that "bigger" has almost always been defined in a comparative way, as in "bigger or better than someone else, or someone else's situation". This question only works well when the comparison is with ourselves or our own situations, and when our answers serve justice rather than exploitation.

If the first question encourages us to be open to new possibilities, and the second one helps us discern what actions we might take for our own flourishing, then the third one helps us to understand much of what is going on around us, especially in our social and political lives. "Cui bono?" is Latin for "Who benefits?" Whenever we are faced with policies, practices, and situations that don't seem to make any sense or tend to make us feel bad about ourselves, if we start to tease out whomever it is who benefits from the way these things are, then the forces and motivations behind the situation start to become clear. This kind of analysis is also the basis of most good mystery novels.

Wherever there is injustice, there are persons, groups, and forces that have an interest in keeping things the way they are. If that's not the case, as in the case of anachronistic laws stating, for instance, where you can tie up your horse in town, there is no controversy in repealing those kinds of laws. Where there is opposition, though, it's probable that someone thinks they're going to lose out. Figuring out who benefits, how they benefit, and why, helps us to understand why there is opposition to so many policies that seem, on first glance, to be obvious for the common good. It's just that we're not the ones who are currently benefiting from the status quo, and so have little to lose. Clearly understanding these dynamics helps us to strategize how to move forward, whether it is to ensure that people need not be afraid that they will lose what is valuable to them, or if it is a case where injustice and greed must be addressed up front.

Let's take, for example, the feeling of guilt and shame that so many of us, especially women, struggle with. Feeling guilty or shameful is usually thought of as signals that we have done something morally wrong, but in our culture, guilt and shame are more about control, that is, being controlled by others, than they are about being "good." They are instilled in us by those who are in a position of teaching us to be moral persons capable of choosing what's right rather than just mindlessly doing things that may be wrong. But who is it that is determining what is defined as right or wrong? We may have had these morals passed on to us by our parents, but their source is most often the dominant religious ideologies of the culture.

The Abrahamic religions of Judaism, Christianity, and Islam have developed morality far beyond the simplicity of the Golden Rule, that is, "Do to others what you would have them do to you." These religions have elaborated a plethora of rules that we are supposed to live by, supposedly given by God in the Holy Books. By attributing these rules to God, the religions then describe God as the great enforcer, instilling in their followers the fear of punishment by God. This fear includes the ever-present threat of Hell, where one is supposedly tortured for eternity. These rules are presented as ways to avoid doing evil, thus being ways to avoid punishment. So far this seems reasonable, but a large proportion of those rules seem to have to do with personal, especially sexual, relations, while at the same time they have little to say about group or corporate evils such as exploitative corporations and political systems, or racism, sexism, and classism.

A young person caught shoplifting is defined as doing something bad, that is, stealing, but religion has traditionally had little to say about corporations taking the earth's resources without regard for sustainability, clean up, or pollution. Taking without adequate compensation is stealing from the earth and from the future generations who end up cleaning up the mess. Religions instead often laud corporate profit, capitalistic ways of doing business, and successful business people as being materially blessed by God, presumably because of the person's good personal morality. Rarely are successful business people wracked by feelings of guilt and shame regarding their business practices. While this may be the mainstream attitude of many religious organizations, we must also remember that in every age there have been prophets who have railed against these attitudes. Perhaps in the internet age these prophetic voices may have a chance to become louder and louder, challenging us to take prophetic stances against injustice and exploitation.

Yet with this primary focus on personal morality, these religions have encouraged us to examine ourselves relentlessly. This results in taking the finite attention we humans have away from the situations and structures around us and directing it to obsess upon our own actions. How many of us were raised to believe that sex before marriage is a mortal sin? Friends of mine were explicitly taught that sex before marriage is as serious a sin as murder. LGBTQIA2S+ persons have been driven to suicide out of guilt that who they are is an abomination to God. Personal morality is important, but this obsession and extremism with sexual behavior serves to teach people, from their youth, to be focused on self-policing in relationships. Guilt and shame are debilitating. Meanwhile, where is the energy and support to look at the social realities of politics, business, resource extraction, and cleaning up after yourself (pollution)? So, who is it exactly that is benefiting from people obsessed with their personal behavior, too demoralized and exhausted to pay attention to corporate greed or totalitarian governance?

I was raised in a tradition, Roman Catholicism, that has a very unhealthy thread in it, where if you want something, or want to do something, then your very wanting is held suspect, as demonstrating selfishness. We are to want only the good of others, and to forget the self. The teaching that I absorbed was that the best thing I could do for desires that were selfish was to banish them, to never give in to our endemic selfishness. And even if the desires were for things or activities that were morally neutral or even good, then I should still probably forgo it — the very best gift I could give God was to "offer up" to "him" my soul's desires. That if I wanted something, then the best I could do was to give it up as a way of "mortification of the flesh," of turning away from this life and turning toward the spiritual. And this supposedly pleases God. Of course, this interpretation of gifts and "giving up" has only a grain of truth in it, but this was the interpretation handed on to me in my childhood.

It was almost impossible to believe that something I wanted could perhaps actually be a GIFT from the Source without Source, that not only was it NOT sinful, but an honoring of the Creator and of myself to give in to these desires of my physical body for rest, or for play, or for beauty. Add to that the messages that most of us women literally "incorporated" (*corpus* means "body" in Latin), that our worth is in what we do, that our only value is in service, and you get good-hearted persons who literally dare not stop. The person who works herself into the grave — or at least the hospital — wins the prize! For me, it's taken much work, reading, writing, reflecting, consulting with wise women, plus the partial breakdown of my body, to examine and reject that way of thinking as so, so wrong.

Living joyfully and fully within the limits of our own flesh is just as holy as serving someone else. There is no separation between life now and the spiritual. While there may or may not be some sort of "heaven" after this life, this life is where we are now. One of the best ideas of Christianity is that the Great Mystery chose to live a human life, fully, in the person of Jesus of Nazareth, showing the beauty, glory, and potential divinity of all of this world. Jesus taught that the kingdom of God is among us, not (just) in a different life than this one on our dear earth. This is what we're invited to live, now. There's no need to live in guilt, shame, or unworthiness. We can instead contribute to the evolution of human consciousness by fearlessly opening to possibility and radical compassion, that is, passion "with."

Sacred Activism: What is Mine to Be and to Do?

We still live in a world of false dualities, where we think that the personal practice of exploration, free questioning, and discovering both what we passionately love and love to do, is vaguely "selfish," rather than simply a balance and resource to our visible actions in the world. I deeply believe that if we don't make the time for developing this inner life of the self, that at best we are running around in circles simply surviving our lives, or at worst we become the blind foot soldiers of forces of greed and ultimately, destruction of life. It is in the interest of those powerful forces that we remain unconscious, unaware of the consequences of an unexamined life, unaware of the power of our passions to engender a larger and enriched life, cooperation, and a world welcoming to all. No wonder that the world around us keeps us busy and exhausted, distracted from ourselves, and feeling vaguely ill at ease all the time! Who benefits?

What if we each grab hold of whatever freedom we do have to find and to support the qualities within ourselves that bring pleasure, encourage deep love, and stimulate our imaginations to create a better world? There is so much that needs to be changed for the better in this world that wherever you care about something or some group of people, there is plenty to do. When I speak of activism I'm not focusing only on specifically Political Action as in attending demonstrations or leading masses of people in a particular campaign. Activism is any way that you extend your care for this world out beyond your immediate family and immediate survival needs. And small "p" political means to me anything related to our relationships with the peoples and groups that make up our community, however large or small we define that community.

So much of the activism that we're familiar with is fueled by anger, whether righteous or not. But anger is not a sustainable type of fuel. It burns at both ends, towards the object of the anger, but also turns back onto the person who is acting out of the anger. It's exhausting, it eats away at our bodies and minds, it depletes the soul, makes the heart hard and closed, and the child spirit isn't having any fun submerged in all that anger.

Sacred activism is imagining and working for justice that is fueled by deep conviction, love, a desire for unity, and great compassion. Justice is how love is manifested in a public manner. Justice is not about punishment, retribution, or "them" getting what they "deserve." Of course, destructive behaviors and hateful people must be contained in ways that limit the damage they can do, but sacred activism is not about being "right," nor about virtue signaling or taking on only the fashionable causes. It's responding with love and justice to the people and issues within our reach in ways that create a world where we can all thrive, where we can all belong. It's about applying healing to all that we hate, both within ourselves and within the society in which we move and act.

So, what kind of world do you really, really, *really* want to be part of? What are you already involved in that you cherish? What kinds of practices consistently express your passion in the world? What values and behaviors do you want to encourage, and which do you want to abolish, as far as is possible? With whom and with what do you want to ally, and with whom and with what do you want to make peace?

Religious people are often admonished to live their theology with the Bible in one hand and the newspaper in the other. Yet atheists and agnostics often live the greatest faith of all, not in invoking God, but in attempting to live out Truth, Justice, and Compassion – which truly are other names for the Mystery that religious people call God. It's easy to focus on the perceived faults of others, and easy to be distracted by the perceived faults of our allies. We use those faults to excuse us from moving forward together, all while the forces of greed and injustice are also using those perceived faults to divide and conquer, but primarily to distract. It's easier to focus on and accuse our allies of not being as perfect as we want them to be than it is to focus on the real problems. The real problems are huge, and sometimes dangerous to take on. The forces of greed and the people who benefit from these forces do not want to be challenged, and we should not underestimate their determination to continue their ways. We should not be surprised when they try to silence us, divide us, neutralize our actions, or in extreme cases, do us physical harm. But it's our job to keep the focus on the most important things, and not be distracted. We need to be aware and wise, but also not allow ourselves to be frightened into silence.

One of the reasons why I urge us all to focus on that which is within our reach is that with large organizations and national or international issues, it's actually really difficult to find out what's really going on. Misinformation campaigns have consistently been used in history in order to misdirect and neutralize resistance. Where do we find reliable reporting? What is truth, and what is propaganda? Remember that the mouthpiece of the previous Soviet government is the newspaper 'Pravda,' whose name means 'Truth.' Has that newspaper really been the source of truth to the common people of that country?

One of the things that a professor of mine used to say is that whenever you read something in the media, all you *really* know for sure is that someone, somewhere, wants you to believe that a particular something recently happened somewhere. Trying to source accurate information on big topics and sort out relative pros and cons of different actions takes a tremendous amount of time in a world where almost every single person is able to post videos of their personal knowledge and opinions onto the internet. I know a very intelligent person with deep integrity who in retirement spends 12 - 14 hours per day on the internet trying to sort through some important issues, to be seemingly no closer to "the truth," from my point of view, than he was months, even years, ago. As admirable as his persistence and research abilities are, by spending all his available time trying to sort out what's really going on regarding these big issues, he has been effectively neutralized in terms of taking action in the world towards positive change. At least so far.

By focusing instead on the issues within our reach, we have a much better chance of actually knowing what is really going on. We can get to know the people involved in the issues we care about, and more accurately assess whether they are acting in integrity, are in a world of their own imagination, or are power-hungry and controlling. We can, with like-minded others in our own communities, forge coalitions of people, strategize the effective next step, and move forward on our good intentions. We can see the results, and evaluate. All the slow work of talking with others, getting them educated and onboard, and helping each other work through anger or apathy means that huge changes in policy or big results may take a long time, but this slow work educates minds and engages hearts for far longer than the current project. It can slowly create new leaders who make life-long commitments to work for a world that has more justice and more compassion. We can explain to our children and to our friends why we do what we do, educating them in the process and helping them discern what actions they might take themselves. Small steps are okay; any movement forward is good. We need to pace ourselves to make this a way of life rather than take our sense of achievement from whether or not our current project is considered a success. Creating a just and compassionate world is probably going to take longer than a single lifetime!

So, decide consciously how much news you will consume, and from where you will get it. More is not always better, and it's a danger to fall into the thinking that you constantly must do more and more and more. The work needed is more than any of us can do alone. Be aware of what you pay attention to, and take responsibility for that, because we are what we pay attention to. Our lives are made up of all the little things we spend time on; as much as possible, be conscious and intentional about what those little things are. Overcome the feelings of false urgency and the fear of missing out.

Take your time to discover what is the best use of your resources: your attention, your energy and actions, your love and passions. And you find out these things best by exploring and developing your inner life, 20 minutes at a time, where you discover your own passions, resource yourself spiritually and psychologically, sort out all the messages coming at you, let your imagination take you to new vistas where you may see more clearly, and discern what it is that "you plan to do with your one wild and precious life," to quote the poet Mary Oliver.

Some people may claim that doing this — developing your inner life and choosing how you will live and take action for justice and compassion — is only for those with the privilege of time and money to not be overwhelmed by mere survival. I don't believe this is so. Almost every person can find 20 minutes in most of their days to breathe, to rest, to discover more about themselves and their lives in this world. I want to emphasize that just as you need not and should not do every single one of the practices that I have described in this book, but practice only a few, that you need not take up every cause, every project, every issue that is worthy of attention.

Don't go around collecting more and more practices, more and more causes and projects. They may each be a good thing to do, but the point isn't to do everything, but to do that which is uniquely yours to do. Each of us has specific abilities and disabilities. For me, I will probably never hike into the old growth forests, putting my body on the line to keep the land from being clear-cut. I can't hike; I'll never make it to the top of a mountain. I can't even stand for very long.

But I gaze out of my windows, loving my yard filled with wildflowers (weeds?) and the trees sheltering birds and other urban wildlife. I sit on park benches patiently watching the 9 square feet around me. I can become a voice for the preservation of wildlife pathways, and of toxic free plant life that can nourish migrating birds and butterflies. I may not go on demonstrations supporting basic human rights, even though those are important as more rights are taken away through apathy and ignorance than through wars and conflict. Yet I can write letters and proposals to educate and persuade.

None of us needs to do it all, or even any particular action, but we do need to do what is ours to do. And we find that out by listening to our deepest selves, 20 minutes at a time.

A Way of Life —
Offering Our Lives to What is Ours to Be and to Do

So much of what we want in life is interconnected: healing, meaning, action in the outer world, exploration in the inner world, inner and outer freedom, alliances with like-minded people, satisfaction, happiness, using resources responsibly including money and the earth's resources, and self-respect, to name just a few. In addition, we can come to know the invisible worlds of spirituality, dreams, artistic and metaphorical sensibilities, can come to understand a mythical outlook as deeply as we know the consensual reality of daily life. We can take these worlds into account and consult their wisdom for a mutually interwoven rich life that does not deplete ourselves, others, or the world around us. This sense of inner freedom and compassionate engagement can fuel each of us to transform the wounds of the world we live in as well as to heal our own woundedness.

Life does not proceed in a linear way, always progressing to something better. It would be nice if it did, and we do often try to make it so. Grade school progresses to high school, to further training or education, to a career, to marriage, to children, to home ownership, hopefully culminating in a prosperous and healthy retirement. But really, look around you: how many of us have lived that script without interruption, U-turns, or unexpected challenges? Life moves in three dimensions, in circles and spirals, with few clear beginnings and few clear ends. And so there are many, many ways to live a good life, with seasons for just about everything.

So many of our movements for social change, for justice, are fueled by angry and exhausted well-meaning persons whose self-worth seems dependent on however their group defines victory. They work so hard, stretched beyond resilience, where all the sacrifice will only have been worth it *if* the desired outcome is reached. Can't we envision a better way of working towards a better world, where we do our best daily evolving into a better way of being human? Is it possible to live in an intentional way, deeply resourced, and ensouled? Can we have confidence that if any particular campaign fails, we will have more chances tomorrow to work for the outcomes that are better for all?

We need long-term vision with ways to participate in that vision now. Changing the world in these ways does not happen in a mere 4-5 years, the length of the term of a political leader. Perhaps it won't happen in our lifetime. But we each can contribute to a long-term inner turning, just by the way we choose to live our lives, examined, resourced, and joyful. We do what we can and all that we can. Even so, we might run out of time. Facing this real possibility can bring us to despair, but we can also take hope when we remember that there have been huge and lasting changes effected in history. Slavery is no longer tolerated, at least publicly. The public whipping of those who commit crimes is no longer common. Many plagues and diseases have been eradicated. In my own lifetime I have seen big changes in the attitudes towards wearing seatbelts in automobiles as well as towards smoking in public.

I invite all of us to live in such a way that if everyone lived in that way, this world can continue sustainably and we can direct our energies to infinite creativity, pro-social community, and deep contentment. None of us has to do it alone. There are others, allies, to carry on the work. I just have to do what is mine to do, within my reach. While this may sound obvious, it is far easier to talk about than to actually live it. I know.

I worked for many years in the movement to eradicate and heal sexual violence, to the point of exhaustion and near despair. I thought that after a year or so of rest, I'd be back at it. After all, I'd learned so much not only about the issue but on how to change policies, even change laws. I surely didn't want that knowledge and experience to be wasted. My eventual ambition was to be the director of the prevention of violence against women and children office at the United Nations. That office doesn't exist, but I'd hoped that I would be the first to hold the position that I would help to create.

But my life didn't progress in that linear manner: health challenges and then home-educating my son derailed those earlier ambitions. And I then felt, for far too long, that I'd had to abandon "the good fight," and secretly held hopes that someday I'd get back to the front lines. Finally, a friend who had witnessed first-hand my health struggles and my involvement with home-educating families challenged me. She asked how long I was going to pine after a job that seemed further away each day. She asked me why I couldn't be content with living my life with integrity and influencing perhaps only four or five women, but influencing and educating them so deeply that they influence their children in such a way that lives and families are changed forever throughout many generations. They were questions that revealed to me how my desire to be a change agent had a little too much personal ambition mixed in there, and exposed how I wasn't able to see the reality of my life right in front of me. They exposed how unexamined were my assumptions as to how real change is accomplished in the world. But they also made me deeply appreciative of aspects of my life that I had not been previously aware of.

It was as though I'd been reminded that the kaleidoscope through which I'd been looking at life could be shifted, just one turn, to see new patterns and be reminded of the infinity of creativity and possibility. Just one shift to turn a weed into a wildflower. I took these insights into my contemplative practice, into my 20 minutes a day, my sabbaths, my explorations, and realized even more deeply how I could live sacred activism with more integrity in each day of my life. I might be living a smaller life than my ambition had striven for, but it is a sustainable life that is richer, healthier, and happier. It is full of love and community, where every action I take can be a vote for the type of world we will live in in the future.

We all have been held captive by old ideas, old ways of working, and the propaganda of those who benefit by our ignorance and unconsciousness. We've been held captive for so long, we think it's normal. And when there is no escape from this kind of captivity, most of us do adapt and go on, but never remember the freedom of thinking our own thoughts. I have come to know that one of the best ways to escape this captivity is to carve out a regular time and space to examine all that we have been taught and to explore other possibilities with inner freedom and creativity. Though nourishing an inner life is sometimes thought of as a selfish, world-denying, individualistic activity, it is truly a way to unite the inner with the outer. It not only creates resources for all of us in all that we are, but does so in such a way that does not use up the world, but actually creates more of what we so deeply need: love, integrity, community, freedom, depth, imagination, and hope for all those who will come after us.

The holy mystery of life shimmers behind and through every living and natural being and thing. We are capable of developing a conscious and joyful relationship with this mystery. The most important thing, I think, is to hold ourselves and each other in this full mystery of all that we are, appreciating that we are here, now, that we belong with each other, and holding all of this with great compassion and possibility.

Notice the wildflowers in the weeds, and spread those seeds abundantly, 20 minutes at a time.

Acknowledgements

It's not until you write a book that you understand how long it takes, and why the acknowledgements are as long as they are! Many people are involved in the care and encouragement of the author as well as those involved with the editing and technical advice.

First, I express my gratitude and love to my principal teacher with whom I have studied for many years: Dr. Clarissa Pinkola Estés Reyes. "Dr. E" is an example of deep integrity, of attempting to always follow the guidance of Greater, and of sharing the wisdom that comes from that guidance. I strive to become that as well.

I want to deeply thank the many, many friends, colleagues, and acquaintances who over the years have encouraged me to set my ideas onto paper and get them out into the world. Most of us are not aware of how much our casual comments mean to a person, how they plant seeds and provide nourishment in the very long haul of getting those ideas onto the paper. Thank you.

To my beta readers I owe deep thanks; your careful readings, comments, corrections, suggestions and practical help have significantly made this book better. Thank you to Marta Baricsa, Andrew Blair, Ahni Bonner, Liberty Charissage, Jill Ebsworth, Amanda Manning, Kerry Morrison, Stacy Oler, Teri Petz, Lynn Russell, Carol Scott, Julie Surber, and Karina Witbeck. Special thanks to Dr. Jan Beauregard and Pamela Lindsay for their high level of professional expertise offered. Thanks too to Vickie MacArthur for publishing advice that was encouraging when I discovered that most traditional publishers want authors with already very large social media numbers.

Many others have given advice or an encouraging word at just the right time. I apologize that I cannot name everyone who was of help.

Final and deepest thanks go to my dear little family: my spouse Andrew and son Liberty, who never ever doubted that I had this book in me and who supported me in the day-by-day work of a few paragraphs here, a page there, until it was "done done."

Author's bio

CAT CHARISSAGE is a contemplative educator, writer, and artist, helping folks navigate the depth dimensions of their lives through image, word, silence, dream, and embodiment. She believes that the most important work each of us can do is to live out our gifted selves fully, creatively, and freely in a world where we are too often wounded in body and soul, our minds colonized by distractions, commodification, and other people's agendas.

She lives in liminal places between the worlds where spiritual reality meets ordinary life, where word (poetry, prose) meets image (paintings, journals), where wild adventure meets chronic pain, and where prairie meets mountains in western Canada.

She's a student of the wisdom traditions of the world with degrees in theology and education, plus 40-some years' experience in education and healing, especially regarding gender violence and trauma. She is also a longtime in-person student of Dr. Clarissa Pinkola Estés Reyes. Cat has taught in university, high school, professional development, small "Story Circles" and in private mentoring. She is the co-founder of Owl Poetry, a poetry open-mic that has been running for five years in Lethbridge, Alberta, Canada, and is the author of the poetry collection *OPEN TO MYSTERY: POEMS and PAINTINGS.*

www.catcharissage.com

Manufactured by Amazon.ca
Bolton, ON

35143419R00162